DOMESTIC DEPLOYMENT OF THE ARMED FORCES

INTERNATIONAL AND COMPARATIVE CRIMINAL JUSTICE

Series Editors:

Mark Findlay, *Institute of Criminology, University of Sydney, Australia*
Ralph Henham, *Nottingham Law School, Nottingham Trent University, UK*

This series explores the new and rapidly developing field of international and comparative criminal justice and engages with its most important emerging themes and debates. It focuses on three interrelated aspects of scholarship which go to the root of understanding the nature and significance of international criminal justice in the broader context of globalization and global governance. These include: the theoretical and methodological problems posed by the development of international and comparative criminal justice; comparative contextual analysis; the reciprocal relationship between comparative and international criminal justice and contributions which endeavor to build understandings of global justice on foundations of comparative contextual analysis.

Other titles in the series:

Democracy in the Courts
Lay Participation in European Criminal Justice Systems
Marijke Malsch
ISBN 978 0 7546 7405 4

The Disruption of International Organised Crime
An Analysis of Legal and Non-Legal Strategies
Angela Veng Mei Leong
ISBN 978 0 7546 7066 7

Restorative Justice
Ideals and Realities
Margarita Zernova
ISBN 978 0 7546 7032 2

The Criminal Law of Genocide
International, Comparative and Contextual Aspects
Edited by Ralph Henham and Paul Behrens
ISBN 978 0 7546 4898 7

Domestic Deployment of the Armed Forces
Military Powers, Law and Human Rights

MICHAEL HEAD and SCOTT MANN
University of Western Sydney, Australia

ASHGATE

Published by
Ashgate Publishing Limited
Wey Court East
Union Road
Farnham
Surrey, GU9 7PT
England

Ashgate Publishing Company
Suite 420
101 Cherry Street
Burlington
VT 05401-4405
USA

www.ashgate.com

British Library Cataloguing in Publication Data
Head, Michael.
Domestic deployment of the armed forces : military powers, law and human rights. -- (International and comparative criminal justice)
1. Military law. 2. Armed Forces--Operations other than war. 3. Civil defense--Law and legislation. 4. Soldiers--Legal status, laws, etc.
I. Title II. Series III. Mann, Scott.
343'.01-dc22

Library of Congress Cataloging-in-Publication Data
Head, Michael, LL. B.
Domestic deployment of the armed forces : military powers, law and human rights / by Michael Head and Scott Mann.
p. cm. -- (International and comparative criminal justice)
Includes bibliographical references and index.
ISBN 978-0-7546-7346-0 (hardback)
1. Military law. 2. Armed Forces--Civic action. 3. Civil-military relations. 4. Internal security. I. Mann, Scott. II. Title.
K4720.H43 2009
343'.0154--dc22

2009016473

ISBN 9780754673460 (hbk)
ISBN 9780754691259 (ebk)

Mixed Sources
Product group from well-managed forests and other controlled sources
www.fsc.org Cert no. SA-COC-1565
© 1996 Forest Stewardship Council
FSC

Printed and bound in Great Britain by
MPG Books Group, UK

Contents

Preface

As this book was being written, between late 2007 and early 2009, it became increasingly apparent that the world was confronting the worst economic breakdown since the Great Depression of the 1930s. We believe that these conditions underscore the concerns raised in this volume. They make more likely the prospect that governments will use military force domestically in response to the economic, social and political tensions that will be generated by the financial crisis.

As young men, our concerns about the use of the armed forces against civilians arose from several experiences, including the Indonesian coup of 1965–66, the Chilean coup of 1972–73, the Vietnam War, and the consignment of British soldiers to Northern Ireland in 1969. More recently, these concerns have been deepened by the global turn to militarism, both internationally and domestically, in the so-called 'war on terror' declared by the United States in 2001. As we explain, far too little public debate has been held on the historical, legal and constitutional implications of this political shift.

Our thanks go to the University of Western Sydney for allowing us the time to research and write this volume. Such work is essential to a university's mission to inform society and generate debate. We are grateful to Ashgate Publishing, particularly Alison Kirk, for supporting and encouraging publication of the book. Our students in Law Foundation over the past few years have also contributed through their interest and comments.

This is a joint work, but Scott Mann was most responsible for Chapters 6 and 7, and Michael Head for the remainder.

As always, the completion of this book would not have been possible without the love, assistance and support of Mary, Tom, Daniel and Kathleen, and Kay, Jocelyn and Claire.

Michael Head and Scott Mann
Sydney
July 2009

Key Terms

Domestic security A vague and expanding term, not generally officially defined, that refers to any perceived concern relating to public safety, critical infrastructure, environmental problems, vital economic interests and political stability.

Domestic violence An undefined official term, which does not refer to violence in the home, but to unspecified violence that, in the United States and Australia, justifies calling out the armed forces. The term is used in s 4 of article IV of the US Constitution and s 119 of the Australian Constitution.

Martial law Regarded as the suspension of law altogether under conditions of emergency. Martial law declarations can authorise far-reaching military powers, even the right to summarily try and execute individuals, in order to put down civil unrest.

Military aid to the civil community The provision of military personnel, equipment and facilities to perform tasks that are primarily the responsibility of civil authorities, but for which the civilian agencies may lack resources. This includes deployment during natural disasters, and for search and rescue operations, disarming explosives, strike-breaking operations, other law enforcement assistance and ceremonial services, where the use of force is not anticipated.

Military aid to the civil power The use of military combat resources to supplement or supplant law enforcement agencies, where the use of force is anticipated.

Posse comitatus The *posse comitatus* principle originally provided for authorities to organise civilian posses, not militia or regular armed forces, for both war and internal law enforcement. The doctrine arose in the Middle Ages, when the King of England or his local representative, the sheriff, could conscript able-bodied free-men into a posse.

Posse Comitatus Act A US Act, first introduced in 1878, declaring it unlawful to employ any part of the federal armed forces as a posse comitatus, or otherwise, for law enforcement, except under such circumstances as may be expressly authorised by the Constitution or by act of Congress.

Reasonable and necessary force Potentially lethal force which called-out armed forces members are generally regarded as having the legal authority to use if they believe on reasonable grounds that the force is necessary to protect life, prevent serious injury or (perhaps) protect designated property.

Rules of Engagement Rules, usually highly-classified, issued by the military to authorise and specify the levels of force to be used by called-out members.

Superior orders A defence that may be available to called-out military personnel who carry out otherwise criminal acts, under an order given by a superior, where the personnel had a legal obligation to obey the order.

Terrorism Definitions vary, but most are broad. Under Australian law, a 'terrorist act' includes anything done 'with the intention of advancing a political, religious or ideological cause' and with the intention of 'coercing, or influencing by intimidation' any government (including a foreign government) or 'intimidating the public or a section of the public', if the act causes death, 'serious harm' to a person, 'serious damage to property', 'serious risk to the health or safety' of a section of the public or 'seriously interferes with' an electronic, information, financial or transport system (Criminal Code 1995 (Cth) 100.1). The definition excludes 'advocacy, protest, dissent or industrial action', but only if the act is not intended to cause physical harm to a person or 'create a serious risk to the health or safety of the public or a section of the public'.

Introduction: Why this Book?

This book raises a number of significant developments that have received inadequate official, academic and media attention, and are little known to the general public. Among the most important are the following:

- There is an international trend toward establishing greater executive or governmental powers to deploy the armed forces for domestic and political purposes.
- This trend includes Germany and Japan, where military or fascist dictatorships dominated before the Second World War.
- In Italy, another country with a fascist past, 2008 and 2009 saw the government place troops on the streets of major cities in the name of combating crime and illegal immigration.
- In two leading countries, the United States and Canada, for the first time in history, separate military commands have been established, specifically tasked with preparing and conducting internal operations.
- Recent years have witnessed the increasing use of the armed forces in domestic settings, from presidential inaugurations to political summits and major sporting events, as well as to repel asylum seekers.
- In a rising number of overseas operations, from Iraq to the Solomon Islands, soldiers have been actively policing civilian populations.
- Powers have been adopted, in the name of combating terrorism, to authorise the calling out of soldiers against civilians, yet the measures taken go far beyond anti-terrorism.
- Troops can be deployed, including during protests and strikes, on vague and undefined grounds, employing terms such as 'security', 'emergency' and 'domestic violence'.
- Executive decisions can be made to call out the armed forces without effective parliamentary scrutiny, constitutional constraint or legal challenge.
- Once soldiers are deployed, they have sweeping powers, which may include authority to use lethal force, shoot down civilian aircraft, issue orders to civilians, interrogate people, raid premises and seize documents.
- These developments accompany the considerable strengthening of the powers and resources of the police, para-military units and intelligence agencies over the past three decades, a process that has accelerated during the 'war on terror' since 2001.
- Calls are being made in political and military circles for domestic security to become a 'core mission' of the defence forces.

These trends raise a number of critical issues, including the strengthening of the power of the state over citizens; the undermining of democratic and legal rights; the erosion of civilian control over the military; and the growing role of what US President Dwight D. Eisenhower called the 'military-industrial complex'.

This book may prove of particular interest to students, scholars and practitioners of law, as well as to military lawyers and experts. However, it is also directed towards general members of the public, in the hope that it might inform and stimulate much-needed debate on these issues.

Economic Turmoil and Militarism

As this book was being written, in 2008 and early 2009, it became widely acknowledged that the world economy had plunged into its deepest and most systemic breakdown since the Great Depression of the 1930s (International Labour Organization 2009, 6). Under these conditions, there were indications of a shift, with the election of the Obama Administration in the United States, to broaden the concept of 'security'. Instead of terrorism, economic and political instability was becoming the primary focus of concern. In February 2009, America's director of national intelligence, retired admiral Dennis Blair, told Congress that the financial crisis, rather than terrorism, was the foremost security threat to the US (Sevastopulo 2009). Commenting on this testimony in a March 2009 address to a national security conference, Australian Federal Police Commissioner Mick Keelty noted:

> This is a major shift in thinking, especially after ten years in which it could be argued that the term 'National Security' was more often than not used as a synonym for 'counter-terrorism'.... This approach means that 'national security' now encompasses a broad range of principles – which include economic stability and a peaceful international environment. (Keelty 2009)

A credit crisis that began in mid-2007 spread throughout the United States and the world financial system. One after another, major finance houses collapsed or had to be bailed out: first Bear Stearns, the fifth largest US investment bank; then Fannie Mae and Freddie Mac, which account for 80 per cent of new mortgages in the US; investment banks Lehman Brothers and Merrill Lynch; American International Group (AIG), the world's largest insurance company; Washington Mutual and many others in the United States and worldwide.

At the beginning of 2009, the International Labour Organization warned that as many as 51 million workers could be laid off during that year, and referred to growing concerns that 'social tensions may begin to rise' (International Labour Organization 2009, 6). Large-scale unemployment was not the only development pointing to the likelihood of social unrest. The crash of 2008 also decimated the net wealth of households that were already under severe financial strain. In the

United States, where some three million homes had been lost to foreclosures by the end of 2008, the housing price decline since its peak was more than twice that registered during the Great Depression (Federal Reserve 2009).

As in the 1930s, this economic turmoil can be expected to generate not only serious social and class tensions, but also political discontent and challenges to the established order. During the Great Depression ushered in by the Wall Street crash of 1929, such tensions triggered social and political convulsions, as well as conflicts, trade wars and wars between rival national powers. In a number of major countries, notably Italy, Germany and Japan (as well as Spain), these developments led to the establishment or entrenchment of military-backed fascist or totalitarian regimes, and ultimately to the Second World War.

For good reason, therefore, this volume reviews the pre-war rise of militarism and dictatorship in Germany, Italy and Japan and draws attention to disturbing signs that the post-Second World War restrictions placed on the military in those countries are being eroded or overturned. At the same time, this book warns against any complacency towards the possibility of similar trends emerging in the Anglo-American countries, where significant shifts in the military's role and doctrine have occurred in the early years of the twenty-first century. The history of these countries, outlined in Chapter 2, also reveals a marked tendency for the ruling establishment to resort to violent force, including the deployment of troops internally, during periods of fundamental challenge to the prevailing socio-economic order. For all these reasons, it is necessary to be constantly on guard against the re-emergence of militarist tendencies. In the famous words of Thomas Jefferson, the principal author of the American Declaration of Independence, 'The price of freedom is eternal vigilance'.

Chapter 1
An International Trend

Mobilising the military for internal use is normally associated with dictatorial regimes, not democratic ones. In the twentieth century, military methods of rule were most commonly associated with names such as Mussolini, Hitler, Franco, Suharto and Pinochet. However, the introduction of enhanced powers to call out the armed forces to deal with domestic disturbances has become an emerging global trend in the opening years of the twenty-first century. There is a clear need for a review and analysis of this trend, including its implications for legal and political rights.

Calling out the armed forces and placing troops on the streets to deal with civil unrest is one of the most drastic and potentially life-threatening actions that a government or other authorities can take against members of society. Such recourse to the ultimate violent power of the state is likely to be a symptom of intense social antagonisms.

Unfortunately, modern history offers many examples of severe repression by governments that have mobilised the military against the population. One need only recall the extermination of up to one million people in Indonesia in 1965–66 following the army coup led by General Suharto, the killing of thousands in Chile in 1972–73 after the coup of General Pinochet, and the murder of thousands by the Chinese regime after the Tiananmen Square uprising of 1989.

It has commonly been assumed that events of this horrific character cannot occur in Western-style democracies. However, the very fact that new measures have been introduced to facilitate the domestic mobilisation of troops suggests that official preparations are being made for possible clashes involving civilians and soldiers.

This book examines the national and international law, human rights and civil liberties issues involved in Western governments calling out troops for domestic purposes. It probes the changes underway in seven comparable countries: the United States, Canada, Britain, Germany, Italy, Japan and Australia. These countries, which could be regarded as advanced industrial and capitalist states, have been selected for several reasons. Four of them derive their political, constitutional and legal doctrines from the English heritage, which is often regarded as an exemplar of democratic traditions, having emerged out of the overturn of the previously autocratic foundations of the British monarchy. These countries are commonly held up as democratic models, contrasted with dictatorial or totalitarian regimes. The other three countries chosen have post-Second World War constitutional arrangements that enshrine measures intended to provide safeguards against the return of the kinds of military-backed fascist or imperial regimes that took hold of these countries before the war.

No attempt has been made in this volume to examine wider global trends, including the resort to outright or thinly-veiled military dictatorships in an array of former colonial or semi-colonial states, such as Pakistan, Burma, Fiji and Mauritania, and the prominent roles played by the armed forces in China, Russia and Vietnam. Instead, the focus is on asking how and to what degree contemporary advanced democracies differ from other states when it comes to having the power to call out troops to suppress internal unrest.

A number of other questions arise. What parallels and differences can be detected in the developments in the two groups of selected countries since the turn of the century? Can an overall pattern be identified in either group or indeed between all the countries? If so, what are the causes?

There is reason for concern that in both groups of countries the 'war on terror' has been conditioning public opinion to accept the internal deployment of the armed forces, including for broader industrial and political purposes. The turn to militarism abroad, seen in the US-led invasions of Afghanistan and Iraq, has been accompanied by a tendency toward the militarisation of domestic life as well.

In the United States, the Bush administration of 2001–2009 initiated reviews of the *Posse Comitatus Act*, which restricts domestic use of the military. Likewise, a Defence Policy review was undertaken in Canada to make domestic security a core business of the Canadian Forces. The British *Civil Contingencies Act 2004* empowered the government to deploy defence forces in broadly-defined 'emergencies'. In Australia, the Sydney Olympic Games in 2000 provided the initial rationale for legislation giving the federal government explicit and expanded powers to call out troops to deal with 'domestic violence'.

Over the same period, the German government has sought legal means to overcome the post-war constitutional restrictions on internal military operations, while the Japanese government has foreshadowed moves to remove the pacifist clause of Japan's post-war constitution. In Italy, the government deployed soldiers on the streets in 2008, purportedly to fight crime and deal with illegal immigrants. These developments in these three countries are of particular significance because of their pre-Second World War experiences under fascist or military dictatorships.

Little academic attention has been paid to this trend and no existing book examines it on an international scale. The issues raised were last canvassed, in relation to the United States and the UK, more than two decades ago in Rowe and Whelan's *Military Intervention in Democratic Societies* (Rowe and Whelan 1985).

This new volume provides an outline of the many and various constitutional and legal issues involved in calling out the armed forces, for example: (a) blurring the line between police and military functions; (b) giving soldiers 'shoot to kill' and other military-style powers on domestic soil; (c) challenging the separation of powers between the executive, legislature and judiciary; (d) overcoming federal–state–local divisions of responsibility; (e) affording legal immunities and 'lawful orders' defences to military personnel; and (f) overcoming the post-Second World War 'pacifist' clauses.

We also examine the 'war on terror' declared by the US government and its allies since 2001, which has provided the primary official rationale for these provisions. That is, in the main, these changes have been brought forward on the pretext of protecting the public from terrorism or political violence. But is that pretext credible? What exactly is the 'war on terror' and how has it been defined? Are its measures, including the military powers, temporary or do they have long-term implications?

Military call-out powers have been expanded in addition to substantial extensions in the size, sophistication and weaponry of police, para-military and intelligence agencies. These extensions began well before 2001, but have also accelerated since then. Thus, while a creeping militarisation of society and law enforcement has taken place, this process has been accompanied by the boosting and arming of the civilian state apparatus. Although the focus of this book is not on those parallel police and intelligence developments, none of our analysis should be read as an argument for supporting the continuing bolstering of the civilian arm of the state as an alternative to military intervention.

On the contrary, the simultaneous strengthening of the military and civilian 'domestic security' forces deepens the basic issues raised here. Why are all the state powers being intensified? Why are increasingly police-state measures being adopted, ultimately backed by the military option? It seems that despite the proliferation of heavily-armed civilian policing agencies, backed by extensive surveillance forces and technologies, the powers-that-be are anticipating civil disorders or unrest that these agencies cannot control without calling in the armed forces. This dual expansion of the armed force available to the political establishment makes all the more necessary the task of probing the underlying politico-legal implications and socio-economic pressures.

The significance of these issues can be fully assessed only by reviewing the historical record, including the struggles that established the principles of military non-intervention in domestic affairs and civilian control over the armed forces. Among the historical experiences examined in this book are:

- The origins of the traditional taboo on domestic deployment, arguably dating back to the Magna Carta of 1215 and the seventeenth-century struggles against the absolutist monarchy in Britain.
- The early British experiences and the later troubles in Northern Ireland: from the Bristol and Featherstone riots to Northern Ireland, where between 1969 and 1993, the military killed 297 people, often in disputed circumstances.
- The aftermath of the American Revolution and Civil War: the roots of the 'traditional and strong resistance of Americans to any military intrusion into civilian affairs' (*Laird v Tatum*, 408 U.S. 1, 15).
- The lessons of pre-war and post-war Germany and Japan: the internal use of military forces by the Nazi and Japanese imperial regimes; the adoption of post-war constitutional protections.

- Australia's evolution from a military colony to civil society, including the use of martial law and other military powers to suppress convicts, Aborigines and workers, and the deployment of the military for industrial and political purposes in the twentieth century.

Having examined these historical experiences we review the developments in each country in more detail and conclude by canvassing the underlying political and legal issues. What are the legal and democratic implications? How can the use of military powers be subjected to public scrutiny and legal restraints? What lies behind the global trend? What role is played by militarism, counter-terrorism, social polarisation and political instability? What are the reasons for concern, in terms of human rights, civil liberties, rule of law, civilian control of society?

Overview: The International Trend

Italy

Perhaps the most striking development in the early years of the twenty-first century was the 2008 decision of the Italian government to deploy 3,000 troops domestically, ostensibly to crackdown on illegal immigrants and make Italy's cities safer. Following a six-month trial, the government foreshadowed a second phase involving up to 30,000 soldiers.

In mid-2008, the government headed by Prime Minister Silvio Berlusconi proclaimed a state of emergency due to the inflow of refugees by boat across the Mediterranean Sea, and the Defence Minister signed a decree to permit the use of 3,000 troops for domestic purposes. One thousand troops were to be deployed at refugee internment camps, officially called 'identification and classification centres', and another 1,000 at sensitive public places (train stations, embassies, St Peter's Cathedral, and so on), with the remainder assigned to patrol streets in Rome and other major cities, alongside police officers. Armed troops, some in body armour and with automatic weapons, appeared on the streets. Some of the troops had previously served in Afghanistan, Iraq or Lebanon (Michaels 2008; Dinmore 2008).

There was widespread scepticism, both internationally and domestically, in the government's motives, given that crime rates had fallen in Italy and the country already had 230,000 police and *carabinieri*. Media commentators accused the government of seeking to shift focus away from the country's sagging economy. The military deployment was not unprecedented – some 20,000 troops were sent to Sicily in 1992 to combat the Mafia, and soldiers were often seen in Italian cities during the Red Brigades' attacks in the 1970s and 1980s. Nevertheless, the emergency measures were reminiscent of Mussolini's pre-Second World War fascist dictatorship (*Economist* 2008; Arens 2008).

Whereas in the 1930s Jews became scapegoats for fascists, there were signs that gypsies and other immigrants were being demonised as economic and social conditions deteriorated in 2008 and 2009. In early 2009, amid a media campaign against an alleged crime wave involving an influx of Eastern European gypsies, Prime Minister Berlusconi said 30,000 troops would be put on the streets to fight crime. There were also allegations that military units had been deployed to make arrests and break up illegally-erected shacks in Rome (Dinmore and Bianchi 2009).

United States

The September 2001 attacks have provided the pretext for significant changes to the military–civil relationship in the United States. Recent years have seen the establishment of the Northern Command – a Pentagon command dedicated solely to domestic security – the staging of internal war game exercises and the deployment of federal troops for major political events, including the 2008 Democratic and Republican national conventions and the 2009 inauguration of President Obama.

In 2006, President George W. Bush signed into law the *Department of Defense Authorization Act for Fiscal Year 2007*, which substantially eroded the *Posse Comitatus Act*, a longstanding Congressional prohibition on the use of the military for domestic policing. The 2007 legislation amended the *Insurrection Act* to permit the President to 'employ the armed forces … to restore public order and enforce the laws of the United States' in the event not just of 'insurrection, domestic violence, unlawful combination or conspiracy', but also 'natural disaster, epidemic, or other serious public health emergency, terrorist attack or incident, or other condition', where civilian authorities are 'incapable of maintaining public order' and such violence 'opposes or obstructs the execution of the laws of the United States' (10 U.S.C. § 333). The latter phrase could cover many forms of political dissent or industrial disruption.

Following considerable opposition, the 2007 amendment was repealed by the *National Defense Authorization Act for Fiscal Year 2008*. However, the repeal was accompanied by measures to upgrade the status of the National Guard Bureau and strengthen the relationship between it and the Northern Command (Leahy 2008). Another measure adopted in 2007, the National Security and Homeland Security Presidential Directive, permits the President to declare an emergency, which would establish extraordinary powers for the president and vice-president, creating a non-constitutional form of government (US NSPD 2007).

The *Washington Post* reported in 2005 that the Pentagon had developed its first ever war plans for operations within the continental United States, in which terrorist attacks would be used as the justification for imposing martial law on cities, regions or the entire country. A total of 15 potential crisis scenarios were outlined, starting with 'low-end', which the report described as 'relatively modest crowd-control missions', in which the military would deploy a quick-reaction force of as many as 3,000 troops. The *Post* said military lawyers had studied the legal implications of such deployments, which risked coming into conflict with the *Posse Comitatus Act* (*Guardian* 2005).

Canada

The Canadian government has been undertaking a major campaign to elevate the role and visibility of the Canadian military, both abroad and at home. While sending thousands of troops to bolster the NATO-led occupation of Afghanistan, it has heralded a re-definition of the mission of the Canadian Forces. The 2008 national defence strategy committed Canada to a major expansion of the armed forces and asserted: 'Canadians rightly expect their military to be there for them in domestic crises' (Department of National Defence, Canada 2008).

The Defence Policy Statement, *A Role of Pride and Influence in the World*, issued in 2006, first announced a shift in Canadian policy, which would mean making domestic security the primary focus of the Canadian Forces:

> To better protect Canada and Canadians, the Canadian Forces will be reorganized to more effectively and quickly respond to domestic crises, as well as support other Government departments as required. (Department of National Defence, Canada 2006)

Also in 2006, the Canada Command was established to focus on domestic operations, mirroring the US Northern Command, and in 2008, the commanders of the Canada Command and the Northern Command signed a Civil Assistance Plan that allows the military from one nation to support the armed forces of the other during a 'civil emergency' (US Northern Command 2008).

Despite Canada's relatively pacifist image, large-scale Canadian 'aid to civil power' operations have occurred four times in the past four decades: the Front de Liberation du Quebec (FLQ) crisis (1963–70), the 1976 Olympic Games, the Oka standoff (1990) and disaster relief in Manitoba (1997) (Maloney 1997).

Britain

2004 saw the adoption of legislation that potentially expands the scope for domestic military intervention, in the name of responding to emergencies. The *Civil Contingencies Act 2004* replaced the Emergency Powers and Civil Defence legislation (Walker and Broderick 2006). It empowers 'Her Majesty' via an Order in Council to issue sweeping emergency regulations in any event that 'threatens serious damage to human welfare' or 'war or terrorism, which threatens serious damage to the security of the United Kingdom'. These regulations can, *inter alia*, 'enable the Defence Council to authorise the deployment of Her Majesty's armed forces'. The powers can be triggered whenever the governing authorities, namely Her Majesty in Council, are 'satisfied' that an emergency has occurred, is occurring or is about to occur. The regulations can even suspend, modify or override any other Act of Parliament, with the sole exception of the *Human Rights Act* (Walker and Broderick 2006, 63–80, 153–88).

During the debate on the *Civil Contingencies Act*, the government rejected proposals to clarify by statute the military's role. The government argued that a case-by-case approach was needed, and that the government was already sufficiently accountable to parliament (Walker and Broderick 2006, 44–5). The end result is that ill-defined and extensive prerogative and common law powers to call out the armed forces continue to exist, augmented by the 2004 legislation.

Australia

In Australia, legislation was introduced in 2000, and extended in 2006, giving federal governments and the chief of the Australian Defence Force (ADF) explicit peacetime powers to call out the troops if 'domestic violence is occurring or is likely to occur' that 'would be likely to affect Commonwealth interests' or require the protection of a state or territory (*Defence Act 1903* (Cth) ss. 51A–51Y).

The turn toward the wider domestic engagement of the ADF began before 11 September 2001 and the 'war on terror'. The Sydney Olympic Games in 2000 provided the initial rationale for call-out legislation. Both major parties cited the danger of a terrorist incident at the Games to justify the swift passage of the legislation, also without any significant public or parliamentary debate. Six years later, the Melbourne Commonwealth Games became the pretext for the 2006 amendments. No specific terrorist threats were reported to either event and no terrorist acts occurred. Nonetheless, the new powers have remained, without any sunset clauses.

Since the 9/11 terrorist attacks, the declaration of a 'war on terror' and the wars in Afghanistan and Iraq, aspects of Australian society have been increasingly militarised. Thousands of soldiers have been mobilised, on alert, for major sporting events such as the Sydney 2000 Olympic Games, the Rugby World Cup 2003 and the Melbourne 2006 Commonwealth Games (Bergin and Smith 2006, 10). Naval vessels have been dispatched to repel asylum seekers, with powers to fire on boats or transport their passengers to remote islands (Head 2002; Laing 2005, 518–20). Frequent anti-terrorism exercises have been conducted in urban environments, involving heavily-armed troops alongside police and intelligence officers (National Security Australia, National Counter-Terrorism Committee 2003, 95). Deployments have been conducted against civilian populations in Afghanistan, Iraq, Solomon Islands and East Timor (Head 2005, 484–92). The armed forces have been used in highly-publicised shows of strength, including air force jets and helicopters flying overhead during major political events such as the 2002 Commonwealth Heads of Government Meeting at Coolum, Queensland and US President Bush's visit to Australia in 2003 (Bergin and Smith 2006, 10).

Germany

In Germany, like Australia, alleged terrorist threats to major sporting events have been used to attempt to make historic shifts in the relationship between the military and civil society, giving rise to serious constitutional and legal issues. Government ministers and other prominent politicians urged deployment of the German army during the 2006 World Cup football finals, despite the existence of a special police unit capable of dealing with terrorist attacks – the GSG9, established after 11 Israeli athletes were kidnapped during the 1972 Olympic Games in Munich.

In 2006, Germany's highest court declared unconstitutional a law that would have allowed the government to order the shooting down of planes hijacked by terrorists (German Constitutional Court 2006). The Constitutional Court's decision did not end the debate, however. In 2007, the Defence Minister publicly stated that a hijacked plane would be shot down, notwithstanding the court's ruling. The Minister sought to justify such action under the suprastatutory state of emergency (Hufnagel 2008, 109–10). Similar appeals to states of exception characterised German jurisprudence under the Nazi regime (Agamben 2005).

Japan

Since the declaration of the 'war on terror', Japanese governments have moved to erode the so-called pacifist provisions of the post-Second World War constitution. These developments have both international and domestic implications. In 2004, the Koizumi government ordered a deployment of troops to Iraq at the request of the United States. This controversial deployment marked a significant turning point in Japan's history as it was the first time since the end of the Second World War that Japan had sent troops to a war zone, except for minor UN peacekeeping deployments.

Japan's government is preparing for a referendum in 2010 to change the 'pacifist clause' – Article 9 of the Constitution – which declares that Japan will never again maintain 'land, sea, or air forces or other war potential'. The constitutional revision will refer to the Self-Defense Force as a military force for the first time since its establishment. Other changes have involved creating a cabinet-level Defense Ministry.

Domestically, anti-terrorism and emergency laws were adopted in 2002 and 2003. For the first time since the Second World War, emergency provisions allowed for the suspension of basic rights when military attacks or other emergencies occurred or were expected to occur (Sugita 2002).

A shift in the military's role, both internationally and domestically, was outlined in the inaugural 2007 speech by the first Defense Minister, Fumio Kyuma:

> In recent years, the missions of the Self-Defense Forces have been not only the defense of our nation, but its missions have expanded into response to disasters

> inside and outside Japan, international peace cooperation and more. (Japan Ministry of Defense 2007)

These remarks pointed to a concerted effort to engage Japanese military personnel in extensive overseas operations, often in civilian areas, under the banner of peacekeeping, while further acclimatising domestic public opinion to widespread use of the Self-Defense Force internally in the form of disaster relief missions.

The Context: The 'War on Terror', Militarism and Rising Social Tensions

The international character of the shift toward using the armed forces for domestic security makes it all the more important to examine critically the rationale and content of the measures. Moreover, the internal changes have been accompanied in each instance by expansions of the armed forces for external interventions, in the context of a turn to militarism by the United States and its allies, most notably in the Middle East.

In the opening years of the twenty-first century, a number of governments have used the threat of terrorism as a pretext to erode such vital principles as free speech, freedom of political association, prevention of arbitrary detention and the right to seek asylum. These measures have profound implications for civil liberties, as well as for the future of international covenants, such as the International Covenant on Civil and Political Rights. These global human rights instruments have proved largely irrelevant in curbing such powers.

Governments in many countries followed the lead of the Bush administration in the United States by declaring that the 11 September 2001 terrorist attacks required an indefinite 'war' against terrorism abroad, accompanied by the curtailment of legal rights at home. Despite criticism by civil liberties groups, governments introduced severe anti-terrorism measures, including detention without trial and proscription of organisations (for a comparison of the United States and British legislation see Hancock 2002, 2–8). Amnesty International condemned the Bush administration, for example, for breaching the International Covenant on Civil and Political Rights and other international protocols against arbitrary detention and inhuman treatment of prisoners (Amnesty International 2002).

While the 'war on terror' has provided the common justification for both the domestic and overseas militarisation of policy, there are reasons to conclude that the roots of the militarising trend lie deeper in growing socio-economic and geo-political tensions. As mentioned in the Introduction, and examined further in Chapter 10, we have once again entered a period of history that is marked by economic breakdown, social inequality and great power rivalries.

It should be noted that the justifications offered for greater military intervention in domestic affairs go well beyond terrorism. They include 'fighting crime', repelling or detaining asylum seekers and dealing with 'emergencies'. For example, a 2008 'Strategic Insight' published by the Australian Strategic Policy Institute called for the Rudd government to consider making disaster response a 'core business' of the Australian Defence Force (Templeman and Bergin 2008, 12).

Some scholars have argued that concerns about the elevated role of the military in society are exaggerated or even unwarranted because one must trust elected governments to use the military for legitimate purposes only. For example, Norman Laing, an Australian barrister with military experience has suggested that calling out the Australian Defence Force would not be 'the end of civilisation' because 'the ADF will only ever be deployed for a legitimate purpose' and 'one must have faith in those elected representatives to undertake such a responsibility' (Laing 2005, 521). Ironically, Laing's article began by recalling the protests against the Vietnam War and President Richard Nixon's invasion of Cambodia, and the use of the Ohio National Guard to shoot down four innocent students at Kent State University in 1970 (Laing 2005, 507–8).

Laing said there was concern in 2000, when the initial military call-out legislation was brought forward, that the ADF would be deployed onto Australian streets to disperse such protestors if they too caused serious civil disturbance. However, the author argued that this 'fear and paranoia' subsided over the following four years because: 'The current climate of terror has created an overriding and shifting attitude towards the ADF being called out' (Laing 2005, 509). This line of reasoning underscores the concern that Australian governments, with bipartisan support, have promoted and utilised 'the current climate of terror' to overcome public opposition to the deployment of the ADF on the streets.

Is it safe simply to say 'one must have faith' in elected governments? The opening years of the twenty-first century have already seen troops dispatched to invade a country and put down domestic resistance – in Iraq – on the basis of information supplied by intelligence agencies, security services and government leaders that was subsequently acknowledged to have been false. After the collapse of the falsifications used to justify the US-led invasion – 'weapons of mass destruction', 'nuclear stockpiles' and Saddam Hussein's supposed links to terrorism – one is entitled, perhaps even obliged, to approach the entire 'war on terror' with considerable scepticism.

Moreover, a 'war' of indefinite duration has been declared on vaguely defined 'enemies' whose only identifiable characteristic is that they pursue a certain set of tactics: acts of individual violence that can attract an array of disoriented and disaffected political, religious and ethnic currents. It is beyond the scope of this book to investigate the root causes of terrorism, but it must be said that the label is notoriously open to political dispute and abuse. After all, today's primary 'terrorist' targets – Al Qaeda-linked groups – were yesterday's 'freedom fighters' in the guerrilla war against the Soviet-backed regime in Afghanistan (Blum 2002, 155). Likewise, Saddam Hussein was once a close ally of Washington, particularly during the fratricidal Iran–Iraq war of the 1980s (Blum 2002, 133–4, 145–6).

The 11 September 2001 outrages in New York and Washington were reprehensible but there is ample evidence that they provided the pretext for the implementation of plans prepared in certain Washington political circles much earlier – during the 1990s – for the conquest of Afghanistan and Iraq (Bacevich 2002). The Middle East and Central Asia, as is well known, contain the largest proven concentrations of oil and natural gas reserves in the world. For all their claims to be exporting democracy to the Middle East, Washington and its allies have for decades financially, diplomatically and militarily supported dictatorial regimes like the Saudi monarchy and the Gulf kingdoms (and previously the Shah of Iran), in the interests of dominating the resource-rich and strategically critical region (Shalom 1993, 63–88). The latest US-led interventions in the region, followed by the establishment of US military bases throughout Central Asia, have added weight to the evidence that Washington's underlying ambition is to secure hegemony over this entire vital expanse.

Domestically, there is no more reason to believe that the same US-allied governments are primarily motivated simply by the need to protect ordinary people from terrorism. On the face of it, none of the new powers were necessary to protect ordinary people against terrorism. In most jurisdictions, any conceivable terrorist activity, such as murder, bombing, hijacking, kidnapping and arson, was already a serious crime under existing law. Moreover, the police and intelligence services hardly needed new powers to detect terrorists. They already had powers to tap phones, install listening devices in offices and homes, intercept telecommunications, open people's mail, monitor on-line discussion, break into computer files and databases, seize computers and use personal tracking devices (for details see Head 2002b).

The official rationale for the anti-terrorism measures asserts that the 'war on terrorism' requires a 'new framework' for considering civil liberties and the rule of law. For instance, in 2004, Australian Attorney-General Philip Ruddock stated:

> The war on terror is like no other war in living memory. This is a war which may have no obvious conclusion, no armistice and no treaty. Victory in this war will not necessarily be measured by territory gained or regimes toppled. In this war victories will be measured by disasters averted and democracy strengthened. This war's victories will be measured by citizens feeling safe in their homes. This war's victories will be measured in the steadfastness and resolve of Australians to be cognisant of, but not to fear, a potential terrorist threat …
>
> Our Constitution, one of the world's oldest and most stable, provides us with a mechanism to protect our country and at the same time protect civil liberties through human security laws. In enacting such laws we are not only preserving traditional notions of civil liberties and the rule of law, but we are recognising that these operate in a different paradigm. If we are to preserve human rights then we must preserve the most fundamental right of all – the right to human security. (Ruddock 2004)

While insisting that the government was upholding the Constitution, civil liberties and the rule of law, the minister asserted that these now operate in a new paradigm: the right to human security, which is said to be the most fundamental right of all.

Ruddock loosely defined 'human security' as encompassing human rights, good governance, access to education and health care and opportunities for individuals to fulfil their potential. All these, the minister asserted, depended upon a secure environment. Thus, in the name of defending civil liberties and the rule of law, they are said to no longer have any independent or absolute existence. Instead, they have been subsumed under another concept, human security. Making 'citizens feel safe in their homes' has become the chief criterion for the unknown duration of the current 'state of war'.

Despite the sweeping breadth of such claims, much of the debate and analysis in academic publications concerning the 'anti-terrorism' legislation begins with the proposition that a balance must be struck between 'national security' and 'civil liberties'. According to this approach, the only disagreement concerns where the balance should lie. By this measure, some inroads into civil liberties must be accepted. There is good cause to question this assumption, however.

For powerful historical reasons, fundamental democratic rights should be regarded as absolute. They embody centuries of deep-going political struggles. In British law, civil liberties – such as habeas corpus, the presumption of innocence, the requirement of proof beyond reasonable doubt for a criminal conviction, freedom of association and free speech – were substantially forged in the conflict against the absolutist monarchy, from the Magna Carta of 1215 and culminating in the English Civil War of the 1640s and the so-called Glorious Revolution of 1688. Among these fundamental rights is freedom from detention without trial, as the US Supreme Court, by a six to three majority, commented in June 2004, in ruling that Guantanamo Bay detainees, including two Australians, David Hicks and Mamdouh Habib, could seek writs of habeas corpus in US courts. The majority judgment, delivered by Justice Stevens, suggested that at stake were democratic conceptions dating back nearly 800 years to the Magna Carta of 1215:

> Executive imprisonment has been considered oppressive and lawless since John, at Runnymede, pledged that no free man should be imprisoned, dispossessed, outlawed, or exiled save by the judgment of his peers or by the law of the land. The judges of England developed the writ of habeas corpus largely to preserve these immunities from executive restraint. (*Rasul v Bush*; *Al Odah v United States* (2004) 542 U.S. (Cases no. 03-343, 03-334) quoting Jackson J in *Shaughnessy v United States ex rel. Mezei*, 345 U.S. 206, 218–219 (1953) (dissenting opinion))

Likewise, as explored in Chapter 2, the right of citizens to live free of military intervention in society, especially in civilian political affairs, has been fought for through centuries of conflict against absolutism, dating back at least to 1215. Justice Douglas of the US Supreme Court referred to this historical record in the 1952 Youngstown case, when he stated 'our history and tradition rebel at the thought that the grant of military power carries with it authority over civilian affairs' (*Youngstown Sheet and Tube Co. v Sawyer*, 343 U.S. 579 at 632). Today, it will be argued in this volume, it is necessary to go further and state unequivocally: Genuine democracy is impossible, and freedom of political opinion and communication a chimera, unless members of society are free from the fear of the mobilisation of the armed forces against dissent and discontent.

Chapter 2
The Troubled Historical Record

In societies with a British background, there is a political and legal principle opposing the use of the military to suppress domestic unrest – an objection that dates back to the Magna Carta of 1215, and was reestablished or reinforced by the seventeenth-century struggles against the absolutist monarchy in England. Moreover, the principle is lodged in deeply felt public sentiment, based on accumulated historical experience.

According to a number of studies, King John's pledge in Chapter 39 of the 1215 charter that no free man would be taken, imprisoned or destroyed except by the 'law of the land' had been demanded at Runnymede specifically because the King had enforced his will by military means instead of civilian processes. Chapter 39 was invoked in 1327 against Edward II's resort to force by knights in arms (Engdahl 1985, 5).

Nevertheless, the Tudors and early Stuarts reasserted a royal prerogative to use 'martial law' against their subjects in times of supposed necessity, including to suspend or supersede the ordinary law, inflict summary punishments and suppress civil disorders by military force. These practices provoked parliament to draw up the 1628 *Petition of Right*, which declared them contrary to the law of the realm, and, in particular, the Magna Carta (Engdahl 1985, 6). The *Petition* demanded that Charles I remove the 'great companies of soldiers and mariners [who] have been dispersed into diverse counties of the realm … against the laws and customs of this realm and to the great grievance and vexation of the people'. The *Petition* is regarded as making it unconstitutional for the Crown to impose martial law on civilians, at least by way of the old prerogative claim (Holdsworth 1902).

Charles I's continued claim to prerogative use of troops helped precipitate the English Revolution and civil war in 1642. As a result of the 1688–89 settlement between the monarchy and the parliament, the *Bill of Rights* declared it illegal for the Crown to suspend laws, or raise or keep an army without parliamentary consent (Greer 1983, 580). More generally, after the 'Glorious Revolution' of 1688–89, military force was seen as a grave threat to civil government, and its subordination to civilian rule was established as a 'constitutional priority' (Greer 1983, 592). The *Riot Act 1714* called for civilian officials and posses (the posse comitatus) to disperse mobs and put down civil unrest, and authorised civilian personnel to use any force necessary to do so, but made no provision for the use of military force. A different act passed the same year authorised the use of militia, but only to deal with 'insurrection' or 'rebellion' as well as 'invasion' (Engdahl 1985, 6–7).

However, subsequent British history demonstrated a recurring resort to military force in every period in which the political establishment felt seriously threatened by any mass political or industrial movement.

English Riots and Strikes

During the late eighteenth and early nineteenth centuries, the emergence of protests fuelled by the conditions of the Industrial Revolution and the growth of the working class frequently caused the British authorities to resort to the military as riot controllers (Greer 1983, 581). Magistrates called for military assistance with increasing regularity, and in 1732 the Secretary of War informed the Attorney General that such requests were always granted. The author Henry Fielding, who was principal magistrate at London's Bow Street from 1748 to 1754, described the *Riot Act* as 'the most necessary of all our laws for the preservation and protection of the people' because the English 'mob' had established itself as the Fourth Estate of the realm. The magistrate 'alone with the soldier barred the way of the riotous mob' (Babington 1990, 7, 11).

During the second half of the eighteenth century, soldiers killed hundreds of rioters as industrial disputes, anti-machinery protests and food riots spread. As a result, 'mistrust of the military when employed in assisting the civil authorities was endemic throughout the country' (Babington 1990, 12–18, 36). By the late eighteenth century, the use of military force had caused such popular discontent that the Secretary at War warned magistrates against too readily calling out troops:

> Frequent use of soldiers to suppress civil commotions has an evident tendency to introduce military government, than which there cannot be a more horrible Evil in a State. (Greer 1983, 592)

Nonetheless, in effect, successive governments, with the eventual acquiescence of parliament, relaxed the principle that the Secretary at War should approve any troop call-out by a magistrate. As a result of the rising civil unrest, the courts elaborated a common law right and duty of magistrates to opt for military intervention. In a series of statements in his dual role as a judge and parliamentarian toward the end of the eighteenth century, Lord Mansfield resurrected the feudal posse comitatus doctrine, which had been effectively extinguished in the seventeenth century. Posse comitatus arose in the Middle Ages, when both law enforcement, including the suppression of riots, and the waging of war was conducted by the king or his local representative, the sheriff, conscripting able-bodied free-men into a posse (Greer 1983, 578–81). Lord Mansfield insisted that this disused power could be resumed by local magistrates and justices of the peace. The principle, however, was effectively transformed from one of mobilisation of civilian volunteers to one of military deployment – the original posse comitatus doctrine was premised upon civilian posses, not militia or regular armed forces.

In 1781, the chief London magistrate, Brackley Kennett, was charged with criminal breach of duty for refusing to read the *Riot Act* and order military intervention to put down the Gordon Riots. For several days, anti-Catholic protesters, after being turned away from parliament, had confronted authorities, burning down buildings (including Mansfield's house). Eventually, the King convened the Privy Council, which issued an order for the armed forces to act without waiting for magistrates. Some 15,000 troops moved into London and, as a result, an estimated 285 rioters were killed (Babington 1990, 21–31). For his reluctance to call in the troops, Kennett was convicted and fined £1,000. Lord Mansfield instructed the jury:

> The common law and several statutes have invested justices of the peace with great powers to quell riots, because, if not suppressed, they tend to endanger the constitution of the country; and as they may assemble all the King's subjects, it is clear they may call in the soldiers, who are subjects and may act as such; but this should be done with great caution. (Greer 1983, 582)

Responding to those who denounced this doctrine as reminiscent of the 'martial law' prerogative claimed by the Tudors and Stuarts, Mansfield sought to distinguish between the use of troops in a military capacity and their roles as citizens, in the nature of the posse comitatus:

> The persons who assisted in the suppression of these tumults are to be considered mere private individuals acting as duty required … The King's extraordinary prerogative to proclaim martial law (whatever that may be) is clearly out of the question … The military have been called in – and very wisely called in – not as soldiers, but as civilians. (Engdahl 1985, 11, citing Cobbett (ed.))

Despite this distinction, which insisted that called-out soldiers were not above the law of the land, the Mansfield doctrine, as it became known, provided little protection for ordinary people against military violence, as the 285 deaths in London indicate.

One of the most notorious mobilisations of the military against civilian protesters was the Peterloo Massacre of 1819. Cavalry troops charged into a crowd of 60,000–80,000 people gathered at St Peter's Field, Manchester for a public meeting, which had been declared illegal, to demand parliamentary representation. Shortly after the meeting began, local magistrates called on the military to arrest the speakers on the platform and to disperse the crowd. Mounted soldiers charged into the crowd with sabres drawn, killing 15 people and injuring 400–700, including women and children (Reid 1989). Whereas the arrested speakers were charged with sedition, found guilty and jailed, a test case against four members of the armed forces ended in acquittal, because the court ruled that their actions had been justified to disperse an illegal gathering (Reid 1989, 204). Nine days after the massacre, the Home Secretary, Lord Sidmouth, conveyed to the magistrates the thanks of the Prince Regent for their action in 'preservation of the public peace' (Farrer and Brownbill 2003; Babington 1990, 46–58).

Citing a range of sources and authorities, one scholar noted the alacrity with which both the parliament and the judiciary were prepared to cast aside the constitutional principle against military intervention in the face of rising social unrest, which reached new heights during the Chartist movement for voting and other basic rights.

> [I]t is debatable whether the eventual acquiescence of Parliament in the 'Mansfield doctrine' constituted sufficient authorisation for the valid revival of the magistrates' common law duty. The judiciary, however, refused to consider the constitutional dimension and blithely built upon the *posse comitatus* principle without regard to its shaky foundations. Civil libertarian reservations about the increasing use of the army in riots seem to have been overwhelmed by the general establishment view that what was good for the maintenance of public order was desirable and, therefore, legal. The fear of disorder had by this stage largely replaced the spectre of military intervention in civil affairs as the *bete noir* of the status quo. (Greer 1983, 583)

Following the defeat of the 1831 parliamentary reform bill, riots broke out in Bristol. Soldiers dispersed the rioters, killing 12 people and wounding about a hundred (Babington 1990, 75–84). These riots gave rise to the last English case in which calling out the troops was directly examined. In *R v Pinney* ((1832) 5 Car & P 254; 170 ER 962) the mayor of Bristol and nine aldermen were prosecuted by the Attorney-General for breaching their common law duty to assemble a sufficient force to put down three days of riots, during which thousands of people, some allegedly armed with 'iron bars, iron crows, pickaxes, hammers, pieces of wood, and bludgeons' broke open a jail and forced the release of prisoners. A military major advised the mayor that it would be 'imprudent to put arms in the hands of young troops'. The jury found the defendants not guilty.

The law report of *R v Pinney* also records Tindal LCJ's *Charge to the Bristol Grand Jury* after the riots. Lord Tindal insisted that soldiers had a duty, as citizens, on their own authority, to do their utmost to 'put down riot and tumult'. Two officers who had refused to order the troops to fire without a magistrate's sanction were found guilty of neglect of duty, causing one to commit suicide. The third officer, who had fatally shot a boy during an incident, was acquitted of manslaughter. Lord Tindal instructed the Grand Jury that if the shot was 'discharged in the fair and honest execution of his duty, in endeavouring to disperse the mob', the killing was justified and amounted to accidental death only (170 ER 962, 969; Babington 1990, 84).

During this period, social tensions were so acute that it was widely recognised that summoning military personnel could inflame rather than subdue disturbances. Commentators were aware that the appearance of uniforms could provoke the crowd to further violence, especially since certain military units, for example the yeomanry, were identified with the propertied classes against whom the riots in this era were generally directed. The opposite could also, ironically, be the case. Other army units often identified with, and on occasion even joined, the rioters (Greer 1983, 585).

These considerations, which were also bound up with the development of industrialised society and the emergence of a large working class, fed into the creation of a modern police force, dating from Sir Robert Peel's *Metropolitan Police Act 1829*. The establishment of police forces, first in London and then in other centres, also initially met with great public hostility (Babington 1990, 59–84), Although the primacy of the police for enforcing public order gradually became established, the army continued to play a significant role, particularly in putting down protests demanding the right to vote. The rise of the Chartist movement led to the creation of police forces across the country, but between 1834 and 1848 armed militia were still called out frequently (Babington 1990, 100). In 1839, for instance, troops opened fire in Newport, Wales, killing at least 22 people (Babington 1990, 104–5).

As late as 1888, the Secretary of State for War listed 'the effective support of the civil power in all parts of the United Kingdom' as the principal duty of the British army. Another episode that illustrated the continuing power of magistrates to call out the troops without reference to the Home Office was the Featherstone Colliery Riots of September 1893. Four people, including two bystanders, were killed when an infantry captain ordered soldiers to fire on striking coal miners and their supporters after a local magistrate had read the proclamation from the *Riot Act 1714*. The 1893 *Report of the Select Committee on the Featherstone Riots* exonerated the captain and his troops, saying 'The necessary prevention of such outrage on person and property justifies the guardians of the peace in the employment against a riotous crowd of even deadly weapons' (Whelan 1985, 272). However, the committee warned that 'officers and soldiers are under no special privileges and subject to no special responsibilities as regards this principle of the law'. The taking of life must be shown to be necessary and resort to military assistance must be the 'last expedient' of the civil authorities, but when such a call was made, it was stated, 'to refuse such assistance is in law a misdemeanour' (United Kingdom Parliamentary Papers 1893, 381; Babington 1990, 122–32).

From the beginning of the twentieth century, the creation of larger police forces meant that troops were deployed less frequently to control riots. Nevertheless, military interventions continued to occur, and so did fatalities. In mid-1906, a detachment of infantry was sent to patrol the Belfast docks to protect strike-breakers. After a mutiny in police ranks in sympathy with the strikers, soldiers patrolled city streets throughout the summer and opened fire on a pro-strike rally, killing two people and wounding at least five (Babington 1990, 133–4).

A parliamentary select committee in 1908 was told that during the previous 30 years, the military had been called out on 24 separate occasions in England and Wales (Babington 1990, 135; Jeffery 1985, 52). While insisting that the power to call out the troops must continue, the committee recommended that police forces should be 'so organised and administered as to obviate to the utmost possible extent any necessity for resorting to military aid' (Jeffery 1985, 53).

Even so, in 1910 troops were called out at Tonypandy, South Wales during a coal strike, and a miner died from a baton blow. Home Secretary Winston Churchill took personal charge of the operation, issuing an unprecedented order placing all police and army forces under the command of an army general (Babington 1990, 137–40). The next year, troops were mobilised in Cardiff, London and Liverpool to help suppress strikes by seamen and dockers, and opened fire on striking workers at Liverpool, killing two. Two naval gunboats and a cruiser were sent to the Mersey and large contingents of soldiers took up positions in the city (Babington 1990, 140–41). During a rail strike later that year, the *Riot Act* was read a number of times, troops charged a crowd at Chesterfield with bayonets fixed, and at Llanelli in Wales soldiers killed two men when a scab train was held up (Babington 1990, 141). After telling the House of Commons that an unprecedented challenge to government authority existed, Churchill sent out telegrams to police chief constables in all the affected areas informing them that the procedures for requesting military assistance via a magistrate had been suspended and that army commanders had complete discretion to use their troops as they saw fit. Churchill came under criticism for instituting a type of martial law, yet the law officers contended that his measures were justified under the circumstances as the soldiers were merely exercising their rights and duties as ordinary citizens (Babington 1990, 142).

In 1912, Tom Mann and four other men were imprisoned for calling upon soldiers not to act against strikers. For publishing a pamphlet urging soldiers to 'refuse to murder your kindred' and 'help us win … the world for workers', they were convicted of incitement to mutiny (Babington 1990, 142). Ireland remained another focus of military activity – in 1914, a detachment of soldiers fired at an unarmed crowd, killing three people and wounding 32 (Jeffery 1985, 53, 60).

After the First World War, armed military units were called out when half the Liverpool police force went on strike in 1919. Four battalions and a troop of tanks were deployed, and two alleged rioters were shot, one fatally. At the height of the confrontation, the HMS Valiant steamed up the Mersey, carrying 8 × 15 inch guns (Bramall 1985, 79–80). At the subsequent inquest into the death, the coroner's jury returned a verdict of 'justifiable homicide' (Babington 1990, 146). According to Babington, the operation was a landmark because:

> [T]his was the last occasion on which the Riot Act was ever read, before its repeal in 1967. It was also the last occasion to date on the British mainland on which soldiers either shot a rioter or charged a mob with fixed bayonets. (Babington 1990, 144)

During this period, soldiers were mobilised more often during industrial disputes, most notably in the British general strike of 1926 (Laybourn 1993), although the decisions were made by the British government through the Home Office, not by local magistrates (Greer 1983, 586–7). There were intense debates within the British government and the military high command between 1919 and 1926 over whether to use regular troops, part-time Reserves, volunteer Territorial Army members and/or specially-recruited Civil Guards or Constabularies against the strikes that erupted in the wake of the First World War. Churchill, now the Secretary of State for War, led the charge for using troops, but there were no fundamental differences over using military force, if need be, to prevent any threat of social revolution. One historical account noted:

> The industrial scene was volatile. Grievances arising out of demobilization procedures, and the prospect of widespread unemployment for returning troops, not to mention – at least in the eyes of the government – the example of the Bolshevik Revolution, led to a situation in which the inevitable readjustments to the strains in society which the war had magnified but not initiated loomed as threatening challenges to the existing order. (Dennis 1981, 706)

Another historian underscored the impact of the October 1917 Soviet Revolution:

> Although talk of revolution had been in the air during the unrest of the pre-war years, the possibility and danger of actual revolution were vividly brought home to politicians and generals in Britain by the Russian Revolution and the violent unrest which swept across Europe at the end of the Great War. 'Our real danger now,' wrote the Chief of the Imperial Staff, 'is not the Boches but Bolshevism'. (Jeffery 1985, 54)

On occasions, troops were used in highly visible displays of strength, designed to intimidate striking workers and their supporters. In the 1919 Glasgow general strike, troops occupied the city centre and set up machine gun posts in the City Chambers. During strikes in 1920 and 1921, the army chief, Sir Henry Wilson, ostentatiously moved units, including tanks, into industrial areas. In the 1926 British general strike, when the government wished to open the strike-bound London docks, the military commander first marched a battalion of guards, 'with drums beating', through the East End to occupy the docks. Throughout the general strike, tanks and armoured cars drove into militant districts to 'impress' local residents (Jeffery 1985, 63). No less than 26 battalions were called out for civil duties during the nine-day strike, before it was ended by the Trades Union Congress. Soldiers patrolled railway lines, guarded buildings and installations, broke blockades, dispersed mass pickets and escorted food convoys, but as far as possible were kept in the background (Babington 1990, 149–50).

In the debates over using troops, the chief concerns in official and military circles were essentially tactical: whether sufficient soldiers could be deployed, given Britain's continuing interventions abroad; the possibility that any recourse to military violence could worsen popular discontent; and doubts about the reliability of troops under those circumstances. Given that many rank and file soldiers, if not officers, are drawn from the working class, this latter issue loomed large. Fear of 'revolutionary' unrest within the army in 1919 prompted the War Office to circulate a questionnaire to the commanding officers of all units in the United Kingdom to assess the political allegiances of their troops. Officers were asked to investigate whether the soldiers were affected by internal or external agitation, whether they would 'respond to orders for assistance to preserve the pubic peace' and whether they would 'assist in strike breaking'. In one incident in 1921, members of a naval reserve battalion declared that nearly all of them were trade union members and 'would lay down their arms if called upon to use them upon their fellow workmen' (Jeffery 1985, 60).

For these reasons, there was considerable discussion about forming para-military 'third forces', whether called 'citizen guards' or 'special constabularies' (Jeffery 1985, 55). In the end, the early collapses of the general strike in Glasgow in 1919, the railway strike later that year, and the 1926 general strike made the large-scale use of the armed forces unnecessary, but not before the War Office had taken the decision, in 1926, to use regular troops, and recruit 300,000 men to a generously-paid para-military Civil Constabulary Reserve (Dennis 1981, 713–22).

Amid these debates, came one of the worst civilian mass killings carried out by the British armed forces. In the massacre at Amritsar in India on 13 April 1919, the city's military commander, General Dyer, ordered his troops to fire without warning on a prohibited meeting of between ten and twenty thousand people, killing 379 and wounding more than 1,200. The incident inflamed anti-British sentiment across India, but Dyer was commended by his military superiors and treated lightly by the British government after the Army Council strongly opposed his dismissal. He was retired from active service, but not dismissed, let alone prosecuted (Jeffery 1985, 56–7). The Army Council's stand in the Dyer case illustrated another issue in mobilising the armed forces: such interventions can become a threat to civilian rule (see Chapter 10).

In summary, the turmoil from the late eighteenth century through to the early twentieth century demonstrated the propensity of the British authorities to call out the armed forces against civilians if the establishment felt threatened, and the readiness of the courts to sanction such operations. From a slightly different angle it could be concluded that serious discussion and preparations in ruling circles for domestic use of the military occurred at times when those in authority regarded the possibility of a social revolution or uprising as a real danger.

Surges of military operations, primarily against strikes, occurred in the late 1940s and early 1970s, also periods of considerable industrial and political turbulence. For Clement Attlee's post-war Labour government, strike-breaking became 'second nature', with soldiers mobilised in 1945, 1947, 1948, 1949 and 1950 (Hennessy 1985, 98). Two decades later, troops were deployed as strike-breakers in the Glasgow Fire Brigade strike of 1973, the Glasgow dustmen's strike of 1975, and the firefighters' strike of 1977–78, when some 20,000 military personnel were mobilised (Bramall 1985, 71). In 1972–73, the Heath government declared a state of emergency to combat a coal miners' strike and drew up a list of

16 key industries for which, in the event of strikes, using military labour might be a possibility (Hennessy 1985, 99–100).

During a 1974 miners' strike, which triggered the defeat of the Heath government, military exercises were conducted, involving the SAS, at London's Heathrow Airport. Tanks and armed soldiers appeared around the airport. Although the exercises were conducted in the name of combating threats of hijacking and other forms of terrorism, Field Marshal Lord Carver, the Chief of the Defence Staff, later admitted that 'fairly senior' officers had discussed plans for a military takeover in the midst of that political crisis (Vallely 2002). His comments appeared to refer to a 1974 series of articles in *The Times*, which reported that the main topic of conversation in officers' messes had been 'what would the British armed forces do if faced with a stalemate political situation, such as we may well have after the next election, with the extreme left pushing for power' (Dorrill and Ramsay 1992; Leigh 1998).

A decade later, following terrorist attacks in Europe, one of the largest ever security operations involving the military was mounted at Heathrow. Infantry and tanks patrolled the airport perimeter while officers of the Metropolitan Police D11 firearms unit were stationed inside terminals, armed with sub-machine guns (Babington 1990, 201). Meanwhile, in 1980, an SAS unit had stormed the Iranian embassy, ending a siege and killing five hostage-takers (Babington 1990, 205).

Throughout this period of upheaval, from the late 1960s to the defeat of the 1984–85 miners' strike, the British military, drawing on its experiences in previous anti-colonial struggles and in Northern Ireland, developed a counter-insurgency manual, *Army Land Operations Manual, Volume III: Counter-Revolutionary Operations*, setting out procedures for when the British government called upon the army to aid police. The ideas in the manual corresponded closely to those of a high-ranking army officer, Sir Frank Kitson (McCulloch 2001, 176). Kitson's main thesis was that the army would have to be engaged in fighting 'subversion' and 'insurgency' in Britain. He defined subversion broadly to include 'the use of political and economic pressure, strikes, protest marches and propaganda' (Kitson 1971, 3). In his view, the military had to be prepared to intervene decisively to suppress opposition and uphold the existing order:

> If a genuine and serious grievance arose, such as might result from a significant drop in the standard of living, all those who now dissipate their protest over a wide variety of causes might concentrate their efforts and produce a situation which was beyond the power of the police to handle. Should this happen the army would be required to restore the position rapidly. Fumbling at this juncture might have grave consequences even to the extent of undermining confidence in the whole system of government. (Kitson 1971, 25)

Particularly from the 1970s, traditional civil policing methods also gave way to the use of heavily-armed riot and para-military police units, such as the Special Patrol Group (SPG). In 1986, for example, the British government announced the purchase of 24 bullet-proof Land Rovers, 80 protected personnel carriers and 1,500 long truncheons for police use. Specialist units were trained to use sub-machine guns, CS gas and rubber bullets (Babington 1990, 197–202). Despite the establishment of these kinds of 'third forces' alongside the military and ordinary police, the opening of the twenty-first century saw renewed moves to strengthen powers to call out the troops, suggesting that the powers-that-be are preparing for another period of intense and unpredictable disturbances (see Chapter 5).

One theme that runs through this troubled history is the readiness of governments and other authorities to exploit vague and elastic phrases such as 'emergency', 'essential' and 'security' to intervene militarily, or to act without clear legal authorisation and, if necessary, obtain retrospective indemnity. No less than seven Indemnity Acts were passed in Ireland between 1796 and 1800 to protect the authorities against legal liability for their unlawful acts (Lee 1984, 222). Whelan traced this trend and gave some examples, one of which was the British government's media announcement during the 1926 general strike:

> All ranks of the Armed Forces of the Crown are hereby notified that any action which they may find is necessary to take in an honest endeavour to aid the Civil Power will receive, both now and afterwards, the full support of His Majesty's Government. (Whelan 1985, 289–90)

Another example was Attorney-General Sir Hartley Shawcross's advice during the 1949 docks strike about the doubtful legal enforceability of the emergency regulations:

> I do not think that matters … I have advised that this risk should be taken and that the Regulations should cover matters on which action is required without due regard to the niceties of the law. In an emergency the Government may have, in matters admitting of legal doubt, to act first and argue about the doubts later, if necessary obtaining an indemnification Act. (Whelan 1985, 289–90)

Shawcross's phrase, 'without due regard for the niceties of the law', illustrates the propensity and capacity of governments to dispense with the finer points of the 'rule of law' when confronted by serious political, social or industrial challenges to the established order.

Although the 1974 Heathrow operation was officially justified as a precaution against terrorism, the legal authority of the government to use the army was not clear (Lee 1984, 211). The editor of the *Criminal Law Review* proposed that resort be had to the royal prerogative to address the legal vacuum:

> If on a future occasion the legal powers of police and soldier prove inadequate, reliance may, in the last resort, have to be placed on the Royal Prerogative governing emergencies. That power, with its requirements of compensation,

> may be an acceptable means of filling in gaps in statutory and common law powers. (Lee 1984, 211–12)

Martial Law

Notwithstanding the 1628 *Petition of Right*, British law has also been prepared to support recourse to the imposition of martial law, which is, in essence, the suspension of law altogether. Martial law declarations can pave the way for setting loose far-reaching military powers, including the right to summarily try and execute individuals, in order to put down civil unrest. After the final defeat of the absolute monarchy in 1688 and up until the nineteenth century, martial law was regarded as an emergency suspension of the rule of law, strictly confined to cases of necessity in times of war, not in times of peace when ordinary courts were open (Hale 2000, 26–7; Capua 1977). Yet, this view seemed to shift somewhat during the nineteenth century.

At the beginning of that century, Blackstone conceded that the rules regarding the power to declare martial law were unclear and capricious. Writing in 1809, he said martial law was 'built upon no settled principle, but is entirely arbitrary in its decisions'. Indeed, it was 'in truth no law but something rather than allowed as law, a temporary excrescence bred out of the distemper of the state' (Blackstone 2001, 413). Writing toward the end of the nineteenth century, however, Dicey asserted that the right to invoke martial law is 'a right inherent in government' (Dicey 2005, 543–5). To this day, according to *Halsbury's Laws of England*, martial law applies 'when a state of actual war, or of insurrection, riot, or rebellion amounting to war, exists' (Hailsham 1973, vol. 8(2), para. 821). Other authorities contend that a modified form of martial law can be declared in cases of internal insurrection or disorder that is beyond the power of the civil authorities to quell, applying the same test of necessity as applies to 'military aid to the civil power' (Wade and Phillips 1970, 409; Dicey 2005, 543).

Doubt exists as to the legal basis of martial law. It is said to be either an example of a common law right to employ force to repel force or, alternatively, a royal prerogative (Hailsham 1973, vol. 8(2), para. 821). Despite this fundamental uncertainty, the Privy Council in the 1902 *Marais* case on appeal from the Cape Colony, extended the doctrine of martial law to apply even where the ordinary civilian courts were still sitting (*D F Marais v The General Officer Commanding the Lines of Communication and the Attorney-General of the Colony* [1902] AC 109). Martial law has been somewhat loosely described as 'the right to use force against force within the realm in order to suppress civil disorder' (Heuston 1964, 152). This formulation could justify dictatorial measures.

According to de Smith (a leading late-twentieth-century authority on English constitutional and administrative law), if martial law arises, it is generally thought that the officer commanding the armed forces will become all-powerful and his actions 'non-justiciable and, for the time being, absolute, subject only to consultation (if this is feasible) with the civil power' (de Smith 1981, 511). 'Non-justiciable' means that the courts have no power to scrutinise the lawfulness of the actions taken.

Two Irish cases, *R v Allen* ([1921] 2 IR 241) and *R v Strickland* ([1921] 2 IR 317), maintain that the ordinary courts have jurisdiction to decide whether the state of disorder warrants martial law, but there is no precise and settled body of law for answering that question, which seems to depend on judging whether order could be restored only by handing over power to the military authorities. If the courts decide that martial law is warranted, then the military's actions will not be reviewable, at least not until the courts decide that the disorder has been pacified. Legal action could be brought against the military for manifestly unreasonable conduct and possibly for unnecessary use of force against people or property, but the law is unclear (de Smith 1981, 512). In de Smith's opinion, the legal uncertainty is academic in any case, because indemnity legislation would almost certainly be passed to exonerate those who acted in good faith to suppress an uprising (de Smith 1981, 514). Indeed, the British parliament passed such an Act of Indemnity to cover the 1920 declaration of martial law in areas of Ireland (Rowe 1985, 200).

Northern Ireland

Over the past four centuries, military aid to the civil power in the United Kingdom has been most frequently applied in Ireland. British rule there was also maintained in more modern times through a para-military force, the Royal Irish Constabulary. During the Easter Uprising of 1916 and the 1919–21 civil war, the army's role was to suppress open insurrection and, later, guerrilla war. But the army also assumed riot control duties often enough for the Irish Command to issue a tactical instructions booklet, covering both potential and actual force. The methods to be used against potential force included military patrols to strike 'a terror in the locality, so as to prevent crime being perpetrated', while the tactics for actual violence included firing on crowds (Jeffery 1985, 61–3).

In the last three decades of the twentieth century, the British establishment had a major and ultimately unsuccessful experience with the deployment of armed forces to Northern Ireland. That experience offers salutary lessons about the potential for military intervention to lead to heavy civilian casualties and an intensification of violent civil conflict. Of course, Ireland was not a purely internal matter, given that the Irish people had been fighting British domination for four centuries. But following the partition of Ireland in 1921, the six counties of Northern Ireland, also known as Ulster, remained part of the United Kingdom. The subsequent conflicts in Ulster were bound up with the discrimination suffered by the generally working class Catholic minority (about one-third of the population), although their grievances were also centrally related to the demand for the reunification of an independent Ireland, a demand opposed by the generally better-off Protestant unionists and loyalists, who largely controlled the local police, the Royal Ulster Constabulary (Jeffrey 1996).

Street violence escalated in 1968–69 following the formation of the Northern Ireland Civil Rights Association, which campaigned against discrimination and for equal civil and democratic rights. After one night of rioting in August 1969, which left 10 civilians dead and 145 wounded, the British Labour government decided to send in the army. The government announced: 'The General Officer Commanding Northern Ireland has been instructed to take all necessary steps, acting impartially between citizen and citizen, to restore law and order. Troops will be withdrawn as soon as this is accomplished' (Hamill 1986, 7; Geraghty 1998, 22). Thirty years later, the troops were still there, though their duties had shifted from 'public order' to 'counter-terrorism'.

Three turning points arose that poisoned relations between the army and the Catholic minority, and provoked armed resistance, primarily led by the Irish Republican Army. The first came in July 1970, when the army imposed a three-day curfew in the Catholic suburb of Falls Road in Belfast, and conducted house-to-house searches (Hamill 1986, 34–40). The second was the introduction of internment without trial in August 1971, with the initial detention of 346 Catholics (Hamill 1986, 56–70). The third was 'Bloody Sunday' in January 1972, when soldiers of the Parachute Regiment killed 13 unarmed civilians during a demonstration in Derry against internment (Bell 1993, 256–75).

The army quickly lost support among residents, yet the British government poured more troops into the province. From an initial deployment of 3,000 troops, the numbers peaked at 21,688 in July 1972, and were still at 12,000 when finally withdrawn in 1998 (Dewar 1997, 105). The mobilisation worsened the situation, at great cost to the population, with the number of civilians killed by the security forces growing from 10 in 1969 to 83 in 1972, before falling back to 10 in 1992 (Sutton 1994, 206). The total number of shootings (by all sides) in Northern Ireland grew from 73 in 1969 to 10,631 in 1972, and was still 348 in 1994 (CAIN Web Service n.d.).

The Northern Ireland exercise in 'military aid to the civil power' also led to the erosion of legal and democratic rights, not only in Northern Ireland but in Britain as well. Official secrecy was imposed on many crucial aspects of the operation, including the number of deaths attributable to the security forces, the number of such killings that resulted in criminal proceedings and the army's Rules of Engagement. Various measures were taken to shield soldiers from prosecution, providing *de facto* immunity. Investigative journalists who sought to obtain data and documents were threatened with prosecution under the *Official Secrets Act* (Geraghty 1998, Chapters 7–8; Rasmussen 1999).

Finally, the Northern Ireland experience illustrates the difficulty of holding anyone, including members of the armed forces, legally accountable for the conduct of the military, even where deaths occur. Between 1970 and 1979, although the army killed 186 people in Northern Ireland, only 28 soldiers were prosecuted for offences involving shooting between 1972 and 1976, of whom 13 were convicted.

One soldier was convicted of manslaughter, but his conviction was quashed on appeal (Rowe 1985, 201). After one solder was acquitted of murder, the House of Lords was asked to provide an advisory opinion. The Law Lords said the 'reasonableness' of force was a question of fact for a jury. Lord Diplock stated that a jury ought to take into account that a soldier may have to make a split-second decision to open fire or not (*Reference under s 48A of the Criminal Appeal (Northern Ireland) Act 1968 (No. 1 of 1975)* [1976] 2 All ER 937). During the 1990s, one private was convicted of murder, when he fired a fatal shot into the back of a passing car (*R v Clegg* [1995] 1 AC 482), yet the British government released him on licence and he was ultimately acquitted after a series of re-trials (Watt 2000).

The American Revolution

The British struggles against absolutism, followed by the American overthrow of British military rule, led the founders of the United States to regard domestic military intervention with profound repugnance. One Congressional Research Service report identified an 'Anglo-American tradition against military involvement in civilian affairs' (Doyle 2000, 1). The American experience began with the repeated use of British military troops to suppress disorders in the colonies, including the Boston massacre of 1770, when the army fired upon anti-colonial demonstrators, killing five (Engdahl 1971; Doyle 2000, 4). Engdahl, who examined this record in some detail, commented:

> The American colonists of the mid-eighteenth century were British subjects who considered themselves heirs to the liberties that had been won through the struggles of what was then relatively recent English history. Increasingly, however, they came to perceive the King of their time as hostile to the liberties thus claimed. (Engdahl 1985, 3)

The 1776 Declaration of Independence spelled out the anti-militarist stance of the United States in unequivocal terms. It condemned the King's use of armies to cause 'death, desolation and tyranny … totally unworthy … of a civilized nation' and specifically attacked the keeping of a standing army in peacetime (Hammond 1997). The Declaration denounced the King for 'protecting [British troops] by a mock trial, from punishment for any murders which they should commit on the inhabitants of these States' (clause 17) and for affecting to 'render the military independent of and superior to the civil power' (clause 14).

When the US Constitution was proposed in 1787, it met opposition on several grounds, but the most controversial was the provision for a standing army. In order to enforce the principle of civilian control, the Constitution restricted military appropriations to two years, designated the President as the Commander-in-Chief and empowered Congress to regulate the armed forces (Article 1, section 8, clauses 12 and 14; Article 2, section 2). At the same time, the Constitution forbade the states to maintain regular armed forces and its 'Guaranty Clause' provided only that the United States should protect the states against invasion and – upon the application of a state legislature or executive (when the legislature could not be convened) – 'domestic violence' (Article 4, section 4).

Despite these protections, there was considerable agitation against the spectre of military law enforcement. As a result, the First Amendment guaranteed individual rights, the Fourth Amendment enshrined freedom from unreasonable search and seizure and the Fifth Amendment insisted that 'No person shall … be deprived of life, liberty, or property without due process of law' (Engdahl 1985, 4–5). These provisions were regarded as bulwarks against military power. The founding fathers regarded the military's authoritarian nature as antithetical to democracy and a potential threat to any democratic system of government (Hammond 1997, fn 42).

Following the experiences of the Civil War and the Reconstruction period, in which military methods, including martial law, were applied in the South, Congress repudiated law enforcement by military means by adopting the *Posse Comitatus Act* of 1878, which declared:

> From and after the passage of this Act it shall not be lawful to employ any part of the Army of the United States as a *posse comitatus*, or otherwise, for the purpose of executing the laws, except in such cases and under such circumstances as such employment of said force may be expressly authorized by the Constitution or by act of Congress.

Thus, the Act not only ended the practice of using troops as a posse (pursuant to the British Mansfield doctrine), it prohibited all military involvement in domestic law enforcement, except with express constitutional or Congressional authority. No room was left for calling out the troops via presidential or executive orders or regulations, unless they had explicit constitutional or Congressional approval.

In two decisions in the 1970s, the US Supreme Court recalled these principles. In 1972, Chief Justice Burger invoked the 'traditional and strong resistance of Americans to any military intrusion into civilian affairs. That tradition has deep roots in our history …' (*Laird v Tatum*, 408 U.S. 1, 15). Two years later, speaking on behalf of the court, Burger CJ observed that 'the decision to invoke military power has traditionally been viewed with suspicion and skepticism since it often involves the temporary suspension of some of our most cherished rights …' (*Scheuer v Rhodes*, 416 U.S. 232, 246).

Nevertheless, US history displays a similar pattern to British history – when the ruling establishment fears serious social or industrial unrest it is quite prepared to defy or erode these principles and resort to military intervention, whether by the national armed forces or the National Guard (the National Guard is not covered by the *Posse Comitatus Act*, because it is a state-based militia – see Hammond 1997). By one estimate, federal troops were used for domestic operations, including riots and civil disorders, more than 200 times in the two centuries from 1795 to 1995 (Brinkerhoff 2002).

Military forces, usually state militia, were frequently called upon between 1875 and 1925, and again in the early 1970s, to break strikes, sometimes with deadly consequences. During the 1877 railroad strike, for example, 45,000 militiamen were mobilised in 11 states, and more than 100 strikers were killed and several hundred were wounded. In another instance, President Cleveland sent federal troops to 'preserve order' in Pullman, Illinois, in 1894 (Jacobs 1985, 130–31). In 1970, President Nixon declared a postal strike to be a national emergency, and dispatched 30,000 troops to replace strikers in New York, claiming that the strike threatened 'survival of a government based on law' (Hammond 1997; Jacobs 1985, 137). In 1981, President Reagan used troops to replace striking air traffic controllers, effectively crushing the PATCO union, and the military has also been utilised to break strikes by coal miners (Hammond 1997).

Political and social movements have also been targeted. At the height of the urban riots of the 1960s, troops were sent into Detroit and other cities (Hammond 1997). During the anti-Vietnam War movement, four students were shot dead at Kent State University in 1970 after Ohio Governor James A. Rhodes sent National Guard troops to the campus at the request of the local mayor (Bills 1988; Caputo 2005). A month later, President Nixon established the President's Commission on Campus Unrest, known as the Scranton Commission, which he charged to study the dissent, disorder and violence breaking out on college and university campuses across the nation. The Commission issued its findings in a September 1970 report that concluded that the Ohio National Guard shootings were unjustified (US President's Commission 1970). No-one was held to account, however (see further Chapter 9).

Far from recoiling from military intervention, in 1972 the increasingly embattled Nixon administration promulgated a new set of regulations, 'Employment of Military Resources in the Event of Civil Disturbances', asserting legal authority for substantial military intrusions into domestic affairs, and reducing prior safeguards against misuse (Engdahl 1985, 2–3). The regulations purportedly derived their legality from federal statutes dealing with insurrections, unlawful obstructions and domestic violence (Title 10 U.S.C. ss 331, 332, 333), whose current form and revived use are discussed in Chapter 3. Further, the regulations asserted three additional sources of legal power. The first was a sweeping concept of an inherent executive emergency power to 'preserve public order'; the second was a purported executive power to protect federal property and functions; the third related to the Secret Service (Engdahl 1985, 19–31).

In 1973, at Wounded Knee a Native American village in South Dakota, the Nixon administration employed the military in a situation not even contemplated by those regulations. After several score supporters of the American Indian Movement, some armed, moved into the village, federal officials cut off access, beginning a 71-day siege. No uniformed military personnel were visible, but the Directorate of Military Support was involved from the first day, a brigade of the

82nd Airborne was placed on alert, air force reconnaissance flights were conducted and, at one point, hundreds of troops were placed on six-hour alert, although ultimately not deployed (Engdahl 1985, 35–6). Courts rejected arguments that the operation breached the *Posse Comitatus Act*, on the basis that there had been no direct 'active' use of the army, only the 'passive' provision of military equipment and supplies (Hammond 1997). Some of the Native Americans, who were charged with interfering with federal officers, ultimately succeeded in having the charges dismissed because the *Posse Comitatus Act* had been violated by giving the military observers too much influence over civilian law enforcement decisions regarding negotiations, use of equipment and the policy on the use of force (Hammond 1997; Jacobs 1985, 222).

Also during the 1970s, evidence came to light of another aspect of military intervention into domestic politics – widespread military intelligence surveillance of civilians, notably political activists. Law suits failed to provide a judicial remedy. In *Laird v Tatum* (408 U.S. 1 (1972)), the case cited above, the US Supreme Court, while invoking a principle against 'military intrusion into civilian affairs', ruled that the plaintiffs, who suspected they had been placed under surveillance, lacked standing. The court found that they had not shown any direct injury and that mere knowledge of military investigative activity fell short of a 'chilling' of their First Amendment free speech rights. In what amounted to a 'Catch-22' situation, the judges refused to order the military to stop collecting information about civilians unless they could prove that they had been harmed by what the military was doing (Jacobs 1985, 223–6; Doyle 2000, 13). The decision effectively gave a green light to the use of the armed forces to spy on citizens. It also illustrated the willingness of US courts to accept military interventions, even while formally adhering to an opposing principle.

In 1992, the first President Bush invoked provisions that permit the president to call out troops to suppress 'insurrections' or 'unlawful obstructions, combinations, or assemblages, or rebellion against the authority of the United States' that 'make it impracticable to enforce the laws of the United States in any State or Territory'. About 4,000 soldiers and Marines were dispatched to Los Angeles at the request of California Governor Pete Wilson after the outbreak of riots sparked by the acquittal of four police officers who assaulted Rodney King. These troops were deployed in addition to 10,465 national guardsmen and 1,717 federal law enforcement officers. A study of the deployment concluded that the heavily-armed soldiers operated largely outside civilian control and that, although the troops killed no one, a 'bloodbath' could have easily resulted (Rasmussen 1999).

Federal troops have also been mobilised many times for disaster relief, a practice that authorities argue does not violate the *Posse Comitatus Act*, because no civilian law enforcement is involved. However, such operations have the potential to spill over into law enforcement and also create a climate for military intervention into civilian areas. Previous operations have included soldiers patrolling urban areas, confronting looters and even providing election facilities, as happened after Hurricane Hugo in Florida in 1992, a quintessentially civilian political role (Hammond 1997).

Over the past three decades, the domestic use of troops against civilians has continued through the deployment of the military for the 'wars' on drugs and terrorism, and for immigration border patrols. The consequences of sending soldiers, trained to kill, to guard the Mexican border were tragically illustrated in 1997 when Marines killed an innocent 16-year-old boy, a local shepherd, near the border (Hammond 1997; Trebilcock 2000). Since 2001, far-reaching claims of presidential, executive or 'Commander-in-Chief' powers to call out the troops and authorise military surveillance have been pursued under the guise of combating terrorism. These current developments are examined in Chapter 3.

Australian Experiences

Although lacking America's revolutionary tradition, the Australian colonies of Britain also inherited a deep aversion to the domestic deployment of troops. Despite, or perhaps because of, their early history as subjects of military rule, the settlers increasingly developed antagonism to military intervention. After reviewing the archival records of a number of twentieth-century Australian episodes in which the issue of military action against civilians was raised, one study concluded:

> The distrust of the use of armed forces in domestic affairs is a long British tradition. The domestic use of armed forces in the early days of the penal settlement, the structure of the Australian population and its experience until the formation of the Federation, apparently, did nothing to weaken that tradition. (Beddie and Moss 1982, 72)

Martial law was invoked several times during the nineteenth century against convicts, Aborigines and workers (Lendrum 1977; Windeyer 1979). Governor King declared martial law in 1804 in New South Wales to suppress an 'Irish insurrection'. Many participants in the revolt were tried by court-martial and a number were hanged (Lendrum 1977, 40). Another NSW Governor, Darling, rejected the urging of his Attorney-General to declare martial law in 1826 to use the military against Aborigines who were resisting seizures of their lands. Darling was of the view, however, based on advice from the British Secretary of State Lord Bathurst, that he could use troops against Aboriginal people without such a declaration, as if they were 'open enemies' against whom war could be declared (Lendrum 1977, 42).

Two of the most barbaric declarations of martial law came in 1828 and 1830, when Governor Arthur of Tasmania mobilised troops to drive Aborigines from settled areas. Arthur twice invoked martial law even though Aboriginal retaliation against their dispossession had taken the form of isolated attacks, not a general war (Lendrum 1977, 41; Calder 2008, 127–50). In 1840, Governor Gawler of

South Australia cited martial law, although not formally declared, as well as the war of law, as the legal justifications for the summary execution of two Aboriginal people rounded up by troops in the Coorong area, near the mouth of the Murray (Lendrum 1977, 29, 34). As late as 1867, British authorities sent regulations to the Australian colonies providing for declarations of martial law, although it seems that these regulations were not put into practice (Clark 2007, 17, citing *Proposed Rules on the Subject of Martial Law*, SAPP No. 107 of 1867).

In his work, *Emergency Powers*, Lee 'hazards a guess' that the power to resort to martial law continues in Australia as a creature of the common law. Despite the uncertainty involved, Lee considers that, while legislation is generally preferable, the doctrine of martial law should not be buried 'for in the face of an extraordinary crisis it may come in useful ... it may be better to rely on a "shadowy, uncertain, precarious something" than nothing at all' (Lee 1984, 224). This argument would seem to justify dispensing with the rule of law. The words quoted by Lee are taken from a nineteenth-century English judgment, where Cockburn CJ stated: 'Martial law when applied to the civilian is no law at all, but a shadowy, uncertain, precarious something, depending entirely on the conscience, or rather on the despotic and arbitrary will of those who administer it' (*R v Nelson and Brand* (1867) F Cockburn Sp Rep 86).

Without resorting to martial law, in 1854, soldiers were used alongside police to mount an attack on the Eureka Stockade, which gold miners had erected to resist the efforts of the authorities to collect licence fees. About 30 miners and four soldiers were killed in the ensuing battle at Ballarat, and many more were injured (McCulloch 2001, 36). The great strike struggles of the 1890s saw troops mobilised against specific demonstrations and gatherings, with orders to shoot to kill strikers and their supporters. In one incident, Colonel Tom Price issued the following instruction to a volunteer unit during the extended Australian maritime strike of 1890:

> Men of the Mounted Rifles, one of your obligations imposes upon you the duty of resisting invasion by a foreign enemy, but you are also liable to be called upon to assist in preserving law and order in the colony ... To do your work faintly would be a grave mistake. If it has to be done effectively you will each be supplied with 40 rounds of ammunition, leaden bullets, and if the order is given to fire, don't let me see any rifle pointed in the air; fire low and lay them out so that the duty will not have to be performed again. (McKinlay 1979, 377)

These experiences left bitter memories in the minds of ordinary working people. The Department of Defence website's history of the Australian armed forces states:

> During the late 1880s and early 1890s, Australia's economy worsened, leading to reduced funding for the colonial armies and to the possibility of internal unrest. In 1890, during the Great Maritime Strike, the Victorian police expected

> rioting on a scale beyond their control. Six hundred troops including 200 from the Victorian Mounted Rifles were called out, and their presence in Victoria Barracks did much to dampen the threat. In the following year, the Queensland shearers withheld their labour when the pastoralists, refusing to recognise the Shearers' Union, began importing non-union labour from other colonies. The ensuing confrontation was deemed sufficiently serious to call out 1442 members of the Queensland Defence Force and send them to centres where the unionists were concentrated. By May 1891, the strike was virtually over, without the employers having conceded freedom of contract to the strikers. The troops received the thanks of the Queensland Parliament but earned the long held suspicion of several sections of the Australian community. (Department of Defence, Australia 2004)

The turmoil of the 1890s led to s 119 being inserted in the Constitution, to allow the military to be mobilised against 'domestic violence' when requested by a state government, at least where there was an 'uncontrollable situation' (Blackshield 1978, 6). In the early years of the twentieth century, Australian state governments requested military intervention on at least six occasions, to deal with such anticipated incidents as 'general strike riot and bloodshed', 'disturbances', wharf strike 'violence', 'labour troubles' and the 1923 Victorian police strike (Beddie and Moss 1982, 8–39). On each occasion, the Federal Government declined on the basis that the state police were capable of dealing with the threat (although troops were sent to guard federal buildings, including post offices, during the 1923 Victorian police strike) (Lee 1984, 201). Only one of those requests – by Queensland in 1912 – was formally made under s 119. Perhaps as a result of the legal and political difficulties experienced in invoking s 119, the section has never been applied.

During the Brisbane general strike of 1912, Prime Minister Andrew Fisher rejected the Queensland government's request for troops, saying the situation could be controlled by police. Fisher also considered that the use of the military would have inflamed the discontent (Beddie and Moss 1982, 13–14). This decision is considered to have created a precedent for the proposition that s 119, which states that the Commonwealth 'shall' protect a state against domestic violence if the executive of the state applies for it, leaves the Federal government a discretion to send in the armed forces or not (Beddie and Moss 1982, 15–16). Federal Attorney-General Billy Hughes also argued, probably incorrectly, that the Queensland application was defective because the request required a proclamation by the Governor of the state (Beddie and Moss 1982, 16–18).

Several of these episodes saw troops mobilised partially or assembled in substantial numbers without a formal call-out. During the conflicts over conscription, in Tasmania from 1916 to 1917, following a request from the Premier, military units were placed on alert, arrangements were made with magistrates to call out troops, and machine guns were requisitioned to be mounted on trucks (Beddie and Moss 1982, 21–3). In the 1923 Victorian police strike, the dispatch of army, air force and naval units to protect federal buildings (Melbourne was then the temporary national capital) was designed as a 'show of force'. The intimidating effect was reinforced by the presence of naval warships in Port Phillip Bay and the creation of a 'Special Constabulary Force' commanded by former general, Sir John Monash (Beddie and Moss 1982, 34–7). Moreover, the Melbourne operation established a precedent for the Federal government to deploy the armed forces domestically to protect its own interests (Beddie and Moss 1982, 37–8). During the 1928 waterfront dispute at Port Adelaide, the Defence Department issued ammunition and military equipment to the police, and special constables sworn into 'The Citizens' Defence Brigade' commanded by an army lieutenant-colonel were provided with rifles, ammunition and bayonets (Beddie and Moss 1982, 38–9).

Beyond the six formal requests for military intervention, plans existed for joint military–police operations against working people and political activists. In one recorded instance, in 1919 the army Chief of Staff held a meeting in Melbourne with senior NSW and Victorian police to discuss a cooperative response to any 'Bolshevik revolutionary action' launched under the cover of an industrial dispute. 'The Army was to provide military equipment, groups of picked men with machine guns and aeroplanes with bombs' (McCulloch 2001, 44).

Apart from establishing legal and political precedents for the informal use of the military to deal with civil unrest, these experiences illustrate how readily industrial disputes can ignite or intersect with broader popular unrest, with the potential to draw troops into armed conflicts with members of society in highly politically-charged circumstances. The use of troops to break strikes does not require them to be formally called out – the argument being that their mobilisation does not involve the use of force – but such deployments, as noted in Chapter 1, may be 'highly controversial and may involve coercion, if not enforcement' (Beddie and Moss 1982, 78).

Troops were mobilised to break strikes on several occasions during the second half of the twentieth century, with Labor governments playing a leading role. In 1949, troops were initially mobilised to unload an Indian ship blacklisted by the unions, and then sent to work in open-cut coal mines. Troops carried weapons in their road and rail movements and to guard their camps, but worked unarmed, under police protection (Beddie and Moss 1982, 39ff.). During the operation, soldiers threatened to break camp unless they were supplied with beer, and the Vice Chief of General Staff expressed fears of 'disturbances' involving the troops.

By sending in soldiers against the coal miners' strike of 1949, the Chifley Labor government set a precedent that the Menzies government extended to establish a plan for systematic military involvement in breaking strikes under the cover of maintaining 'essential services' and defeating 'communism'. The secret military plan, codenamed Operation Alien, continued from 1950 to 1955, even after the High Court ruled unconstitutional the government's use of the defence power to outlaw the Communist Party, and a subsequent referendum to ban the party was defeated (Louis 1992, 1–18).

Under the direct control of Prime Minister Menzies, Operation Alien was launched shortly after the Communist Party Dissolution Act became law in October 1950. Its taskforce, which included high-ranking military officers, senior departmental officials and the assistant general manager of the Shell Company, adopted a model based on the handling of the 1926 British general strike (Louis 1992, 3–4). Ministerial authorisation was given for the army to be used in stevedoring, in all states, coal mining and transport, even though legal experts offered conflicting opinions on the employment of troops in peacetime (Louis 1992, 6). Large numbers of troops were placed on standby for use on the waterfront and between mid-1951 and March 1952, soldiers loaded strikebound ships at Williamstown, Geelong and Sydney (Louis 1992, 8–10).

In 1953, arrangements were made to send hundreds of troops to load ships at six ports affected by union action, although in the end the only one affected was the sugar port of Bowen (Louis 1992, 14). The people of Bowen were 'awakened by the first of seven flights to land on the airfield at the outskirts of town' and 'feared that an air-borne invasion had occurred' (Louis 1992, 1). The deployment inflamed the situation, triggering wider protest strikes and the likelihood of national stoppages. Local businesses refused to supply the army and work only resumed when the government agreed to withdraw the troops (Louis 1992, 2). By some interpretations, the Bowen intervention was a miscalculation (Beddie and Moss 1982, 50; White 2005, 449). The evidence suggests it was part of a wider scheme adopted by the Menzies government to provoke strikes by 'communist'-led unions, launch prosecutions and pursue its efforts to outlaw the Communist Party despite the defeat of the 1951 referendum (Louis 1992, 2–7). 'Operation Alien' was used once more in 1954, when troops loaded a ship with war *matérial* for the French government in Vietnam, and was not disbanded until late 1955 (Louis 1992, 18).

In 1970–71, the Gorton Government called out the Pacific Island Regiment (PIR), part of the Australian Defence Forces (ADF), to suppress secessionist agitation in Papua New Guinea, then an Australian colony, administered under a United Nations Trusteeship. Since no state government request was involved, s 119 of the Constitution could not be invoked, and recourse to the defence power was problematic, since Papua New Guinea was not regarded as a foreign country. Moreover, the agitation that alarmed the government was a political movement seeking to end Australian rule. It seems that on legal advice, Defence Minister Fraser insisted on the issuing of a secret Order-in-Council, signed by the Governor-General, to authorise the call-out, but its constitutionality remains questionable (Ward 1997, 13; Beddie and Moss 1982, 55). There were additional concerns in cabinet that military violence could bring UN condemnation and that the use of the PIR might provoke riots that the PIR could not control, requiring troops to be sent from Australia (Beddie and Moss 1982, 58). Detailed instructions were given to the territory's Administrator, including the requirement, spelled out in the Australian Military Regulations that 'in the event of troops being ordered to fire the fire will be effective' (Beddie and Moss 1982, 60). He was given the power to issue intervention orders before seeking further ministerial approval (Beddie and Moss 1982, 55). Ultimately, the troops were not actually used, but officials argued that the call-out decision, which was publicly broadcast, could also provide a powerful 'show of force' deterrent (Beddie and Moss 1982, 51–61).

The threat of military intervention was also present during the constitutional crisis of 1975. Governor-General Sir John Kerr reportedly held his own meetings, as the titular Commander-in-Chief of the ADF, with senior defence officials before dismissing the Whitlam government (Coxsedge, Caldicutt and Harant 1982, 35, 96). On November 6, five days before the dismissal, Kerr allegedly met with the secretary of the Defence Department, who afterward stated publicly that the government's suggestion of an investigation into the role of the US satellite communications bases at Pine Gap and Nurrungar in central Australia posed 'the greatest risk to the nation's security there has ever been' (Coxsedge, Caldicutt and Harant 1982, 35). Two days later, another senior defence official briefed Kerr about CIA allegations against the Whitlam government and a day later, Kerr visited the Defence Signals Directorate for a briefing (Coxsedge, Caldicutt and Harant 1982, 96). A former Whitlam government cabinet minister alleged that Kerr secretly placed the armed forces on alert after the dismissal (Watching Brief 1986; Workers News 1976). Nevertheless, no troops were seen on the streets, and eventually the widespread strikes and protests that greeted the dismissal subsided after Whitlam and Australian Council of Trade Unions (ACTU) president, Bob Hawke, appealed for workers to go back to work.

The most dramatic military deployment occurred in 1978 when Prime Minister Fraser and the New South Wales Premier Wran called out nearly 2,000 soldiers in Sydney and the New South Wales Southern Highlands towns of Bowral and Mittagong after an explosion outside the Commonwealth Heads of Government Regional Meeting at the Sydney Hilton Hotel. To this day, the question of who was actually responsible for the bomb blast remains clouded in uncertainty and controversy. Following the collapse of two police prosecutions, there is no evidence that it was an act of terrorism (Head 2008). Nevertheless, the mass media and the federal and state governments immediately declared that the 'age of terrorism' had arrived in Australia. Two ensuing reports by Justice Hope (Hope 1977 and Hope 1979) and one by former London police chief Sir Robert Mark (Mark 1978) recommended a significant boost to the powers of the Australian Security Intelligence Organisation (ASIO), the establishment of the Office of National Assessments (ONA), the formation of the Australian Federal Police (AFP), wider domestic use of the army's Special Air Services (SAS), and the creation of 'anti-terrorist' and SWAT-style squads in state police forces.

Mark's report also revealed that Crisis Policy Centres had been set up to facilitate the provision of 'military aid to the civil power'. These were police–military 'nerve centres', run by the Protective Security Co-ordination Centre (PSCC), which included representatives of the Prime Minister's National Security Council, the ONA, ASIO and the Australian Secret Intelligence Service (ASIS, the external intelligence service), the military and the federal and state police (Mark 1978).

In 1983, the Hawke Government authorised RAAF flights over Tasmania to photograph work being conducted by the Tasmanian government in breach of Commonwealth regulations and in 1989, the same government authorised the dispatch of troops to combat protesters at the Nurrungar joint Australian–United States military satellite base. Both deployments generated political controversy and legal uncertainty, particularly with regard to the potential use of soldiers to confront demonstrators outside the Nurrungar base perimeter (Ward 1997, 14–18).

During the first decade of the twenty-first century, the military has been deployed in civilian settings with unprecedented regularity, and often on a very large scale. Operation Gold for the 2000 Sydney Olympics was the second largest ADF operational deployment since the Vietnam War (after the INTERFET deployment to East Timor in 1999), while Operation Acolyte for the 2006 Melbourne Games was 'the largest ADF operation mounted in support of an Australian domestic event since 9/11' (Bergin and Smith 2006, 4, 6).

The Australian record, like that of Britain and the United States, indicates that it would be unwise to assume that the armed forces will not be used to put down civil or industrial unrest. Rather, a pattern emerges of governments calling in the military for support during periods of upheaval.

Chapter 3
United States: Eroding Protections against Military Intervention

Through the 1776 Revolution, the United States took the lead in enunciating opposition to military interference in civil affairs. However, that principle has been increasingly subverted, particularly since 2001.

In overthrowing British colonial rule, the American people inherited and defended a deeply-felt hostility to the use of the armed forces to suppress discontent. A Congressional Research Service report on the *Posse Comitatus Act* remarked:

> Americans have a tradition, born in England and developed in the early years of our nation, that rebels against military involvement in civilian affairs. It finds its most tangible expression in the nineteenth century *Posse Comitatus Act*. (Doyle 2000, 1)

As late as 1985, a legal expert could still write with some justification that:

> To the conscience of the nation that fancies itself as the world's greatest democracy, the idea of military intrusion into the affairs of civil government is profoundly repugnant. (Engdahl 1985, 1)

Even then, however, Engdahl warned that new foundations had been laid for military intervention within the United States during the Nixon administration of 1969–74, when regulations were introduced to authorise the use of troops against civil disturbances. Despite such concerns being expressed in academic and civil liberties circles, those foundations have been revived and extended since the terrorist attacks of 2001.

While the principle of civilian supremacy over the military is enshrined in the US Constitution, which provides that the President is the Commander-in-Chief, that provision has been interpreted in recent years to produce the opposite effect: the expansion of executive power and the concentration of political power in the hands of the President, resting on the military. The most well-known examples have been the assertion of presidential authority to order the military incarceration of individuals, including US citizens, as 'enemy combatants' at Guantanamo Bay and elsewhere, secret renditions of people to be tortured in other countries, and military surveillance of domestic telecommunications without judicial warrants.

At the same time, the *Posse Comitatus Act* has been eroded to the point that one US Army Reserve lawyer has described its effect in impeding the use of the military for 'homeland defense' as a 'myth' (Trebilcock 2000). Moreover, in 2002, the Pentagon established the Northern Command (NorthCom), giving the armed forces an unprecedented focus on domestic operations across the North American continent, and developed plans for military deployments during political crises. As part of NorthCom, in 2008, for the first time ever, an active duty regular army combat unit was assigned to full-time use inside the United States (Cavallaro 2008).

Meanwhile, the military has played an increasingly visible role in domestic political events. For example, NorthCom forces were on high alert during President Barack Obama's 2009 inauguration, increasing air defences and deploying chemical attack experts and medical units. In total about 11,500 military personnel took part: approximately 4,000 National Guard members provided support to local law enforcement, boosting security on the National Mall and around Washington, with an additional 7,500 troops under federal control, including emergency medical teams and experts in chemical attacks (Barnes 2008).

Erosion of Civilian Control of the Military

Beneath these developments is a tendency toward a reversal of the relationship between the military and civilian rule.

In his 1961 farewell speech, President Dwight D. Eisenhower urged the American people to beware the undue political influence of the 'military-industrial complex'. He warned: 'This conjunction of an immense military establishment and a large arms industry is new in the American experience. The total influence – economic, political, even spiritual – is felt in every city, every Statehouse, every office of the Federal government.'

Half a century on, that complex is far larger and more powerful than it was in Eisenhower's time. By 2007, the Pentagon commanded an annual budget of more than three quarters of a trillion dollars, which exceeded the military budgets of every other country combined, and operated more than 1,000 bases in 132 countries. It is a military that has engaged in repeated military interventions over the past three decades, including in Grenada, Nicaragua, Haiti, Somalia, Libya, the former Yugoslavia, Afghanistan and Iraq, often to overturn foreign governments. Its senior commanders have wielded *de facto* political power over entire populations in Afghanistan and Iraq (Van Auken 2007).

Likewise, the corporate side of the military-industrial complex has mushroomed, benefiting directly from military contracts and indirectly from the global assertion of American strategic and commercial interests. Led by Lockheed-Martin and Halliburton and the giant weapons and aerospace contractors, the 'complex' also includes the oil and energy conglomerates, the big construction, engineering and public utility companies, and the biotechnology corporations. Other prominent firms include Boeing, Carlyle Group, General Atomics, General Electric and Northrop Grumman Corporation (Louis 1992, 1–18; Singer 2003; Chalmers 2004).

Those who have studied the American military establishment have issued warnings about its transformed role over the past period. One review by a military historian, Richard H. Kohn, concluded that 'in recent years civilian control of the military has weakened in the United States and is threatened today':

> The issue is not the nightmare of a coup d'etat but rather the evidence that the American military has grown in influence to the point of being able to impose its own perspective on many policies and decisions. What I have detected is no conspiracy but repeated efforts on the part of the armed forces to frustrate or evade civilian authority when that opposition seems likely to preclude outcomes the military dislikes. (Kohn 2002)

Examples cited by Kohn included the public Joint Chiefs of Staff opposition to the Clinton administration's proposal to abolish the ban on open homosexual service, in which the chiefs floated rumours of their own and dozens of other resignations, encouraged their retired brethren to arouse Congressional and public opposition, and then more or less openly negotiated a compromise with President Clinton, their Commander-in-Chief.

Also among the 'continuous stream of incidents and controversies' were the undermining and driving from office of Secretary of Defense Les Aspin in 1993, followed by the humiliating withdrawal of his nominated replacement; controversies over the retirements of at least six four-star flag officers; and bitter arguments over readiness, budgets, and whether and how to intervene with American forces abroad, from Somalia to Haiti, Bosnia and Kosovo, and over national strategy generally. In other cases, senior officers spoke out publicly on whether the United States should sign a treaty banning the use of land mines; on whether American forces should be sent into the Balkans in the 1990s; and on whether the United States should support the establishment of the International Criminal Court (Kohn 2002).

During the presidential election crisis of 2000, the chief legal officers of two of the largest commands in the Army and Air Force issued warnings that resentment over Gore campaign challenges to military absentee ballots in Florida could boil over into open contempt. Democratic Party presidential candidate Al Gore dropped his challenges, saying he would not wish to take office in conflict with the military (Kohn 2002; Grey 2001). This back-down cleared the way for George W. Bush to become President, a result that was sanctioned by the Supreme Court in its five-to-four vote in *Bush v Gore* (531 U.S. 98 (2000)) to halt the counting of votes in Florida, a ruling in which the majority denied that citizens had any federal constitutional right to vote for the President.

While the US Constitution contains measures to ensure civilian power over the military, Kohn issued the following warning about the façade of civilian control:

> If one measures civilian control not by the superficial standard of who signs the papers and passes the laws but by the relative influence of the uniformed military and civilian policy makers in the two great areas of concern in military affairs – national security policy, and the use of force to protect the country and project power abroad – then civilian control has deteriorated significantly in the last generation. In theory, civilians have the authority to issue virtually any order and organize the military in any fashion they choose. But in practice, the relationship is far more complex. Both sides frequently disagree among themselves. Further, the military can evade or circumscribe civilian authority by framing the alternatives or tailoring their advice or predicting nasty consequences; by leaking information or appealing to public opinion (through various indirect channels, like lobbying groups or retired generals and admirals); or by approaching friends in the Congress for support. They can even fail to implement decisions, or carry them out in such a way as to stymie their intent. The reality is that civilian control is not a fact but a process, measured across a spectrum – something situational, dependent on the people, issues, and the political and military forces involved. We are not talking about a coup here, or anything else demonstrably illegal; we are talking about who calls the tune in military affairs in the United States today. (Kohn 2002)

Kohn argued that this development was unprecedented in American history. Five decades of warfare had created

> something entirely new in American history – a separate military community, led by the regular forces but including also the National Guard and reserves, veterans organizations, and the communities, labor sectors, industries, and pressure groups active in military affairs. More diverse than the 'military-industrial complex' of President Eisenhower's farewell address forty years ago, this 'military' has become a recognizable interest group. Also, it is larger, more bureaucratically active, more political, more partisan, more purposeful, and more influential than anything similar in American history. (Kohn 2002)

In 2006, Kohn was joined by three other scholars to produce a discussion article, 'Coup d'état: Military Thinkers Discuss the Unthinkable', which was published in *Harper's Magazine* (Bacevich 2006). Andrew Bacevich, a professor of international relations and former career officer, commented:

> The question that arises is whether, in fact, we're not already experiencing what is in essence a creeping coup d'état. But it's not people in uniform who are seizing power. It's militarized civilians, who conceive of the world as such a dangerous place that military power has to predominate, that constitutional constraints on the military need to be loosened. The ideology of national security has become ever more woven into our politics. It has been especially apparent since 9/11, but more broadly it's been going on since the beginning of the Cold War. (Bacevich 2006)

Bacevich pointed out that the use of the US military against American citizens was not a hypothetical scenario, but had already taken place with the domestic spying operation mounted by the National Security Agency (NSA), which is part of the military.

It would be wrong to regard these developments purely as products of the Clinton and Bush administrations of 1993 to 2009. President Obama elevated three recently retired four-star officers to top government positions, an unparalleled representation of the military in a Democratic administration. He appointed General James Jones, retired Marine Commandant, as his National Security Adviser; General Eric Shinseki, retired Army Chief of Staff, as Secretary for Veterans Affairs; and retired Admiral Dennis Blair as Director of National Intelligence. There were further signs of military readiness to defy civilian authority. General Raymond Odierno, the US commander in Iraq, held a press conference in early 2009, just after the commencement of the Obama administration, in which he dismissed Obama's campaign pledge to withdraw one brigade a month and all US combat troops within 16 months. Obama's pledge would still leave behind tens of thousands of 'non-combat' forces, but Odierno went further, announcing that the speed and level of combat troop withdrawals would be determined by the military according to its assessment of the security situation on the ground in Iraq (Grey 2009).

Undermining the Constitution?

Both the Declaration of Independence and the Constitution embody a principle, based on the 'Anglo-American tradition', opposing domestic military mobilisation against the citizenry. As noted in Chapter 2, the Declaration of Independence indicted the King for rendering 'the military independent of and superior to the civil power'.

The Constitution restricts military appropriations to two years, designates the President as the civilian Commander-in-Chief and empowers Congress to regulate the armed forces (Article 1, section 8, clauses 12 and 14; Article 2, section 2). Its 'Guaranty Clause' provides that the military may only be used to protect a state against 'domestic violence' if requested by a state legislature or executive, when the legislature cannot be convened (Article 4, section 4).

It is also possible to see in the First, Second, Third, Fourth and Fifth Amendments, with their promises of individual rights, a civilian militia, freedom from the quartering of troops, freedom from unreasonable search and seizure and no deprivation of life, liberty or property without due process, an underlying constitutional principle barring the use of a standing army to interfere in civilian affairs (Doyle 2000, 12).

There is some judicial support for this proposition. Members of the Supreme Court seemed to acknowledge a larger constitutional principle in both *Youngstown Sheet and Tube Co. v Sawyer* (343 U.S. 579 (1952)) and *Laird v Tatum* (408 U.S, 1 (1972)). In *Youngstown*, Douglas J, after noting the President's role as Commander-in-Chief, added: 'But our history and tradition rebel at the thought that the grant of military power carries with it authority over civilian affairs' (324 U.S. at 632). The court struck down an attempt, via a presidential order, to use the armed forces to seize and operate the country's steel mills, which were threatened by a nationwide strike. The court held that the President's constitutional and statutory powers as President and Commander-in-Chief were not sufficient to support such an executive order, when Congress had specifically refused to grant such authority by statute. That decision still leaves considerable scope for military intervention where Congress has not expressly taken an opposing stand (Doyle 2000, 15).

In *Laird v Tatum*, the Court commented that the 'philosophical underpinnings' of the Constitution explained 'our traditional insistence on limitations on military operations in peacetime' (408 U.S. at 15–16). Nevertheless, the court refused to order the military to stop collecting information about civilians. It held that a claim that First Amendment rights were chilled was non-justiciable unless citizens could show evidence of specific harm or the realistic threat of specific harm.

Likewise, in 2008 the Supreme Court refused to hear an appeal brought by the American Civil Liberties Union and other groups challenging the Bush administration's warrantless domestic wiretapping programme, conducted by the NSA, a military agency. The wiretapping programme began in 2001 but was first revealed to the public through a media leak in 2005. The programme, the full details of which are still not known, included domestic spying in breach of the Foreign Intelligence Surveillance Act (FISA). In 2006, a US District Court judge ruled that the programme violated the First and Fourth Amendments, the separation of powers and FISA.

When that ruling in *ACLU v NSA* was overturned on appeal, the challengers were caught in a 'Catch-22' situation. The government refused to identify the individuals targeted by the NSA programme on the grounds that the information was secret. However, the appellate court upheld the government's argument that only those who could prove they had been specifically targeted by the programme could have standing to sue. The Supreme Court rejected a further appeal without comment.

The courts have long been reluctant to recognise the authority of military tribunals over civilians (Doyle 2000, 12). This view was upheld, albeit in a limited manner, in the Guantanamo Bay habeas corpus cases that challenged the constitutionality of the military commissions established to try 'enemy combatants'. In 2004, the Supreme Court, by a majority of six to three, ruled that Guantanamo Bay detainees could seek writs of habeas corpus in US courts. The majority judgment, delivered by Stevens J, suggested that at stake were democratic conceptions dating back nearly 800 years to the Magna Carta of 1215 (*Rasul v Bush*; *Al Odah v United States*, 542 U.S. 466 (2004)).

Four years later, in *Boumediene v Bush* (553 U.S. __ (2008)), the Supreme Court ruled five to four that Guantánamo detainees could immediately file habeas corpus petitions in US district courts challenging the legality of their confinement. Most had been held at the US naval base under brutal conditions, often enduring solitary confinement, water-boarding and other coercive techniques or torture, for more than six years, without having the merits of their cases reviewed by a court of law. However, the ruling did not question the executive branch's ability to declare someone an 'enemy combatant', a power the Supreme Court upheld four years earlier in *Hamdi v Rumsfeld* (542 U.S. 507 (2004)).

Later in 2008, a five-to-four decision by the US Court of Appeals for the 4th Circuit backed the Bush administration's contention that the President has such power. In *Al-Marri v Pucciarelli* (4th Cir. July 15, 2008), the court effectively overturned a decision reached by a three-judge panel of the same court in 2007 which had compared the assumption of such sweeping powers to military rule and the oppression of the American colonies by King George III. The appellate ruling denied habeas corpus to Al-Marri, a legal resident of the United States before the White House declared him an enemy combatant in 2003 and ordered the military to detain him in a Navy brig in South Carolina. The government claimed that the Authorization to Use Military Force (AUMF) resolution passed by Congress in 2002 gave the President the power to carry out such detentions. Alternately, it asserted that the Commander-in-Chief has unchallengeable authority to imprison anyone without charges for the duration of a global war on terror.

Overall, the courts have failed to enunciate a wider constitutional principle against military intervention, even in the context of the *Posse Comitatus Act*, where the judges have generally avoided any examination of its possible constitutional underpinnings (Doyle 2000, 13–14). Thus, in *United States v Walden* (490 F.2d 372 at 376), the court said 'we do not find it necessary to interpret relatively unexplored sections of the Constitution in order to determine whether there might be constitutional objection to the use of the military to enforce civilian laws.'

It therefore seems that military action must violate one of the explicit constitutional prohibitions or guarantees, such as habeas corpus, the right to jury trial, freedom of expression and freedom from unreasonable searches and seizures, before courts will object. This means that a president has substantial leeway, both as chief executive, charged with seeing that laws are faithfully executed, and as Commander-in-Chief, to mobilise the armed forces.

The Supreme Court has made it clear that the President does not require express Congressional or statutory authorisation to exercise such powers. If an emergency threatens the freedom of interstate commerce, transportation of the mail or some other federal government responsibility, he may call upon 'the army of the Nation, and all its militia … to brush away the obstructions' (*In re Debs*, 158 U.S. 364 at 381).

Such rulings have left the way open for increasingly aggressive assertions of presidential, executive and prerogative powers to use military personnel and resources against civilians, flying in the face of the clear intent of the Constitution. In effect, the role of Commander-in-Chief has been transformed from a guarantor of civilian supremacy over the military, to an instrument for utilising the armed forces against civil unrest and political dissent.

Constitutional presidential authority has been asserted to provide a broad basis for the mobilisation of military forces under the banner of homeland security.

Particularly since 2001, the White House has asserted that the executive powers of the President and his position as Commander-in-Chief support wide-ranging exceptions to the *Posse Comitatus Act*. Defense Department regulations assert another 'constitutional' exception to the Act, founded on the 'inherent right of the US Government … to ensure the preservation of public order and to carry out governmental operations … by force, if necessary'.

Stated so sweepingly, this 'federal functions exception' has the capacity to swallow the rule (Hammond 1997). Expanding federal authority over areas formerly reserved to the states, such as transportation, commerce, education and civil rights, has widened the scope of federal functions. During the 1960s, presidential authority provided the basis for sending troops to the South to enforce school de-segregation (Trebilcock 2000).

The Guaranty Clause

The Constitution provides one explicit avenue for authorising domestic military intervention. Its language presents potential obstacles to presidential power to deploy the armed forces. The Guaranty Clause provides:

> The United States shall guarantee to every State in this Union a Republican Form of Government, and shall protect each of them against Invasion; and on Application of the Legislature, or of the Executive (when the Legislature cannot be convened) against domestic violence.

By distinguishing between invasion and domestic violence, the clause is clearly intended as a limitation on the President's executive power to send in federal troops. There must be a request by the state. Four obvious questions arise. First, what is domestic violence? It is not defined by the Constitution, nor has it been defined by legislation or judicial interpretation. Second, when can a state governor request military aid without waiting for the state legislature? Third, is the federal government obliged to accede to an application? Fourth, can a president send in federal troops without a state request?

'Domestic violence' is a vague term. Presidents have interpreted it to justify military interventions against 'an assemblage of rioters', 'mobs' and widespread violence (Bassiouni 1971, 372–3). Clearly these interpretations are broad enough to cover political protests and other forms of dissent that fall far short of armed violence. Only in one instance, in 1903, was a governor's request for troops denied because the disturbance did not amount to an 'insurrection'. In 1967, Attorney General Ramsey Clarke sent letters to all governors indicating that 'serious domestic violence' was needed, but the addition of the word 'serious' hardly clarified anything (Bassiouni 1971, 373).

The requirement for an application from the state legislature has been read as preventing a governor requesting troops while the legislature is in session.

If the legislature is not sitting, however, presidents have not insisted on waiting for the legislators to gather to make a request. On the face of it, the wording of the Guaranty Clause seems to limit unilateral action by a governor to when it is impossible to convene the legislature. In practice, most presidents have only required that there be difficulty in convening the legislature. On a few occasions, presidents have rejected requests because the language of the application was not unequivocally asking for intervention, as distinct from recommending it (Bassiouni 1971, 368–9).

Despite the Constitution's imperative phraseology – 'shall protect' – the clause has generally been treated as leaving the President discretion to withhold aid. Pleas for troops have been rejected because a president thought the danger exaggerated or the state forces adequate to deal with the situation. The precedents indicate that a state must fully utilise all its forces, including its National Guard, before federal troops will be dispatched (Bassiouni 1971, 374–5).

Even though the Guaranty Clause specifically sets a state application as a precondition for deploying troops, it seems to have been accepted that this proviso only applies if there is no independent or concurrent federal interest in maintaining order. At least, legal opinion appears to allow for presidential executive or Commander-in-Chief powers to protect substantial federal interests, regardless of any state request (Bassiouni 1971, 375–6).

Eroding the *Posse Comitatus Act*

On its face, the *Posse Comitatus Act* (PCA) stands as a strict prohibition against using the military for civilian law enforcement, complete with criminal penalties for violation. Its entire text, in its current form, states:

> Whoever, except in cases and under circumstances expressly authorized by the Constitution or Act of Congress, willfully uses any part of the Army or Air Force as a posse comitatus or otherwise to execute the laws shall be fined under this title or imprisoned for not more than two years, or both. (18 U.S.C. section 1385)

Congress has essentially left the PCA unchanged since 1878, and buttressed it with an additional proscription against the use of the armed forces to make arrests or conduct searches and seizures. Section 375 of 10 U.S.C. forbids the Secretary of Defense making regulations that permit direct participation by military personnel in 'a search, seizure, arrest, or other similar activity'.

It appears that no prosecution has ever been conducted for breach of the PCA, however. Moreover, the dearth of judicial interpretation has left its parameters 'substantially untested' (Hammond 1997). In addition, growing numbers of major and minor exceptions have been created, some by Congress and some by the courts. The cumulative result has been to blur the line between police, para-military and military intervention, undermine civilian control of the military and expose the population to the dangers of deadly force and *de facto* dictatorship. The following outline seeks to trace the erosion of the PCA to the point where 'reality bears little resemblance to the myth' and the PCA 'is more of a procedural formality than an actual impediment' to the domestic mobilisation of the armed forces (Trebilcock 2000).

In the first place, while the Act applies today to Army, Air Force, Navy and Marines, and their Reserve components, it does not cover the Coast Guard and the National Guard, at least as long as the National Guard is operating exclusively under the control of a state (Doyle 2000, 42–3). Only when federalised by presidential authority does the Guard become subject to the PCA. This exception gives the authorities access to 'huge military manpower resources' (Trebilcock 2000). The courts have also said that the PCA has no extra-territorial effect. It therefore does not prevent the military from conducting operations with law enforcement agencies abroad or mounting its own operations against civilians, including US citizens and residents, overseas (Hammond 1997).

Secondly, the courts have interpreted the PCA as only barring 'active', rather than 'passive' engagement in law enforcement. 'Execution of the laws' includes the arrest and detention of criminal suspects, search and seizure activities, restriction on civilian movement through the use of blockades or checkpoints, gathering evidence for use in court and the use of undercover personnel in civilian law enforcement. From the cases arising from the 1973 Wounded Knee confrontation, the courts have developed three tests:

1. whether military personnel have been in 'direct active use' in civilian law enforcement;
2. whether the use of the military 'pervaded the activities' of the civilian officials;
3. whether the military subjected 'citizens to the exercise of military power which was regulatory, prescriptive or compulsory in nature' (Doyle 2000, 37).

Thus 'direct active' participation in making arrests has been deemed a violation of the PCA, but not taking a supporting role. Military personnel may be involved in planning law enforcement operations, as long as actual arrests of suspects and seizures of evidence are carried out by civilian personnel. Courts have held that providing supplies, equipment, training, facilities and certain types of intelligence information does not contravene the PCA (Trebilcock 2000; Hammond 1997). This semantic and artificial distinction ignores the reality that troops engaged in supposedly passive support roles can and will be called upon to use force against civilians if operations encounter resistance or other difficulties that threaten to exceed the capacities of the police or civilian authorities. Courts have also ruled that aerial photography and visual search and surveillance by the military do not breach the PCA.

Thirdly, aspects of the language of the PCA can serve to narrow its scope. It is restricted to 'willful' misuse of the military. Although the few judicial interpretations of that requirement are somewhat conflicting, it seems that a court would not convict for anything less than deliberate disregard of the PCA, with the authorities acting with the knowledge that their conduct was unlawful (Doyle 2000, 35). This approach leaves considerable scope for government or military figures to argue that they acted innocently, thinking that their activities were within the boundaries set by the PCA. Courts have treated the phrase 'execute the laws' as confined to civilian laws, and allowed military personnel to perform military duties in a manner that assists civilian law enforcement – as long as the primary purpose of an activity is a military one. For example, a court permitted naval military police investigators to act as undercover informants in a civilian police drug operation near a naval base, for the purpose of minimising the flow of drugs into the base (Doyle 2000, 33).

Fourthly, because the Act is a statutory creation, not a constitutional prohibition, it can and has been repeatedly circumvented by subsequent legislation. This has happened particularly since 1980, when the Reagan administration directed the Department of Defense to utilise naval and air assets for the 'war on drugs'. Congress subsequently approved this tasking, and extended it to immigration control, customs and tariff enforcement (Trebilcock 2000). By 1989, the military was designated the 'single lead agency' in the drugs war, a classic instance of mission creep. The Pentagon embraced new missions like drug interdiction as a means of boosting budget levels and improving public relations. In 1993, the Department of Defense budget included more than $1.4 billion for drug-related missions (Hammond 1997).

The undermining of the PCA has been a bipartisan process. In 1995, for example, within one week of the bombing of a federal building in Oklahoma City, President Clinton proposed an exception to the PCA to allow military involvement in investigations related to 'weapons of mass destruction' (Hammond 1997).

The other most prominent Congressional exceptions to the PCA relate to: insurrections, espionage, terrorism and civil disturbances, natural disasters, nuclear materials, protection of national parks, investigation of crimes against the President or others in the line of succession, civil rights, fishery conservation, internationally protected persons and quarantine (Hammond 1997, fn 130; Doyle 2000, 20–23).

Another exception is the Uniform Code of Military Justice. The code gives the military the inherent right to maintain good order and discipline over its personnel through law enforcement, prosecution and punishment. As such, the code gives jurisdiction to the military to enforce both military and civilian laws against its own personnel (Trebilcock 2000, fn 5). These provisions may permit the military to protect its personnel from prosecution in civilian courts for alleged abuses of power committed during domestic operations.

The most direct threat to civilian politics comes from the Civil Disturbance Statutes (10 U.S.C., sections 331–5), which allow the President to call up the armed forces and the National Guard (state militia) to suppress challenges to the political order, ranging from insurrections to 'domestic violence'. Section 331, covering insurrections against states, says:

> Whenever there is an insurrection in any State against its government, the President may, upon the request of its legislature or of its governor if the legislature cannot be convened, call into Federal service such of the militia of the other States, in the number requested by that State, and use such of the armed forces, as he considers necessary to suppress the insurrection.

Section 332 deals with various threats to federal authority, from unlawful combinations to rebellions:

> Whenever the President considers that unlawful obstructions, combinations, or assemblages, or rebellion against the authority of the United States, make it impracticable to enforce the laws of the United States in any State or Territory by the ordinary course of judicial proceedings, he may call into Federal service such of the militia of any State, and use such of the armed forces, as he considers necessary to enforce those laws or to suppress the rebellion.

Section 333 goes further to cover 'interference with State and Federal law':

> The President, by using the militia or the armed forces, or both, or by any other means, shall take such measures as he considers necessary to suppress, in a State, any insurrection, domestic violence, unlawful combination, or conspiracy, if it –
>
> (1) so hinders the execution of the laws of that State, and of the United States within the State, that any part or class of its people is deprived of a right, privilege, immunity, or protection named in the Constitution and secured by law, and the constituted authorities of that State are unable, fail, or refuse to protect that right, privilege, or immunity, or to give that protection; or
>
> (2) opposes or obstructs the execution of the laws of the United States or impedes the course of justice under those laws.
>
> In any situation covered by clause (1), the State shall be considered to have denied the equal protection of the laws secured by the Constitution.

In 2006, the Bush administration succeeded in securing Congressional support for amendments that extended these powers. One amendment effectively widened the scope of section 333 from 'insurrection, domestic violence, unlawful combination, or conspiracy' to 'natural disaster, epidemic, or other serious public health emergency, terrorist attack or incident, or other condition' if the authorities of the state 'are incapable of maintaining public order'. In part, the Bush administration justified the change as a response to the monumental failings of the Hurricane Katrina relief operation in 2005. Expert commentators described the amendments as an unhelpful diversion from the government's political embarrassment over the Katrina debacle, in which the military actually played a substantial part (Banks 2005).

In 2007, amendments were reversed. Democrat Senator Patrick Leahy opposed them, partly to defend states' rights and to strengthen the role of the National Guard. He said the amendments 'make it easier for presidents to declare martial law' and 'make it unnecessarily easy to assert federal authority over national guard elements without the consent of governors'. President Bush initially vetoed the reversion to the original PCA, but later signed the reversal into law, in exchange for measures expanding the military budget, giving the National Guard higher status at the Pentagon, and a closer relationship with the Northern Command, and directing the Pentagon to work with the Guard in homeland defence planning (Leahy 2008). Thus, in the name of civil liberties, Congress overturned the PCA changes, but bolstered the National Guard's substantial part in domestic military deployments. Moreover, the reversion still left the PCA in a severely eroded condition. In addition, President Bush attached a signing statement that he did not feel bound by the repeal (Goodman 2008).

The Bush administration's moves dovetailed with the National Security Presidential and Homeland Directive (NSPD 51, HSPD 20), promulgated in 2007. In the event of a 'catastrophic emergency', which the President can declare without Congressional approval, NSPD 51 would institute virtual martial law under the authority of the White House and the Department of Homeland Security. It would suspend constitutional government under the provisions of Continuity in Government, leaving extraordinary powers in the hands of the President and Vice-President. 'Catastrophic emergency' is loosely defined as 'any incident, regardless of location, that results in extraordinary levels of mass casualties, damage, or disruption severely affecting the US population, infrastructure, environment, economy, or government functions'. 'Continuity of Government' is defined as 'a coordinated effort within the Federal Government's executive branch to ensure that National Essential Functions continue to be performed during a Catastrophic Emergency'.

After surveying the whittling away of the PCA, military reserve lawyer Trebilcock concluded:

> The erosion of the *Posse Comitatus Act* through Congressional legislation and executive policy has left a hollow shell in place of a law that formerly was a real limitation on the military's role in civilian law enforcement and security issues. (Trebilcock 2000)

Growing Political Use of Armed Forces

When President Obama's 2009 inauguration featured a visible military presence, it built upon a growing trend. In effect, the PCA has been eroded by the common use of military forces as security for essentially civilian events. 'National Security Events' covered by NorthCom have included sports events, State of the Union addresses, G-8 summits, presidential inaugurations and funerals, and political conventions (Ehling 2008). During the 1996 Atlanta Olympics, more than 10,000 US troops were deployed, partially on the pretext of deterring terrorism. No questions were raised about infringement of the PCA, even though these troops would have been central to a massive law enforcement emergency if a terrorist attack had occurred (Trebilcock 2000).

It has become customary for the military to be involved in the security for the national conventions of both the Republican and Democratic parties. For the 2004 Republican National Convention, 307 federalised National Guard troops were fielded, in addition to 1,247 state-level soldiers, and provided military aircraft to enforce no-fly zones (Ehling 2008). In 2008, the Department of Homeland Security declared the conventions of both the Democratic and Republican parties 'National Special Security Events'. This designation placed the department and the Secret Service in charge of overall security and brought in an array of national police, military and intelligence agencies. For the Democratic convention, in addition to 1,500 heavily-armed police officers, more than 1,000 National Guard troops were activated. Elements of the US Coast Guard were placed in charge of intelligence operations in designated areas, while the North American Aerospace Defense Command and the Northern Command also participated, in part to provide 'air cover'. Such operations at party conventions not only amount to military intrusion into political affairs but also serve to help entrench the two-party monopoly of the political system.

The Establishment of NorthCom

As part of a global reorganisation of the Pentagon, the creation of the Northern Command in 2002 set a new focus for the US military. Alongside the invasions of Afghanistan and later Iraq, for the first time a specific Pentagon command was established for domestic military intervention. NorthCom's stated mission was to defend the US 'homeland' and assist federal, state and local authorities.

Another step was taken in 2008, when for the first time a regular army combat unit was deployed for full-time use inside the United States. The 4,000-strong 1st Brigade Combat Team of the 3rd Division was placed under the command of US Army North, the Army's component of NorthCom. The unit had spent nearly three out of the previous five years in Iraq, leading the assault on Baghdad in 2003 and carrying out house-to-house combat in the suppression of resistance in the city of Ramadi. It was the first brigade combat team to be sent to Iraq three times (Cavallaro 2008).

While active-duty units previously had been used in temporary assignments, such as the combat-equipped troops deployed to Los Angeles to suppress riots in 1992 and to New Orleans in the wake of the 2005 Hurricane Katrina, it was the first time that an army combat unit had been given a dedicated assignment on US soil. The Pentagon's official announcements stressed the role of specialised units in a potential response to terrorist attacks, but the mission exceeded terrorism. *Army Times*, a specialist military publication, reported that 'they may be called upon to help with civil unrest and crowd control'. The article noted the connection and continuity between the unit's operations in Iraq and its domestic task: 'The 3rd Infantry Division's 1st Brigade Combat Team has spent 35 of the last 60 months in Iraq patrolling in full battle rattle, helping restore essential services and escorting supply convoys. Now they're training for the same mission – with a twist – at home' (Cavallaro 2008).

According to military officials quoted by *Army Times*, the deployment that began with the 1st Brigade Combat Team was to become permanent, with different units rotated into the assignment on an annual basis. *Army Times* reported that the 1st BCT would be kitted out with 'the first ever nonlethal package that the Army has fielded'. The publication reported, 'the package includes equipment to stand up a hasty road block; spike strips for slowing, stopping or controlling traffic; shields and batons; and, beanbag bullets'. Without explanation, the newspaper later retracted that portion of their report, stating that NorthCom said the weapons package was intended only for use in Iraq.

Army doctrine and rules of engagement for civil disturbance and 'riot control' planning have long recommended equipping troops with 'non-lethal weapons' for 'operations other than war'. In 2000, the Center for Army Lessons Learned, located at Fort Leavenworth, Kansas, issued a primer on the subject, entitled *Civil Disturbances: Incorporating Non-Lethal Technology, Tactics, Techniques and Procedures* (Burghardt 2002).

In October 2008, the American Civil Liberties Union filed a Freedom of Information request for information from the government about the *Army Times* report. The ACLU said: 'This deployment jeopardizes the longstanding separation between civilian and military government, and the public has a right to know where and why the unit has been deployed' (ACLU 2008). ACLU requested the Departments of Justice, Homeland Security and Defense to immediately make public all legal opinions, executive orders, presidential directives, memos, policy guidance and other documents that authorise the deployment of military troops for domestic purposes.

Two months later, in December 2008, the *Washington Post* reported that the Pentagon had begun to implement plans to make 20,000 troops available to NorthCom on a full-time basis by 2011. The additional soldiers were to be assigned as they completed assignments in Iraq or Afghanistan. Bert B. Tussing, Director of Homeland Defense and Security Issues at the US Army War College's Center for Strategic Leadership, told the *Post* that the plan 'breaks the mold' by assigning an active-duty combat brigade to the Northern Command for the first time. Previously, the military required the command to rely on troops requested from other sources (Hsu and Tyson 2008).

According to the *Post*, Deputy Defense Secretary Gordon England signed a directive in late 2007 providing $556 million over five years to fund the programme. Paul McHale, Assistant Defense Secretary for Homeland Defense, said the use of 20,000 troops in a domestic deployment 'would have been extraordinary to the point of unbelievable' before the terrorist attacks of 11 September 2001, according to the text of a speech given to the Center for Strategic and International Studies, a Washington think tank, quoted by the *Post*. He described the new policy as 'a fundamental change in military culture' (Hsu and Tyson 2008).

The Department of Defense Directive 3025.12, 'Military Assistance for Civil Disturbances (MACDIS)' provides for far-ranging use of the military against civil unrest:

> Ensure continuous planning by the DoD Components, both in the Department of Defense and in cooperation with civil government agencies for MACDIS operations that may be required during any time or condition of peace, war, or transition to war, including any national security emergency. …
>
> The President is authorized by the Constitution and laws of the United States to employ the Armed Forces of the United States to suppress insurrections, rebellions, and domestic violence under various conditions and circumstances. Planning and preparedness by the Federal Government and the Department of Defense for civil disturbances are important due to the potential severity of the consequences of such events for the Nation and the population. The President has additional powers and responsibilities under the Constitution of the United States to ensure that law and order are maintained. ('Military Assistance for Civil Disturbances [MACDIS],' Department of Defense Directive, No. 3025.12, February 4, 1994, pp. 1, 3)

DoD 3025.12 also states: 'Under reference (r), the terms "major disaster" and "emergency" are defined substantially by action of the President in declaring that extant circumstances and risks justify Presidential implementation of the legal powers in those statutes.' In other words, at least as far as the Pentagon is concerned, the 'circumstances' in which troops can be deployed are 'defined substantially' by the President.

Use of Deadly Force

If troops are called out, civilians appear to have little protection against the use of force, including lethal force. None of the statutory exceptions to the PCA define or limit the powers of military personnel. Instead, these critical issues are left in the hands of the Pentagon. DoD 3025.12 directed the Army Secretary to 'promulgate orders, rules, and regulations, as appropriate, to govern all MACDIS operations in which the use of force or deadly force is or can be authorized'. The Secretary was also tasked with ensuring that all task force commanders 'promulgate supplemental rules of engagement and rules for the use of force'.

The Rules of Engagement for the 1992 Los Angeles riots deployment set three preconditions for the use of deadly force: (a) all other means have been exhausted; (b) there is no significantly increased risk of death or serious bodily harm to innocent persons; and (c) one or more of the following purposes exists: self-defence, prevention of a crime, defence of others, detention or prevention of escape of persons (Rasmussen 1999). These provisions left the way open for wide use of lethal force. A study of the operation noted that 'all other means have been exhausted' implied that non-lethal weapons were available to soldiers, but that was not the case. Few non-lethal riot and crowd control resources were distributed, nor did the soldiers (with the exception of some National Guard units) have any training in the use of non-lethal equipment. In one instance, on receiving a request to 'cover me', marines fired more than 200 bullets into a house with young children inside (Rasmussen 1999).

The study pointed out that decisions on the Rules of Engagement 'were left to all intents and purposes in the hands of the military' and the enforcement of those rules was 'at best haphazard'. Task force commanders devised the rules and Arming Orders, based on existing Department of Defense operational plans and regulations. There was no evidence that the relevant civilian authorities, the mayor and state governor, provided any input into the rules or how they were enforced. There was also substantial evidence that different units operated at different arming levels, and that this was widely known at the time (Rasmussen 1999).

Military Plans and Exercises

Since the formation of NorthCom in 2002, plans have been drafted and exercises conducted for large-scale internal troop deployments, usually under the banner of counter-terrorism preparedness.

According to a report published by the *Washington Post* in 2005, the Pentagon had developed plans for operations within the continental United States, in which terrorist attacks would be used as the justification for imposing virtual martial law on cities, regions or the entire country (Graham 2005). The article cited sources working at the NorthCom headquarters, located in Colorado Springs, Colorado. These classified plans outlined 15 potential crisis scenarios, ranging from 'low-end', which the article described as 'relatively modest crowd-control missions', to 'high-end', after as many as three simultaneous catastrophic mass-casualty events, such as a nuclear, biological or chemical weapons attacks. In each case, the military would deploy a quick-reaction force of as many as 3,000 troops per attack. More troops could be made available as needed. At the time of the article the plans were due to be sent to the Defense Secretary for approval. Military lawyers had studied their legal implications, and canvassed the use of the

National Guard, which is exempt from the PCA, to detain people. The plans also involved the military's intelligence agencies and the article described NorthCom's 'Combined Intelligence and Fusion Center, which joins military analysts with law enforcement and counterintelligence specialists from such civilian agencies as the FBI, the CIA and the Secret Service'.

Exercises have also been conducted to test domestic military capacities. One example is Exercise Vigilant Shield 2008, which was officially described as 'a Chairman of the Joint Chiefs of Staff-designated, North American Aerospace Defense Command (NORAD) and US Northern Command (USNORTHCOM)-sponsored, and US Joint Forces Command-supported Department of Defense exercise for homeland defense and defense support of civil authorities missions'. At various locations across the United States and the Territory of Guam, NORAD and NorthCom, along with the Pacific Command, the Department of Homeland Security and local, state and other federal responders exercised their 'response abilities against a variety of potential threats'. The purpose was said to be to 'provide local, state, tribal, interagency, Department of Defense, and non-governmental organizations and agencies involved in homeland security and homeland defense the opportunity to participate in a full range of exercise scenarios that will better prepare participants to prevent and respond to national crises' (US Northern Command 2007).

On occasions, residents of US cities have been confronted by armed troops conducting exercises in urban areas. In February 2008, a company of Marines arrived in Toledo, Ohio, carrying M16 rifles and wearing camouflage uniforms to carry out foot patrols, drive military vehicles through city streets, and engage in mock gunfights and ambushes with blank ammunition. However, the mayor ordered the Marines to leave because the sight of armed soldiers patrolling city streets would 'frighten people' (Reindl 2008).

During the 2008 Vibrant Response exercise at Fort Stewart, Georgia, three units of NorthCom's Consequence Management Response Force (CCMRF, pronounced 'sea-smurfs'), including two combat units from the 1st Brigade Combat Team, 3rd Army Division and the elite 82nd Combat Aviation Brigade, participated in mock drills designed to 'coordinate with local governments and interagency organizations such as the Federal Bureau of Investigation and the Federal Emergency Management Agency', according to a report on the website of US Northern Command News (US Northern Command 2008b).

Further, a report published by the US Army War College's Strategic Studies Institute in November 2008 indicated that Pentagon planners are preparing for a serious domestic crisis that could require the use of armed force to quell social struggles at home. Entitled, *Known Unknowns: Unconventional 'Strategic Shocks' in Defense Strategy Development*, the monograph stated that one of the key contingencies for which the US military must prepare is a 'violent, strategic dislocation inside the United States', which could be provoked by 'unforeseen economic collapse', 'loss of functioning political and legal order' or 'purposeful domestic resistance or insurgency' (Freier 2008, 31–2). The report stated:

> Widespread civil violence inside the United States would force the defense establishment to reorient priorities *in extremis* to defend basic domestic order … An American government and defense establishment lulled into complacency by a long-secure domestic order would be forced to rapidly divest some or most external security commitments in order to address rapidly expanding human insecurity at home. (Freier 2008, 32)

In other words, domestic unrest could erupt on such a scale that it threatened the entire established order and forced the Pentagon to call back its forces from overseas expeditions, such as those in Iraq and Afghanistan, for use against dissidents, protesters and other perceived enemies. The document continued:

> Under the most extreme circumstances, this might include use of military force against hostile groups inside the United States. Further, DoD [the Department of Defense] would be, by necessity, an essential enabling hub for the continuity of political authority in a multi-state or nationwide civil conflict or disturbance. (Freier 2008, 33)

The phrase, 'an essential enabling hub for continuity of authority', suggests either a government resting directly on the armed forces or some kind of military dictatorship.

Conclusion

The 'war on terror' declared in September 2001 has accelerated processes leading toward a greater mobilisation of the US military, both at home and abroad. Actions such as the overturning of the governments in Afghanistan and Iraq not only gave the military direct experience against civilian populations but were accompanied by intensive preparations for domestic use of the armed forces, also in the name of combating terrorism. For the first time in US history, an entire command, NorthCom, was established for internal use.

In the process, basic constitutional principles have been transgressed and the only specific legislative protection against military intervention, the *Posse Comitatus Act*, has been further eroded, both in law and practice. At the root of these developments has been a corrosive undermining of civilian supremacy, described by one former military officer as a creeping *coup d'état*. A resurgence of social and class tensions, as witnessed in Los Angeles in 1992, could see troops called out against civilians in a manner not experienced since the American Revolution itself.

Chapter 4
Canada: Making 'Domestic Security' a Core Mission

Like their British and American brethren, Canadians have long displayed antipathy to the use of the armed forces on home soil. One Canadian military historian notes:

> The application of military force by a democratic government within the confines of its own borders, and in some cases against its citizenry, has long been a controversial and politically sensitive topic. (Maloney 1997, 135)

In 1935, for example, when the Ontario government requisitioned the military to deal with a depression-era disturbance, the government was soundly defeated at the following year's election (Lerhe 2004, 9).

To some extent that underlying sentiment finds expression in law. The *Constitution Act* of 1867 established a military-civilian demarcation. While the armed forces ('militia, military and naval service and defence') were placed under the exclusive jurisdiction of the federal government by subsection 91(7), law enforcement and public safety were placed in the hands of the provinces.

Military operations against civilian populations, including French colonists and the Aboriginal peoples, featured heavily in the early history of Canada (CBC and Gillmor 2001, Vol. I). Moreover, troops were used regularly against striking workers in the early years of the twentieth century (Heron 1998; Fudge and Tucker 2004). By the late twentieth century, however, Canada had established an international image of a less militarist society than its much more militarily powerful southern neighbour, the United States (CBC and Gillmor 2001, Vol. II).

Since the advent of the 'war on terror' in 2001, the US-led invasions of Afghanistan and Iraq, and with the growth of global economic, strategic and military tensions, this image has been substantially repudiated. Prime Minister Stephen Harper summed up the shift in his message at the front of the 2008 Canada First Defence Strategy, where he wrote of 'rebuilding the Canadian Forces into a first-class, modern military', 'keeping our citizens safe and secure' and 'ensuring that Canada can return to the international stage as a credible and influential country' (Department of National Defence, Canada 2008, 1).

Citing a new period of global instability, military rearmament by competing foreign powers and 'challenges on the home front', the 2008 national defence strategy committed Canada to a substantial expansion of the Canadian Forces (CF), with the ambition of sustaining major operations simultaneously both abroad and internally. Notably, of the six core missions defined in the national defence strategy for the CF, three explicitly related to domestic security operations in civilian settings: supporting major international events such as the 2010 Vancouver Winter Olympics and the G-8 summit of the same year; responding to terrorist attacks; and supporting civilian authorities during crises.

The document projects a more active domestic role for the CF, asserting that 'Canadians rightly expect their military to be there for them in domestic crises'. Annual military spending was to be increased to more than $30 billion by 2025–26, treble the 1986–87 level, and the number of CF personnel from about 82,000 in 2000–2001 to 100,000 by 2027–28 (Department of National Defence, Canada 2008, 3, 7, 11, 14).

Groundbreaking steps have been taken to prepare to use these expanding forces internally. In 2006, the Canada Command was established to focus on domestic operations, and in 2008 the Canada Command and its US counterpart, the Northern Command, signed a Civil Assistance Plan (CAP) that allows the military of each nation to support the other during 'civil emergencies', including terrorist incidents and 'criminal activity'.

During the same period, thousands of Canadian troops have been deployed to Afghanistan, while the elite SAS-style Joint Task Force Two (JTF2) has been used in Iraq, Haiti and possibly other countries. This turn to a more aggressive military posture internationally is likely to increase the possibility of domestic military intervention for a number of reasons. In part, such operations generate a political and military climate of opinion more favourable to greater utilisation of the armed forces. At the same time, public opposition to militarism, as witnessed by the large demonstrations across Canada and globally in 2002 and 2003 against the Iraq war, may well fuel political discontent that may ultimately be met with military might. The 'blooding' of soldiers in operations against civilians abroad may also make the political and military establishment more confident that the CF has the capacity, training and internal resolve needed to confront citizens at home.

Canada's entire civilian national security apparatus has been transformed since 2001. The term 'national security' or a close equivalent, such as 'security of Canada', now appears in more than 30 Canadian statutes, often creating new government powers or limiting government obligations (Forcese 2008, 6–7). Overarching responsibility has been vested in the Department of Public Safety and Emergency Preparedness, established in 2005, which goes by the name Public Safety Canada. The Minister of Public Safety has been given wide-ranging coordination powers and is specifically charged with exercising 'leadership relating to public safety and emergency preparedness'. The department hosts the Government Operations Centre, an interdepartmental and interagency body tasked with coordinating responses to 'anything – real or perceived, imminent or actual, natural disaster or terrorist activity – that threatens the safety and security of Canadians or the integrity of Canada's critical infrastructure (Forcese 2008, 77–8).

Constitutional Issues

Like the American and Australian Constitutions, the Canadian constitutional instruments embody the principles of civil/military demarcation and civilian control over the military. The *Constitution Act 1867*, s 91 (7) gave the federal legislature jurisdiction over 'Militia, Military and Naval Service, and Defence', thus reserving military matters to the national government. By contrast, ss 92 (14) and (15) placed law enforcement in the hands of the provinces. These provisions at least implicitly reserve to the provinces control over civilian law enforcement and limit the power of the federal government to intervene militarily. However, s 91 (27) allocated criminal law to the federal sphere, and the federal government has residual authority over matters not assigned exclusively to the provinces. The Supreme Court of Canada has interpreted the latter power as permitting the national parliament to legislate for national emergencies (Forcese 2008, 63).

Contradictory possibilities are thrown up by section 15 of the *Constitution Act*: 'The Command-in-Chief of the Land and Naval Militia, and of all Naval and Military Forces, of and in Canada, is hereby declared to continue and be vested in the Queen.' This provision today arguably vests command in civilian hands, via the vice-regal representative, the Governor-General, appointed by the federal government. However, the section also leaves open the possibility of the Governor-General exercising the old royal prerogative powers of the British monarchy to deploy the armed forces without the authority, or even against the wishes, of an elected government. (This possibility is discussed in Chapter 7, dealing with the similar situation in Australia).

Canadian courts have also recognised the continued existence of the royal prerogative as a source of executive power, encompassing 'the powers and privileges accorded by the common law to the Crown'. Legislation can override or abrogate prerogative powers, but only if the statute makes this clear by explicit language or necessary implication. Some court rulings would suggest doubt may still exist about whether a legislative scheme has replaced prerogative powers (Forcese 2008, 67–8).

Canada has two statements of basic rights, although neither expressly prohibits or curtails the domestic mobilisation of the Canadian Forces to suppress political or social unrest. The *Canadian Charter of Rights and Freedoms* and the *Canadian Bill of Rights* do not allow for abridgement of rights during emergencies, but they do permit parliament to circumscribe at least some of the rights. Section 33 of the *Charter* allows the federal and provincial legislatures to exclude most *Charter* provisions by stating that a statute operates 'notwithstanding' the *Charter*. No parliament has utilised this power in an emergency situation, but it remains possible for this happen in a crisis (Forcese 2008, 35, 120–22).

Otherwise, section 1 of the *Charter* guarantees the rights and freedoms set out in it 'subject only to such reasonable limits prescribed by law as can be demonstrably justified in a free and democratic society'. This protection is far from absolute. In the event of a crisis involving military deployment, the issue of what are 'reasonable limits' may well arise. In *Operation Dismantle v Canada Inc* ([1985] 1 S.C.R. 441), Wilson J of the Supreme Court said the concept of 'right' used in the *Charter* had to 'take account of the fact that the self-contained political community which comprises the State is faced with at least the possibility, if not the reality, of external threats to both its collective well-being and to the individual well-being of its citizens' (at 489–90). While these remarks related to external threats, a similar claim could be made about internal threats.

Section 2 of the *Charter* recognises 'fundamental freedoms' of conscience and religion; thought, belief, opinion and expression; peaceful assembly; and association. Other sections set out certain democratic, mobility, equality and legal rights, some of which may limit military powers. For example, a person cannot be deprived of the 'right to life, liberty and security of the person' except 'in accordance with the principles of fundamental justice'. Everyone has the rights 'to be secure against unreasonable search or seizure' and 'not to be arbitrarily detained or imprisoned'.

These provisions can restrict violations of democratic rights, at least where the rules of procedural fairness have not been followed. In *Suresh v Canada (Minister of Citizenship and Immigration)* ([2002] 1 S.C.R. 3, 2002 SCC 1), the Supreme Court ruled that deportation to face torture was generally unconstitutional and therefore Suresh was entitled to a fair hearing with procedural safeguards before being deported. However, the Canadian courts have generally treated military and national security considerations as overriding procedural fairness (for example, *Chiarelli v Canada (Minister of Justice)* [1992] 1 SCR 711). Moreover, the phrases 'reasonable limits', 'unreasonable' and 'arbitrarily' in the *Charter* leave considerable scope for military intervention, provided it is authorised by legislation, common law or judicially-recognised prerogative powers. In a number of cases, the Supreme Court has suggested that the right to life, liberty and security of the person can be tempered or violated in times of war, national emergency or other security exigencies (Forcese 2008, 37).

Similar issues arise with the *Canadian Bill of Rights*, which declares 'human rights and fundamental freedoms' that include life, liberty, security of the person and enjoyment of property, except where deprived by due process of law. Other rights listed in section 1 of the *Bill* are equality before the law and the protection of the law; and the freedoms of religion, speech, assembly and association, and the press. However the protection of these rights and freedoms is far from guaranteed. Section 2 of the *Bill* merely specifies that federal statutes be construed and applied as not to abrogate, abridge or infringe any of the rights or freedoms, unless expressly provided otherwise by an Act of Parliament. Therefore, it remains possible for federal legislation to override these provisions, as happened with the *War Measures Act*, prior to its repeal by the *Emergencies Act* in 1988 (Forcese 2008, 119).

One scholar of Canadian national security law has concluded: 'In Canadian constitutional law, it seems clear that *Charter* protections may be tempered where national security threats are at issue' (Forcese 2008, 35). The same appears to apply to the *Bill of Rights*.

Overview of Legal Mechanisms

Notwithstanding the possible constitutional limits, a remarkable array of legal mechanisms exists for mobilising CF personnel and capacities, including intelligence resources, to deal with civil unrest.

- Part VI of the *National Defence Act* permits the Attorney General of a province to request 'military aid of the civil power' to suppress a 'riot or disturbance'. The request is made direct to the Chief of the Defence Staff – not the federal government – who is obliged by law to execute the request.
- Section 273.6 of the same Act allows the federal cabinet or Defence Minister to authorise the CF to 'perform any duty involving public service'. The section also empowers the cabinet or the minister to authorise CF assistance in any law enforcement matter, provided it is considered to be in the national interest and cannot be effectively dealt with without CF assistance.
- The *Emergencies Act* confers extraordinary powers on the federal Cabinet, allowing it to govern by decree when it perceives the existence of 'threats to the security of Canada', including acts of serious political violence or activities aimed at overthrowing the system of government.
- The Solicitor General of Canada can, under the National Counter-Terrorism Plan and the Canadian Forces Armed Assistance Directions (CFAAD), call for armed assistance by the CF to respond to terrorist incidents or other disturbances affecting national security.
- The federal government can and does use the military in aid of its own responsibilities, such as guarding federal buildings and facilities.
- Various provisions allow for military assistance for disasters and emergencies.
- Assistance can be requested for the Royal Canadian Mounted Police (RCMP) in penitentiaries and customs enforcement.
- Under the 1996 Canadian Forces Assistance to Provincial Police Forces Directions (CFAPPFD), a provincial Attorney General can request assistance through the Department of Public Safety and Emergency Preparedness Canada.
- The *Public Safety Act 2002* strengthened the powers of federal anti-terrorism and national security agencies, including the CF, to share critical information.
- As in Britain, martial law may be declared.

It should be noted that previous powers contained in the *War Measures Act* of 1914 were replaced in 1988 by the *Emergencies Act*. The *War Measures Act* conferred extreme powers on the federal government, allowing it effectively to rule by decree when it perceived the existence of 'war, invasion or insurrection, real or apprehended'. During both world wars, the Act was used to issue detailed regulations limiting the freedom of Canadians of foreign descent. The Act was invoked to authorise a military intervention in a domestic crisis in October and November 1970, when a state of 'apprehended insurrection' was declared to exist in Québec and emergency regulations were proclaimed in response to two kidnappings by the separatist Front de Libération du Québec (FLQ).

Despite Canada's recent pacifist reputation, large-scale military interventions have occurred four times in the past four decades: during the FLQ crisis (1963–70), the 1976 Olympic Games and the Oka standoff (1990), and for disaster relief in Manitoba (1997) (Maloney 1997, 135–52). Lesser mobilisations under the CFAPPFD occurred at Davis Inlet (1994), Gustafsen Lake (1995) and Ipperwash Provincial Park (1995) (Haslip 2002, 2). After reviewing these experiences, a Canadian military historian concluded that the mechanisms for military assistance to civilian authorities were 'extremely flexible' and ensured that 'the military is not overburdened with legalities' (Maloney 1997, 145).

The changes made in 2008 to the national defence strategy suggest that operations against civil unrest are likely to become more prevalent in the coming period. Significantly, an 'aid of the civil power' scenario on the CF's Defence Planning and Management website is based on the prospect of economic and social conflicts producing large-scale unrest and armed insurrections:

> Canada has been suffering through several years of drought and across the country water rationing has been enforced. Minor disputes over access to water have become more and more commonplace, pitting individual against individual and individual against industry. As water has grown more and more scarce, the groups involved in disputes have had time to become organized. The affected region has expanded to include the jurisdiction of two provinces. In at least one case a minor dispute has escalated creating large-scale unrest, including armed insurrections. The situation has reached a point where civilian authorities can no longer cope, and military assistance has been requested under Part XI of the National Defence Act. (Department of National Defence, Canada, Defence Planning and Management 2004)

The website also refers to a restricted document entitled 'Crowd Confrontation Operations'.

CF's intelligence capacity has expanded in recent years, enhancing its collaboration with domestic intelligence agencies such as the RCMP and the Canadian Security Intelligence Service (CSIS). The Department of National Defence also hosts the Communications Security Establishment (CSE), the national cryptologic and signals intelligence agency, giving the military significant capacities to intercept and monitor telecommunications (Forcese 2008, 75).

A Brief History and Five Case Studies

Following the acquisition of Canada in 1760, the British army garrison troops replied to requests for 'aid to civil power' in accordance with their military regulations. In 1868 Canadian laws concerning the police, illegal assembly and riots were enacted, and the *Militia Act* authorised calling out Canadian troops. British practice generally remained the model, although Regulations and Orders for the Canadian Militia replaced the British ones in 1870. In 1924 the power of calling out troops was moved from local authorities to provincial attorneys general.

From 1796 to 1870 British troops, occasionally helped by local militiamen, provided aid to the civil power roughly 100 times. Since then Canadian troops have helped maintain or restore public order 140 times and have helped repress penitentiary riots 20 times. Half the former occurred before 1900, usually because of absence, shortage or improper training of police.

During the years before and after the First World War, soldiers were mobilised whenever strikes threatened the established order. In the words of two prominent labour historians: 'When strikes took the form of mass unrest involving unskilled workers, troops were deployed.' And during 1906, the use of military force 'spiked dramatically', when the troops were called out four times to deal with mass strikes by unskilled workers (Fudge and Tucker 2004, 18, 49).

The most notable strike of this period was the Winnipeg general strike of 1919. The 21 June confrontation with the Mounties and soldiers, following earlier arrests and confiscation of documents, resulted in 30 casualties, including one death. However, the use of troops was not confined to Winnipeg; they were also mobilised during the subsequent Vancouver general strike, against Quebec textile workers in 1920, coal miners in St John's and Halifax in 1922, Sydney steelworkers in 1923 and Nova Scotia miners in 1925 (Heron 1998, 35–6, 67–8, 113).

Since 1933, troops have not been involved in strike-breaking except under the *War Measures Act* (now the *Emergencies Act*) and all call-outs except one have taken place in Ontario and Québec, which are the only provinces not policed by the RCMP. Over half the penitentiary call-outs have occurred since 1962, and in most cases the army did not have to use force. On five occasions, troops have been used against Aboriginal peoples, from the Red River Rebellion of 1870 to Oka in 1990 (Haslip 2002, 4).

During the late 1990s and early years of the twenty-first century, with the development of substantial anti-globalisation and anti-capitalist demonstrations against summits of world leaders, the CF was mobilised regularly to assist police in preventing or suppressing protests at such gatherings. For the 2001 Summit of the Americas in Québec City, some 1,200 CF personnel joined 6,700 police and hundreds of customs officers in the security operation, with another 3,000 soldiers on standby at nearby CF bases. Heavily-armed police used tear gas, water cannon and rubber bullets, with CF troops maintaining a support role (Legras 2001). The 2002 G-8 summit in Alberta saw the largest homeland mobilisation of troops since the 1970 FLQ crisis. More than 6,000 CF personnel and 4,500 police were deployed to enforce a 6.5-kilometre no-go zone around the summit venue, while three anti-aircraft missile batteries were set up and CF-18 fighter jets policed a 150-kilometre no-fly zone (Adelaide 2002).

Five case studies since 1970 underline the broad scope for military intervention against domestic unrest.

Québec Crisis 1963–70

The Québec crisis, which began in 1963, ultimately involved several simultaneous military operations, each relying on a different legal mechanism. The Front de Libération du Québec (FLQ) began a bombing campaign in 1963, with a view to galvanising support for separatism. At that point, the provincial government explored with regional army commanders the possibility of deploying troops. The army commander advised that military intervention would only spread FLQ activity beyond Montréal and that if troops were wanted, a formal request would have to be made for aid of the civil power. No such request was made in 1963, but two were made in 1969 after a further spate of bombings and a substantial pro-FLQ protest in Montréal. On the first occasion in March, a mechanised infantry battalion was deployed to back up police, although its services were not required to disperse the protest. In October, during a civil service and police strike, a battalion was again mobilised on standby, while troops protected federal facilities and conducted mobile patrols (Maloney 1997, 138–9).

In 1970, after the FLQ kidnapped a Québec minister, the provincial Premier asked Prime Minister Trudeau to invoke the *War Measures Act* and 'send in the army'. Trudeau, however, would only agree to a formal aid of the civil power request under the *National Defence Act*. While the Premier apparently vacillated for several days, the army chief drew up a plan for intervention, codenamed Operation Essay, should the Québec government request it. In the meantime, the federal government, through the office of the Solicitor General, requested military assistance for the RCMP to secure federal government buildings in Ottawa, provide armed escorts for federal officials and supply a quick reaction force. Codenamed Operation Ginger, this deployment involved 1,000 soldiers. Once the Québec Attorney General formally requested military aid, some 9,000 troops were placed on alert or dispatched to about 150 sites designated for protection.

After a cabinet debate, Trudeau then went further, invoking the emergency powers of the *War Measures Act*. Trudeau's view was that the *National Defence Act* provisions were too restrictive, because they did not cross provincial boundaries (Maloney 1997, 138–9).

Under the emergency regulations, the FLQ was declared an illegal organisation, normal liberties were suspended, and arrests and detentions were authorised without charge. Ultimately more than 12,000 troops were deployed in full battle order for a massive show of force to the citizens of Montréal. Airborne forces were brought in to conduct special operations, while soldiers conducted cordon and search operations jointly with Québec provincial police. Over 450 persons were detained in Québec, most of whom were eventually released without the laying or hearing of charges.

In all, ten shots were fired, all warnings, without casualties. It could easily have been worse. At one point, Trudeau directed the Vice Chief of Defence Staff to place 'tanks on all the bridges in Montreal and men all over the city to show these pipsqueaks who has the power'. When troops arrived in Ottawa without Rules of Engagement and sought advice from the RCMP on what to do when approached by unknown individuals, they were told 'shoot them, but let us know afterwards so we can clean up the situation' (Lerhe 2004, 10).

The 1970 crisis demonstrated the potential for political misuse of, or interference in, domestic military mobilisations. It also revealed the real danger of fatalities, as well as drastic infringements on civil liberties. In response to criticism, Trudeau later pledged to refine and limit the application of the Act. The Act had not been modified by the time his government was defeated in 1984, but in 1988, the *Emergencies Act* was passed to replace the *War Measures Act* (Lerhe 2004, 11).

1976 Olympic Games

For the 1976 Montréal Olympics, the federal cabinet decided that the legal way to mobilise military support was to have the Solicitor General formally ask the National Defence Minister to provide assistance to the civil authority. In other words, the action was envisaged as preventative, rather than active and involving aid of the civil power. Nevertheless, preparations were made for armed intervention if judged necessary. CF tasks included VIP and site security at all Games venues, and armed response to any situation that developed. The training 'threat scenarios' included demonstrations as well as acts of terrorism. The military deployment, some 16,000 personnel, was deliberately large, designed to act as a visible deterrent. Soldiers carried small arms, but were not in full battle dress as they had been in 1970. Jets and helicopters enforced no-fly zones. However, there were no specific terrorist threats to the Games and no incidents eventuated (Maloney 1997, 140–41).

The 1990 Oka Standoff

In 1990, the Québec government requested aid of the civil power under the *National Defence Act* to dismantle barricades at Oka and Kanewake in Montréal erected by indigenous people, organised by the 'Mohawk warriors', who were protesting against a proposal to extend a golf course across a former burial ground. A small number of protestors, estimated at 50 to 70, were armed. More than 4,400 soldiers and 12 army battalions, including tanks, were deployed in another show of force. Operation Salon was assigned four tasks: remove barricades, restore freedom of movement, remove strong points and restore public order and security. The last task was particularly vague and open to broad interpretation.

Intensive operations ensued, including frequent night patrols, low-level helicopter flights, surveillance aircraft and well-aimed spotlights, some designed to unhinge the insurgents psychologically. Armoured personnel carriers were used to intimidate the indigenous activists into dismantling the barricades (Maloney 1997, 142–4).

Although the mobilisation was requisitioned by the provincial government, in accordance with the Act, the federal Prime Minister signalled that the army would take over the barricades. This intervention cut across the legal procedure, whereby the Chief of Defence Staff (CDS) was meant to respond directly to the provincial Attorney General. During the operation, the CDS sat in on national cabinet meetings, underscoring both the political involvement of the federal government and the close integration of the military high command into the civilian executive. Media releases were also placed under tight political control (Lerhe 2004, 11–12).

The 1997 Red River Flood and 1998 Ice Storm

Two military mobilisations of unprecedented magnitude occurred in 1997 and 1998 in response to natural disasters. A public welfare emergency was declared in 1997 to authorise the deployment of military personnel, and the Manitoba Premier also subsequently formally requested assistance to the civil authority. More than 8,500 soldiers, sailors and airmen participated. The floods were fought in battlefield style, complete with reconnaissance aircraft, ground units, satellite tracking, strategic airlift, military police controlling movements and armed units combating looting (Maloney 1997, 144–5).

For the 1998 ice storm that struck a major portion of Québec and southern Ontario, the federal government mobilised 12,000 troops, the largest such deployment in Canadian peacetime history. The operation revealed the deterioration of civilian emergency services and public utilities, such as Hydro-Québec (Legras 1998).

The 1990s Somalia Affair

Although it was not a domestic deployment, during the mid-1990s, the Somalia Affair highlighted the propensity for military operations against civilians to lead to abuses, particularly when governments authorise aggressive conduct. The CF deployment to Somalia for a US-led mission – Operation Restore Hope – ostensibly for peacekeeping and humanitarian purposes, led to one local teenager, Shidane Arone, being tortured to death by Canadian soldiers, and two Somalis being shot in the back, one fatally. After grisly photos of Arone's torture were leaked to the media, causing public revulsion, the government felt compelled to conduct an official inquiry. Although the inquiry was later controversially cut short, evidence to the inquiry showed that Lieutenant-Colonel Matthieu authorised deadly force against unarmed Somalis inside the Airborne Regiment's compound, exceeding the Rules of Engagement (ROE). To justify his orders, Matthieu cited well-publicised comments of Foreign Affairs Minister Barbara McDougall who 'boasted that soldiers going to Somalia had been provided with ROE that permitted them to shoot first and ask questions later' (Lerhe 2004, 19, citing Commission of Inquiry into the Deployment of Canadian Forces to Somalia 1997, 659–60).

The 'Domestic Security' Focus from 2006

A Defence Policy Statement, *A Role of Pride and Influence in the World*, issued in 2006, announced a shift in Canadian policy, which would mean making domestic security the primary focus of the Canadian Forces:

> Events such as the tragic attacks against our neighbours on September 11, 2001, demonstrate that Canada is also vulnerable to terrorism and threats emanating from failed and failing states around the world. To respond to these threats, the new policy statement sets out a plan to make Canadian security the first priority for the Canadian Forces. To better protect Canada and Canadians, the Canadian Forces will be reorganized to more effectively and quickly respond to domestic crises, as well as support other Government departments as required …
>
> It will require the Canadian Forces to re-examine their approach to domestic operations. Most significantly, the Forces will now view Canada as a single operational area where the best available resources from our maritime, land, air and special operations forces can be brought to bear on a contingency, wherever it occurs. As such, the Canadian Forces will establish a single national operational command headquarters (Canada Command) to respond to domestic crises. (Department of National Defence, Canada 2006)

Accordingly, in 2006, the Canada Command was established to focus on domestic operations. Without any legislative authorisation, that shift was extended in 2008, when the commanders of the Canada Command and the US Northern Command signed a Civil Assistance Plan (CAP) that allows the military from one nation to support the armed forces of the other during a 'civil emergency'. This could mean US troops being deployed against dissenting Canadians, and *vice versa*. US Northern Command commander, Air Force General Gene Renuart, who signed the pact with his Canada Command counterpart, Air Force Lieutenant-General Marc Dumais, described the document as 'a unique, bilateral military plan to align our respective national military plans to respond quickly to the other nation's requests for military support of civil authorities' (US Northern Command 2008, 1).

Although the CAP was presented substantially under the banner of responding to natural disasters, its provisions are not confined to such emergencies. Among the examples cited in the plan were 'effects of a terrorist attack' and 'criminal activity'. Moreover, the use of violent force was envisaged: the plan referred to Rules of Engagement for use of force and stated that, without further oral or written direction, CF personnel were entitled to use force in self-defence, up to and including deadly force. The plan said it did not apply to support for law enforcement, which was to be included in the Canada-United States Combined Defense Plan (Canada Command and US Northern Command 2008, 1, 2, 4).

National Defence Act

Potentially, the *National Defence Act* (NDA) provisions allow for considerable use of the armed forces to suppress domestic political unrest and dissent. The CF is liable to be called out whenever a 'riot or disturbance of the peace, beyond the powers of the civil authorities to suppress, prevent or deal with' occurs or is, in the opinion of a provincial attorney general, 'likely to occur' (NDA s 275). Considerable discretionary powers are placed in the hands of provincial attorneys general and the CF chief. Once an attorney general submits a written requisition, the Chief of the Defence Staff must call out the armed forces, and cannot dispute any statement of fact contained in the requisition. Nor can a provincial government call into question the competence or authority of the attorney general's requisition (NDA s 280).

The Chief of the Defence Staff, in turn, has broad powers to call out such parts of the CF that he or she 'considers necessary for the purpose of suppressing or preventing' any riot or disturbance. These powers are exercised independently of the federal government, although they are 'subject to such directions as the [Defence] Minister considers appropriate in the circumstances' (NDA s 278). Called-out CF personnel automatically acquire all the powers of police officers, which include powers of arrest, search and seizure and use of lethal force, as well as whatever powers they hold as soldiers. They are deemed to have 'all of the powers and duties of constables', in addition to 'their powers and duties as officers and non-commissioned members'. However, they 'shall act only as a military body and are individually liable to obey the orders of their superior officers' (NDA s 282). The latter clause could be interpreted as legally requiring troops to obey superior orders, regardless of whether those orders are lawful.

No time limits are set for call-outs, which can be scaled up or down at the discretion of the CF chief. The CF will remain on duty, in such strength as the Chief of the Defence Staff deems necessary, until the provincial attorney general notifies that the armed forces are no longer required (NDA s 283).

In addition, s 273.6 of the Act allows the federal cabinet or Defence Minister to authorise the CF to 'perform any duty involving public service'. The section also empowers the cabinet or the Minister to authorise CF assistance in 'any law enforcement matter', provided it is considered to be in the national interest and that it cannot be effectively dealt with without CF assistance. Moreover, the section provides a blanket authorisation for law enforcement assistance 'that is of a minor nature and limited to logistical, technical or administrative support'. Thus, s 273.6 is capable of supporting considerable military involvement in civilian affairs. It creates a wide executive discretion to mobilise the CF without public notice or even parliamentary oversight.

Emergencies Act

The *Emergencies Act* permits the Canadian government to rule by executive orders and regulations in any 'national emergency', which is defined broadly as 'an urgent and critical situation of a temporary nature' that 'seriously endangers the lives, health or safety of Canadians' or 'seriously threatens the ability of the Government of Canada to preserve the sovereignty, security and territorial integrity of Canada'. Four kinds of emergency are provided for: public welfare (natural disasters), public order (internal security), international (external threats to security or territorial integrity) and war (war or other armed conflict, real or imminent). Considerable scope exists for domestic military intervention under the other three headings, but 'public order emergencies' explicitly relate to suppressing certain types of political opposition.

A public order emergency, covered by Part II of the Act, is one that arises from 'threats to the security of Canada' as defined by the *Canadian Security Intelligence Service Act*. Section 2 of that statute refers to espionage, sabotage, foreign influenced activities, 'acts of serious political violence' for the purpose of achieving a 'political, religious or ideological objective' within Canada or a foreign state, and activities 'directed toward or intended ultimately to lead to the destruction or overthrow by violence' of the Canadian system of government. Although the definition exempts 'lawful advocacy, protest or dissent', unless linked to any of the proscribed activities, the section leaves considerable scope for emergency rule directed against various forms of political dissent, particularly if they can be depicted as potentially violent.

Once a public order emergency has been declared, the Governor in Council (normally on behalf of the federal cabinet) can issue far-reaching orders, including banning public assemblies, stopping travel and seizing control of public services, and imposing summary convictions for up to six months of imprisonment. There are no unlimited search and seizure powers, previously available under the *War Measures Act*, for a public order emergency, but they remain for an international emergency. Emergency powers can last initially for 30 days and be continuously renewed. Ministers and other personnel exercising emergency powers 'in good faith' are protected from personal legal liability, although government liability and compensation remain. Parliamentary scrutiny is weak and belated: either House of Parliament can revoke an emergency declaration, but only after a delay of at least seven sitting days (*Emergencies Act*, ss 3, 16–26, 47–8, 58–9).

The statute states that it does not confer on the government the power to detain, imprison or intern Canadian citizens or permanent residents 'on the basis of race, national or ethnic origin, colour, religion, sex, age or mental or physical disability' (*Emergencies Act*, s 4). This proviso, however, does not preclude detention on political or ideological grounds, nor does it apply to non-citizens without permanent residency status.

How the Act can be used to trigger military mobilisations can be seen from natural disaster operations. The public welfare emergency provisions of the Act were activated to direct the CF to support provincial and local authorities in the Saguenay floods of 1996, the Manitoba floods of 1997 and the ice storm event of 1998. Because of the lack of adequate civilian emergency services, especially on a national scale, the CF is often depicted as the only agency capable of responding effectively to such calamities (for example, McCluskey 2004). In this way, public opinion is conditioned to accept, and even demand, military interventions.

One limitation on use of the Act, compared to its predecessor, the *War Measures Act*, is that under s 25(3), the Governor in Council cannot declare a public emergency unless requested by a province, or the emergency extends to more than one province. Thus, as with the *National Defence Act*, the power to invoke the emergency powers and call in the troops depends on provincial consent, at least until a wider emergency (beyond a single province) is said to exist. For that reason, there have been calls from within military and police circles for the Act to be amended (Lerhe 2004, 17).

Forcese states that it is doubtful whether the Act could be used, as the *War Measures Act* was in October 1970, to abridge fundamental civil liberties. He explains that the Act's preamble says that the 'special temporary measures' are subject to the *Charter*, the *Canadian Bill of Rights* and 'must have regard to the International Covenant on Civil and Political Rights, particularly with respect to those fundamental rights that are not to be limited or abridged even in a national emergency' (Forcese 2008, 124). However, such preambles are not legally binding and, as previously discussed, the *Charter* and the *Bill of Rights* provide no secure protection of basic rights in the context of an alleged national security emergency.

Forcese acknowledges that the 'fog of war' may cloud the ability of the public and the courts to challenge government actions taken under the banner of an emergency, particularly a political emergency. Forcese cites Ignatieff's warning that emergencies are most corrosive of democracy when they are proclaimed 'on grounds that involve bad faith, manipulation of evidence, exaggeration of risk, or the prospect of political advantage' (Forcese 2008, 116–17). An added difficulty noted by Ignatieff is that the executive invariably claims to hold secret and undisclosable information that justifies the emergency powers (Ignatieff 2004, 51). Referring to the 'war on terror', Ignatieff suggests that 'in a long twilight war, largely fought by secret means, the key issue is maintaining as much legal and legislative oversight as is compatible with the necessity for decisive action' (Ignatieff 2004, 39). However, Ignatieff's proposition leaves considerable room for a government to argue that the need for 'decisive action' takes precedence over, or is not compatible with, civil liberties and legal scrutiny.

National Counter-Terrorism Plan

The Solicitor General of Canada, under the authority of the Government of Canada, is responsible for the National Counter-Terrorism Plan. The plan establishes lines of communication and policy to guide officials in resolving a terrorist incident. It also describes the authorities and responsibilities of federal departments and agencies in a counter-terrorism situation, and outlines the legislation, conventions and agreements to which Canada is a party. The procedures for employing a military unit in a counter-terrorism situation are also detailed in the National Counter-Terrorism Plan.

The Canadian Forces Armed Assistance Directions (CFAAD) establishes the procedures for the request and provision of armed assistance by the CF to the RCMP to resolve disturbances affecting the national interest. Provisions have also been made to ensure that CF resources can be expeditiously positioned close to the site of a disturbance while the situation is developing, and before any armed assistance is authorised.

The CFAAD come into play on the basis of a request by either:

- the Commissioner of the RCMP submitting to the Chief of the Defence Staff for the positioning of a military force in anticipation of a request from the Solicitor General; or
- the Solicitor General of Canada submitting to the Minister of National Defence for the provision of such assistance by the CF to the RCMP, and for the purpose of assisting in suppressing, preventing or otherwise dealing with the disturbance.

CF members engaged in armed assistance activities would be given the status of police officers.

Since 1993, the Canadian Forces have provided the country's federal anti-terrorist forces, replacing the RCMP in that function. Joint Task Force Two (JTF2) is the CF unit responsible for federal counter-terrorist operations. Its mission is to provide 'a force capable of rendering armed assistance in the resolution of an issue or a potential issue that affects national security. While JTF2's primary role is counter-terrorism, its personnel can be employed in any type of military operations, which include, but are not limited to, surveillance, security advice and close personal protection' (Department of National Defence, Canada n.d.). While the unit has a primary focus on counter-terrorism, its roles have expanded over the years and it has likely assumed roles similar to that of the British Special Air Services (SAS) and the United States Delta Force.

The Canadian government has been secretive about releasing any information about the capabilities, organisation and operational missions of the unit. However, some information has appeared (Pugliese 2002). JTF2 states that the year 2001 was an important milestone in its history when the unit was committed to the US-led International Special Operations Forces coalition in Afghanistan. This deployment was the first time that JTF2 was acknowledged to have served in a major combat role outside Canada (Department of National Defence, Canada n.d.).

Wider use appears to be being made of the JTF2. According to the Canadian Broadcasting Corporation (CBC), JTF2 was in Haiti at the time that Haitian president Jean-Bertrand Aristide was ousted from power. The unit protected the Canadian embassy and secured the airport. In 2006, the Pentagon and the British Foreign Office both commented on the instrumental role JTF2 played in rescuing a British and Canadian 'Christian Peacemaker Team' that was being held hostage in Iraq. There has been speculation in the Canadian media on possible JTF2 operational deployments elsewhere, including in conflicts involving native groups in Ontario, Québec and British Columbia and other domestic security operations.

Military Surveillance and Intelligence

The CF and Department of National Defence (DND) have significant surveillance and intelligence capacities that can be used domestically. Defence Intelligence performs a variety of functions, including collecting and analysing material in support of CF's deployments, which may be internal. It also cooperates with the civilian security and police agencies, such as the Canadian Security Intelligence Service (CSIS) and the RCMP in the area of domestic intelligence. DND also hosts the Communications Security Establishment (CSE), a signals intelligence agency that has substantial electronic eavesdropping capacities.

In theory, both the CF's SIGINT Operations Centre (CF-SOC) and the CSE are constrained in intercepting purely domestic communications – that is, they are subject to the provisions of the *Criminal Code* and *CSIS Act* that affect the police and CSIS. However, the *National Defence Act* permits the Defence Minister to authorise interceptions of internal communications in order to obtain 'foreign intelligence', and four such authorisations were in place as of 2006. Even in official circles, doubts exist about whether such intercepts are compatible with the *Charter of Rights and Freedoms* (Forcese 2008, 75, 453–63). Former Chief Justice Lamer, in his 2005–2006 report as CSE Commissioner, complained that 'supporting documentation provided by CSE as part of requests for the Minister's authorization address the underlying foreign intelligence requirements only in general terms' (Forcese 2008, 457).

Vancouver Winter Olympics and G-8 Summit

Two major events in 2010 were to see further major military mobilisations within Canada. According to local media reports, up to 1,800 military personnel were to be housed in six to ten 'austere' temporary camps near venues for the February 2010 winter Olympics around Vancouver. Each camp would accommodate 200 to 800 Department of National Defence (DND) and Canadian Forces personnel between November 2009 and April 2010, according to an August 2008 newsletter from Defence Construction Canada (DCC), a Crown corporation that handles construction and infrastructure projects for DND.

A military spokesman for the Integrated Security Unit (ISU), a joint effort between the RCMP, Vancouver Police, West Vancouver Police and the CF to 'maintain public safety' during the 2010 Games, said the CF would only have a supporting role, though he did not specify what form that support would take.

No details have yet been released of security arrangements for the 2010 G8 Summit to be held at the Deerhurst Resort in Huntsville, Ontario, about two hours north of Toronto. The previous G8 summit, convened in Kananaskis County, Alberta became the object of the largest domestic security operation in Canadian history and the most important homeland mobilisation of Canadian troops since the 1970 October Crisis.

More than 6,000 CF personnel and 4,500 were deployed in Kananaskis and the city of Calgary, which is about 100 kilometres from the summit site. A 6.5-kilometre no-go zone was established around Kananaskis Village and three anti-aircraft missile batteries set up as a last line of defence should a plane evade the CF-18 fighters that enforced a 150-kilometre radius no-fly zone. The only road through Kananaskis County was blocked with security checkpoints (Adelaide 2002).

In preparation for the summit, the Chrétien government introduced legislation in 2001 to amend the *National Defence Act* to allow the Defence Minister to declare any area of land, water or air a 'military security zone'. In effect, the law would have provided another mechanism for domestic military intervention, and given the armed forces considerable powers over civilians. Such zones could have been declared in relation to, *inter alia*, 'property, a place or thing that the Canadian Forces have been directed to protect in order to fulfil a duty required by law'. The CF could 'prohibit, restrict or control access' to a zone, and 'forcibly remove' any person or vehicle found in the zone without authorisation (Bill C-42 (2001)). After considerable public outcry, the provision was withdrawn (Privacy Commissioner of Canada 2002).

Conclusion

In line with the developments across the border in the United States, a major shift has occurred in Canada's military stance and capacity-building, for both overseas and domestic deployment, since 2001. Alongside the dispatch of thousands of troops to front-line fighting in Afghanistan, a dedicated Canada Command has been established to make internal security a major function of the CF, matching and closely coordinating with the US Northern Command.

While the Canadian Constitution embodies a civil–military and federal–provincial demarcation, there are no explicit guarantees in the *Constitution Act*, the *Bill of Rights* or the *Charter of Rights and Freedoms* prohibiting or restricting the use of troops against domestic civilians. Moreover, a surprising variety of legal avenues exist for mobilising the military internally.

Finally, there are good reasons for concern that any serious political disaffection or social unrest in the coming period will be met by military force, and indeed CF 'aid of the civil power' training scenarios suggest that preparations are being made precisely for such eventualities. Both the 1970 Québec crisis and the 1990s Somalia affair reveal how easily such interventions could lead to civilian fatalities, as well as far-reaching violations of fundamental civil liberties.

Chapter 5
Britain: 'Defend the State'

Despite the historical taboo, derived from the Magna Carta and the English Revolution, on using the military against civilians, the armed forces have frequently been mobilised to deal with civil and industrial unrest in the United Kingdom, particularly at times of heightened social and class tensions. Military interventions may well be associated by members of the public with dictatorships, not democracies, but as reviewed in Chapter 2, British history is replete with examples of troops being called out to put down riots, disturbances, protests and strikes.

Although this pattern appeared to recede after the early years of the twentieth century, with the rise of substantial and increasingly heavily-armed police forces, the military option has been kept open, ready for use in times of crisis. Indeed, there is a view that the British military has an inherent and essential role in securing the state against internal political disaffection. One scholar of the subject has argued that 'It is truism that the function of an army is to defend the state' and:

> [D]omestic security is an inescapable responsibility for any army. The 'defence of the state' must include the capability to assist in the maintenance of public order and the suppression of internal unrest, insurrection or even revolution. (Jeffery 1985, 51)

There are several indicators, including the political climate created by the 'war on terrorism' and the introduction of far-reaching emergency powers in the *Civil Contingencies Act 2004*, that preparations are being made for greater recourse to military operations to 'maintain public order' and 'suppress internal unrest'. Like Canada, but even more so, the British government has been an active participant in US-led military interventions since 2001, sending the second largest contingents of troops to both Afghanistan and Iraq. British soldiers have been in the frontlines of house-to-house combat and patrolling of urban populations in both countries. Alongside this turn to military aggression have come moves to facilitate a greater military presence and role domestically.

The 2012 London Olympics will involve a substantial military deployment, alongside an unprecedented police mobilisation. By late 2008, the security budget for the Olympics had risen to £1.5 billion. In addition to thousands of police and security guards, the operation will feature military troops, helicopters and jets. According to one newspaper report:

> The Army is to be drafted in to help protect athletes and hundreds of thousands of spectators from an atrocity … Military helicopters will patrol overhead, and

> jets will be on standby to intercept any suspect private plane heading for the main Olympic stadium in Stratford, east London … The security operation is expected to be largest in peacetime Britain … Unmanned military planes, as used to monitor the Taliban in Afghanistan, could be deployed to monitor suspected terrorist aircraft. (Merrick 2008)

In late 2008, the British government decided, in response to an official report (Prime Minister's Office 2008), to launch a campaign to boost public recognition and support for the military. Among the proposals was an annual day to recognise and celebrate the work of the armed forces community. Another plan was that military servicemen and women be ordered to wear their uniforms in public as often as possible to help raise the profile of the armed forces. While officers would stop short of ordering personnel to wear uniform in public, they would be told to do so 'in all appropriate circumstances' including travelling to and from work on public transport, and at formal and semi-formal public events (Hickley 2008).

It seems that the report and recommendations arose from concerns expressed in media and official circles about public sentiment toward the military, largely because of the conduct of the wars in Afghanistan and Iraq, and about discrimination against members of the armed services. There also appeared to be a broader purpose of bolstering the military in the eyes of the public. The package of measures came 'amid growing concerns that many people in Britain know very little about the armed forces – despite their courage and sacrifice in recent wars – and often do not treat them with the respect they deserve' (Hickley 2008).

During 2008 a White Paper on constitutional reform was published that included a proposal to require parliamentary approval for military deployments abroad (Ministry of Justice 2007). Arguably, this particular proposition was a move to legitimise and legalise war-making decisions because of the controversies surrounding the decisions to join the wars in Afghanistan and Iraq. These engagements had been launched, without any parliamentary vote, let alone public plebiscite, under the royal prerogative, said to be personally exercisable by the Prime Minister. One of the prime movers behind the proposal, Conservative Party shadow minister William Hague, wrote in the *Guardian* 15 May 2007: 'The decision to go to war requires democratic legitimacy – so we must strengthen parliament's ability to challenge the executive on this matter' (Hague 2007).

It must be said that the proposed parliamentary resolution was quite limited, with exceptions for 'emergencies' and 'national security' concerns, as well as for all Special Forces-led operations. These exceptions would cover many recent British military interventions, in which the Special Forces have been given the leading role. But, by contrast, the White Paper on constitutional reform made no specific mention of reducing or defining the scope of the royal prerogative power to deploy the armed forces domestically. That is, there was a marked difference between the recommendations regarding external and internal use of the armed forces. The broader uncodified and vague conventions surrounding the prerogative powers were to be reviewed at some time in the future (Ministry of Justice 2007, 62).

Even the twentieth century had seen military mobilisations during industrial and political crises. The *Emergency Powers Act 1920* gave the United Kingdom government power to declare an emergency by proclamation in certain circumstances. These provisions were invoked 12 times during industrial and political unrest, notably during the 1926 general strike and the 1970–74 period of discontent that eventually led to the defeat of the Heath government (Walker and Broderick 2006, 39). After the 1926 general strike, Military Aid to Civil Power (MACP) provisions were invoked formally only once during the twentieth century, during the 1980 siege of the Iranian Embassy in London. However, guards battalions were put on alert, though not used, during the 'Hunger Marches' of the 1930s Great Depression, plainclothes units of the Special Air Services (SAS) and Royal Military Police undertook patrols within England against the Irish Republican Army (IRA) in the 1970s, and in 1974 there were four highly-publicised but unexplained joint police/military 'exercises' at London's Heathrow Airport shortly before the Heath government resigned (Jeffery 1985, 65).

The latter part of the twentieth century was indelibly stained by a protracted and disastrous attempt to utilise military force to end civil conflict and resistance to British rule in Northern Ireland. Two decades of army deployment against alleged 'terrorist' opponents of British control produced numerous instances in which civilians were killed by troops. By 1998, more than 3,000 people, civilians as well as soldiers, police and prison officers, had lost their lives over 26 years. The toll included the infamous 'Bloody Sunday' events of 30 January 1972. During a disturbance in Londonderry following a civil rights march, shots were fired by the British Army. Thirteen people were killed and another 13 were wounded, one of whom subsequently died (Bloody Sunday Inquiry n.d.).

Despite these bloody experiences in Ireland, 2004 saw the adoption of legislation that potentially expands the scope for domestic military intervention, in the name of responding to emergencies. The *Civil Contingencies Act 2004* effectively replaced the Emergency Powers and Civil Defence legislation (Walker and Broderick 2006, 63–80, 153–88). It empowers 'Her Majesty' by an Order in Council (in ordinary times, this means the senior cabinet ministers) to issue sweeping emergency regulations in any event that 'threatens serious damage to human welfare' or 'serious damage to the environment' or 'war or terrorism, which threatens serious damage to the security of the United Kingdom (s 19). These regulations can, *inter alia*, 'enable the Defence Council to authorise the deployment of Her Majesty's armed forces' and 'make provision (which may include conferring powers in relation to property) for facilitating any deployment of Her Majesty's armed forces' (s 22(3)(l) and (m)). The meaning and significance of these provisions is considered below.

Legal Mechanisms for Intervention

Current government and military policy assumes that considerable powers exist to mobilise armed troops internally to deal with a variety of threats to 'public safety' or 'order'. The 2005 Ministry of Defence document, *Operations in the UK: The Defence Contribution to Resilience*, sets out policy guidelines for Military Aid to the Civil Power (MACP). It states:

> Based under common law, MACP is the provision of military assistance (armed if appropriate) to the Civil Power in its maintenance of law, order and public safety, using specialist capabilities or equipment, in situations beyond the capability of the Civil Power. (Ministry of Defence 2005, 4-1)

According to the guidelines, the legal basis for instructing armed forces personnel to provide MACP in the UK can be one, or a combination, of:

- Section 2 of the *Emergency Powers Act 1964* (plus the *Emergency Powers (Amendment) Act (Northern Ireland) 1964*), which enables the Defence Council to issue instructions to undertake 'work of urgent national importance';
- Part 2 of the *Civil Contingencies Act 2004*, which empowers the Queen or a Senior Minister, in particular circumstances, to issue emergency regulations which can in turn enable the Defence Council to deploy the armed forces;
- a common law tenet that indicates that citizens should provide reasonable support to the police if requested to do so. All members of the armed forces have a duty to provide the support normally expected of the ordinary citizen. The same common law tenet enables a Defence Minister to direct the armed forces, on a case by case basis, to provide specialist support to the police;
- Queen's Regulations, which place an additional duty on military commanders to act on their own responsibility without a request by a civil agency where 'in exceptional circumstances, a grave and sudden emergency has arisen, which in the opinion of the Commander demands his immediate intervention to protect life or property'.

Thus, the guidelines assume or assert that alongside specific statutory provisions, there are potentially far-reaching common law and prerogative or executive powers to justify armed interventions. These can be invoked to deal with 'a varying range of criminal and malicious activities'. The request procedures envisage MACP operations for criminal investigations and major events (Ministry of Defence 2005, 4-2, 4B-2).

Significantly, the document sets out a long list of authorities considered to be a 'Civil Power' that can ask for military aid. A Civil Power is loosely defined as a 'civil authority that has constitutional or statutory responsibility for the maintenance of law and order' (Ministry of Defence 2005, 4-1). The Civil Power is said to include not just government ministers and police forces but also the security and intelligence services, the Government Communications Headquarters (GCHQ), customs, coastguard and serious crimes agencies, as well as maritime, rail and air accident investigation branches.

The Ministry of Defence suggests that the *Emergency Powers Act* and the *Civil Contingencies Act* 'provide a stronger basis for' MACP activity than the common law. It insists that the common law imposes a duty on every citizen, including service personnel, to assist in the enforcement of law and order when requested, where it is reasonable to do so, and that this requirement forms the 'main basis for the MACP mechanism'. However, the guidelines state that this duty is 'difficult to formulate and cannot be relied upon in all circumstances to provide a legal basis for a response, especially if commanders use it without Defence Council authorisation' (Ministry of Defence 2005, 4-2).

Civil Contingencies Act

Under the *Civil Contingencies Act*, emergency powers can be triggered whenever the governing authorities, namely Her Majesty in Council, are 'satisfied' that an emergency has occurred, is occurring or is about to occur. The regulations can suspend, modify or override any other Act of Parliament, with the sole exception of the *Human Rights Act* (Walker and Broderick 2006, 44–5). Even statutes regarded as essential to civil liberties and basic constitutional rights, such as the *Magna Carta 1297*, the *Bill of Rights 1688*, the *Parliament Acts 1911–49* and the *Representation of the People Act 1983*, can be swept aside (Walker and Broderick 2006, 192). Regulations can last for up to 30 days, and can be renewed. They must be laid before parliament 'as soon as is reasonably practicable' and shall lapse after seven days unless both houses of parliament approve them, but in the meantime their effect is immediate. Moreover, even these limited provisions would mean little if parliament could not or did not meet.

Section 19 of the Act defines 'emergency' as follows:

> (1) In this Part 'emergency' means–
> (a) an event or situation which threatens serious damage to human welfare in the United Kingdom or in a Part or region,
> (b) an event or situation which threatens serious damage to the environment of the United Kingdom or of a Part or region, or
> (c) war, or terrorism, which threatens serious damage to the security of the United Kingdom.
>
> (2) For the purposes of subsection (1)(a) an event or situation threatens damage to human welfare only if it involves, causes or may cause–
> (a) loss of human life,

(b) human illness or injury,
(c) homelessness,
(d) damage to property,
(e) disruption of a supply of money, food, water, energy or fuel,
(f) disruption of a system of communication,
(g) disruption of facilities for transport, or
(h) disruption of services relating to health.

This definition covers a very wide range of circumstances, far beyond any perceived threat to human life. Moreover, sub-sections (4) and (5) permit the Secretary of State to rule whether an event or situation poses a threat to human welfare, and to amend the Act itself, subject to subsequent parliamentary approval. These sub-sections read as follows:

(4) The Secretary of State may by order amend subsection (2) so as to provide that in so far as an event or situation involves or causes disruption of a specified supply, system, facility or service–
(a) it is to be treated as threatening damage to human welfare, or
(b) it is no longer to be treated as threatening damage to human welfare.

(5) An order under subsection (4)–
(a) may make consequential amendment of this Part, and
(b) may not be made unless a draft has been laid before, and approved by resolution of, each House of Parliament.

Although the Blair government presented the Act as one concerned primarily with responding to disasters, the 2003 Queen's Speech specifically referred to terrorism, and the proposal was also driven by concerns about civil unrest, including the eruption of fuel price protests and pickets outside oil refineries in 2000 (Walker and Broderick 2006, xiii, 47). The definitions of emergency are extensive, considerably wider than the previous provisions under the 1920 Act and allow for politically 'interventionist stances' toward potential crises (Walker and Broderick 2006, 63–76). Possible threats to 'human welfare' extend to 'damage to property' and disruption to supplies, communications or transport. No criteria are provided for the key tests of 'serious damage to human welfare' and 'war or terrorism, which threatens serious damage to the security of the United Kingdom'. 'Serious' is not defined, nor is 'security'. Ministers are given powers to specify that certain situations or events are emergencies.

Once an emergency has been declared, the authorities can assume 'almost boundless power' (Walker and Broderick 2006, 161). They can, among other things, prohibit assemblies, ban movement, create offences, deploy the armed forces and confer emergency powers on any individual. There are no specific powers of arrest or detention without trial, but the Act's sponsors refused to rule out such detention, which the courts have in the past been prepared to accept, even in peacetime 'civil emergencies' (see *Attorney-General of St Christopher, Nevis and Anguilla v Reynolds* [1980] AC 637).

The scope of emergency regulations is spelt out in s 22:

> 1) Emergency regulations may make any provision which the person making the regulations is satisfied is appropriate for the purpose of preventing, controlling or mitigating an aspect or effect of the emergency in respect of which the regulations are made.
>
> (2) In particular, emergency regulations may make any provision which the person making the regulations is satisfied is appropriate for the purpose of–
> (a) protecting human life, health or safety,
> (b) treating human illness or injury,
> (c) protecting or restoring property,
> (d) protecting or restoring a supply of money, food, water, energy or fuel,
> (e) protecting or restoring a system of communication,
> (f) protecting or restoring facilities for transport,
> (g) protecting or restoring the provision of services relating to health,
> (h) protecting or restoring the activities of banks or other financial institutions,
> (i) preventing, containing or reducing the contamination of land, water or air,
> (j) preventing, reducing or mitigating the effects of disruption or destruction of plant life or animal life,
> (k) protecting or restoring activities of Parliament, of the Scottish Parliament, of the Northern Ireland Assembly or of the National Assembly for Wales, or
> (l) protecting or restoring the performance of public functions.
>
> (3) Emergency regulations may make provision of any kind that could be made by Act of Parliament or by the exercise of the Royal Prerogative; in particular, regulations may–
> (a) confer a function on a Minister of the Crown, on the Scottish Ministers, on the National Assembly for Wales, on a Northern Ireland department, on a coordinator appointed under section 24 or on any other specified person (and a function conferred may, in particular, be–
> (i) a power, or duty, to exercise a discretion;
> (ii) a power to give directions or orders, whether written or oral);
> (b) provide for or enable the requisition or confiscation of property (with or without compensation);
> (c) provide for or enable the destruction of property, animal life or plant life (with or without compensation);
> (d) prohibit, or enable the prohibition of, movement to or from a specified place;

(e) require, or enable the requirement of, movement to or from a specified place;
(f) prohibit, or enable the prohibition of, assemblies of specified kinds, at specified places or at specified times;
(g) prohibit, or enable the prohibition of, travel at specified times;
(h) prohibit, or enable the prohibition of, other specified activities;
(i) create an offence of–
  (i) failing to comply with a provision of the regulations;
  (ii) failing to comply with a direction or order given or made under the regulations;
  (iii) obstructing a person in the performance of a function under or by virtue of the regulations;
(j) disapply or modify an enactment or a provision made under or by virtue of an enactment;
(k) require a person or body to act in performance of a function (whether the function is conferred by the regulations or otherwise and whether or not the regulations also make provision for remuneration or compensation);
(l) enable the Defence Council to authorise the deployment of Her Majesty's armed forces;
(m) make provision (which may include conferring powers in relation to property) for facilitating any deployment of Her Majesty's armed forces;
(n) confer jurisdiction on a court or tribunal (which may include a tribunal established by the regulations);
(o) make provision which has effect in relation to, or to anything done in–
  (i) an area of the territorial sea;
  (ii) an area within British fishery limits; or
  (iii) an area of the continental shelf;
(p) make provision which applies generally or only in specified circumstances or for a specified purpose;
(q) make different provision for different circumstances or purposes.

These provisions mean there are virtually no restrictions on the powers that a government can assume, and enforce via the armed forces. However, emergency regulations cannot require a person to perform military service or prohibit any activity in connection with a strike or other industrial action (s 23(3)).

In a briefing on the legislation, Liberty (the National Council for Civil Liberties) called it 'the most powerful piece of peacetime legislation ever proposed in the UK' and warned that 'it seeks to grant the Government unprecedented powers to make emergency regulations which are unavailable under existing laws'. Liberty expressed concern that 'it is times of emergency that citizens' fundamental rights are at greatest risk' (Liberty, *Liberty's second reading briefing on the Civil Contingencies Bill in the House of Lords*, June 2004, para. 4). Liberty also noted that the present government had sown an increased willingness to declare an emergency, citing the declaration of a 'technical' emergency following the September 2001 attacks in the United States. This declaration enabled the government to derogate from article 5 of the *European Convention on Human Rights*, thereby permitting indefinite detention without trial under the *Anti-Terrorism Crime and Security Act 2001* (Liberty, para. 5).

These views are not isolated. One detailed study of the Act described it as 'the most powerful and extensive peacetime legislation ever enacted', containing within it 'the tools for dismantling civil society', with 'the potential to inflict terrible damage on the constitution of the United Kingdom' (Walker and Broderick 2006, 188, 214). The authors also drew attention to the slim likelihood of any effective parliamentary or judicial review of actions taken under emergency powers. In effect, the legislation provides the framework for extra-constitutional and dictatorial forms of rule, backed by military force.

During the debate on the *Civil Contingencies Bill*, the cabinet rejected calls to clarify by statute the military's role. The government also dismissed a recommendation by a House of Commons Select Committee to define the prerogative power to engage in armed conflict. The government argued that a case-by-case approach was needed, and that the government was already sufficiently accountable to parliament (Walker and Broderick 2006, 44–5). The end result is that ill-defined and extensive prerogative and common law powers to call out the armed forces continue to exist, augmented by the 2004 legislation.

Vague Common Law and Executive Powers

The Ministry of Defence's reference to the common law duty to provide military aid being 'difficult to formulate' points to the uncertain scope and character of this power and the associated legal rights and liabilities of called-out service personnel. As noted in Chapter 2, the last judicial guidance on this subject was provided in 1832 in *R v Pinney* ((1832) 170 ER 962). The mayor of Bristol and nine aldermen were unsuccessfully prosecuted by the Attorney-General for breaching their common law duty to assemble a sufficient force to put down three days of riots. A military major had advised the mayor that it would be 'imprudent to put arms in the hands of young troops'. But in the related case, *Charge to the Bristol Grand Jury*, Lord Tindal insisted that soldiers had a duty, as citizens, on their own authority, to do their utmost to 'put down riot and tumult'. Two officers who had refused to order the troops to fire without a magistrate's sanction were found guilty of neglect of duty, causing one to commit suicide (Babington 1990, 84).

There has been some parliamentary endorsement of the common law duty. The 1893 *Report of the Select Committee on the Featherstone Riots* said resort to military assistance must be the 'last expedient' of the civil authorities, but when such a call was made, 'to refuse such assistance is in law a misdemeanour' (Babington 1990, 122–32).

Apart from the Queen's Regulations, *Operations in the UK* makes no mention of the prerogative powers of the Crown. The relationship between these and the asserted common law tenet remains unclear. The royal prerogative powers are vast in scope – they are said to cover any situation not otherwise dealt with by statute – and may be unreviewable by the courts (*Burmah Oil Co. Ltd. v Lord Advocate* [1965] AC 101; Whelan 1985, 287).

In *Chandler v Director of Public Prosecutions* ([1964] AC 763, 800), Lord Hodson stated: 'The Crown has, and this is not disputed, the right as head of State to decide in peace and war the disposition of its armed forces.' In *Burmah Oil Co Ltd v Lord Advocate* ([1965] AC 75, 100), Lord Reid said: 'There is no doubt that control of the armed forces has been left to the prerogative ... subject to the power of Parliament to withhold supply and refuse to continue legislation essential for the maintenance of a standing army.'

It is remarkable that, some three centuries after the struggle for parliamentary and civilian supremacy over the British monarchy – and in a political system that professes to be democratic – the power of the government to call out the military is said to rest on vestiges of regal authority. In the words of one scholar, the prerogative power to control disorder 'is a dangerous mystery unwarranted in a democratic society' (Whelan 1985, 287).

Nevertheless, these murky powers provided the basis for not only the deployment of troops to Northern Ireland but more 'commonplace' uses of troops to dispose of explosives or in operations against terrorism. For example, there were 957 calls for explosives disposal in 2001, and 431 in 2002, as well as between 30 and 40 requests per year to assist police in anti-terrorism operations (Walker and Broderick 2006, 248). Thus, it appears that a wider internal use of the armed forces became routine in the 'war on terror', even before the *Civil Contingencies Act*, and without substantial public scrutiny or debate.

Another category of military intervention exists, Military Aid to the Civil Community (MACC), which generally covers unarmed assistance in weather or environmental disasters and major accidents, but can extend to shooting down a hijacked civilian aircraft. The Quick Reaction Alert (Interceptor) Force can open fire on such planes with ministerial approval (House of Commons Defence Committee, *Defence and Security in the UK*, 2001–2002 HC 518, para. 45).

Yet another kind of intervention, Military Aid to Other Government Departments (MAGD) comprises maintenance of essential services, often in a strike-breaking role, relying on s 2 of the *Emergency Powers Act*. Between 1984 and 2003, MAGD was invoked 15 times, including against the 1984–85 mineworkers' strike, ambulance and firefighters' stoppages, and fuel pickets in 2000. Soldiers have also set up temporary prisons at times of overcrowding and industrial disputes (Walker and Broderick 2006, 248–9). These operations, while unarmed, contain the potential to spark conflicts with strikers and others that could involve the arming of troops if the police proved unable to contain the situation.

Ordinarily, the Defence Council, which consists of military leaders as well as government ministers and officials, exercises the prerogative powers on behalf of the Crown. The council is based in the Ministry of Defence and is normally chaired by the Secretary of State for Defence. In cases of MACP, a military commander would contact the Ministry of Defence (Counter Terrorism and UK Operations) to seek formal approval from the Minister. Police agreement would be required, but with the advent of the *Civil Contingencies Act*, it has been suggested that, as well as police, regional and emergency coordinators could request military assistance under MACA arrangements (Walker and Broderick 2006, 249–50). However, where military unit commanders receive police or emergency services requests and consider that a 'grave and sudden' emergency demands 'immediate intervention to protect life and property', they are authorised by the *Queen's Regulations for the Army* to respond on their own authority. They must subsequently seek ministerial approval. For MAGD operations, a Defence Council Order must be signed by two members of the council, including a minister (Walker and Broderick 2006, 250).

All these powers and arrangements operate above and beyond the *Civil Contingencies Act*. That is, they can be instigated without any formal declaration of a state of emergency under the Act (Walker and Broderick 2006, 251). Taken as a whole, considerable legal powers are said to exist to authorise calling out the troops to deal with a wide variety of alleged threats to society, including civil unrest, industrial action and acts of terrorism, and these measures have been augmented by the 'almost boundless power' that can be asserted under the 2004 Act.

Legal Powers and Lethal Force

Called-out military personnel have been given no specific statutory powers, but the Ministry of Defence guidelines assert substantial common law powers, including to use lethal force and make arrests. The Ministry states that soldiers must act within the law and have no special legal powers beyond those of the ordinary citizen. Nevertheless, they 'may use reasonable force to prevent crime, including in self-defence'.

Although service personnel 'should not normally' make arrests, 'in certain circumstances there may be no other option'. The Ministry's policy is that soldiers can arrest people even to prevent a breach of the peace, which is defined as an occasion where a person causes harm or appears likely to cause harm to persons or property, or acts in a manner likely to provoke violence to others (except in Scotland, where arrest powers are slightly less). The guidelines state that force is lawful if the immediate object is to prevent crime (including public order offences), to arrest offenders, or in self-defence or the defence of others (Ministry of Defence 2005, 4–3, 4A-1). This is in line with s 3 of the *Criminal Law Act 1967*, which provides:

> A person may use such force as is reasonable in the circumstances in the prevention of crime, or in effecting or assisting in the lawful arrest of offenders or suspected offenders or of persons unlawfully at large.

Military law provides that troops must obey lawful commands. Secret rules of engagement will be approved by Ministers (Ministry of Defence 2005, 4A-2).

These may purport to authorise or even require the application of lethal force, as they did in Northern Ireland.

In the past, both the common law and parliament have condoned deadly force to deal with disturbances. After the Bristol riots that followed the defeat of the 1831 parliamentary reform bill, an officer who had fatally shot a boy during an incident was acquitted of manslaughter. Lord Tindal instructed the Grand Jury that if the shot was 'discharged in the fair and honest execution of his duty, in endeavouring to disperse the mob', the killing was justified and amounted to accidental death only (Babington 1990, 84).

When four people were killed after soldiers fired on striking miners, the 1893 *Report of the Select Committee on the Featherstone Riots* exonerated the commanding officer and his troops, saying 'The necessary prevention of such outrage on person and property justifies the guardians of the peace in the employment against a riotous crowd of even deadly weapons' (Whelan 1985, 272). The committee simply warned that 'officers and soldiers are under no special privileges and subject to no special responsibilities as regards this principle of the law'. The taking of life had to be shown to be necessary (Babington 1990, 122–32).

Secret Preparations

The *Operations in the UK* document reported that the military had 'pre-prepared contingency plans for the use of Service personnel in specific MACP situations', but did not elaborate. Instead, it disclosed an intention to keep MACP preparations and operations hidden from the public as much as possible. The Ministry of Defence emphasised that planning for MACP is likely to be 'highly sensitive'. Due to 'legal and operational security restrictions', 'most MACP support receives no publicity' and 'under no circumstances should any comment be made about UK Special Forces involvement (Ministry of Defence 2005, 4-4, 4-5).

Once called out, service personnel were instructed not to discuss their work with, or answer questions from, members of the press or the public. Even the possibility of arresting prying journalists is raised. 'Except in a situation where arrest under the Official Secrets Act would be permissible, it is not possible to prevent photographers or television cameramen from recording, but Service personnel should not be drawn into conversation' (Ministry of Defence 2005, 4A-3).

Likewise, the document calls for measures to hide from the public any preparations to use lethal force. 'If the potential use of firearms is considered necessary, usually as a last resort in civil disturbances, a force so armed should be kept in reserve and out of sight of those involved in the disturbance.' The Rules of Engagement covering the use of force are also kept secret (Ministry of Defence 2005, 4A-2).

A 2002 Ministry of Defence White Paper signalled an intention to enhance the military's capacity for domestic deployment by establishing Reserve Reaction Forces of, on average, 500 Reserves for each region (a total of 6,000) (Ministry of

Defence 2002, Ch. 5). The Reserves can be mobilised under the *Reserve Forces Act 1996*, s 52, which allows a call-out where 'it appears to Her [Majesty] that national danger is imminent or that a great emergency has arisen'. In a 2003 paper (Ministry of Defence 2003, para. 3.9), the Ministry of Defence reported that 14 Civil Contingencies Reaction Forces were being established, though the numbers have since been depleted by operations in Iraq (Walker and Broderick 2006, 246).

London Olympics 2012

The powers to deploy the military domestically may be tested during the 2012 London Olympics, which were expected to involve a substantial armed forces operation, alongside a large police mobilisation, on the pretext of combating terrorism.

According to a BBC report in April 2008, an extensive closed circuit television (CCTV) network would monitor people in London, combining 10,000 Metropolitan Police Service cameras with thousands of traffic and congestion cameras. The overall network of up to half a million cameras, the largest in the world, was to be controlled from a bomb-proof bunker operated jointly by the military, police and intelligence services (Morgan 2008).

RAF Reaper drones were also to be used for surveillance and intelligence-gathering during the Games, the first time that unmanned aircraft have been allowed to fly over the heavily-populated capital. The drones have infra-red sensors, ground-scanning radars, electronic eavesdropping equipment and high-definition cameras, providing for intensive spying and bugging directed against civilians. In addition, manned fighter aircraft would be stationed at several bases near London to enforce an air exclusion zone and intercept aircraft, with powers to shoot down civilian aircraft regarded as a threat (*Herald* 2008).

The RAF's association with the London Olympics was given a high public profile when the Red Arrows, the RAF Aerobatic Team, performed a fly-past at the 2008 handover ceremony in London at the conclusion of the Beijing Olympics. The military's engagement with the Games was enhanced by the British Olympic Association's selection of the Aldershot Garrison, often described as the home of the British Army, to host the British Olympic team's pre-games preparation and processing camp.

Conclusion

As in the United States and Canada, Britain's involvement in US-led militarism abroad has been accompanied by enhanced military call-out powers at home. Unlike in Australia (see Chapter 7), British governments have thus far not introduced specific legislation authorising call-outs and creating express powers for soldiers. However, the *Civil Contingencies Act* has created substantial military deployment powers and an unprecedented framework for extra-constitutional and dictatorial forms of rule. Moreover, Ministry of Defence policies are based on vague and sweeping common law, executive and prerogative powers that purportedly can authorise the use of troops against a wide range of challenges to 'public order'. Secretive preparations have been made for Military Aid to Civil Power and the 2012 London Olympics are likely to involve a sizeable armed forces contingent.

Throughout British history, troops have been mobilised against civilians in periods of acute political and social conflict, and even though far larger police forces have been created over the past century, it appears that the powers-that-be are preparing for the possible use of the military again in the event of further such convulsions.

Chapter 6
Germany and Italy: Post-War Restraints under Challenge

In both Germany and Italy, official challenges are being made to the restrictions on the use of the military imposed after the Second World War to prevent a return to the militarist and dictatorial practices witnessed under fascism. This chapter focuses on Germany but closes with a brief review of the recent developments and historical issues in Italy.

The Constitution of the German Federal Republic, produced in the aftermath of the Second World War and the holocaust, was originally, like that of Japan, strictly pacifist. There was considerable opposition throughout the country to changes instituted in 1956 which allowed the Republic to have an army and conscription for military service. It was accepted that the newly created armed forces would have a purely defensive role, confined within the borders of the NATO countries. Article 35 of the Constitution specifically prohibited the German military from being deployed domestically except in cases of natural disaster.

After 9/11, following the lead of the United States and Britain, leading German politicians called for increasing involvement of German troops in the war on terror, both internally and externally. A political consensus also came to support a limited peacekeeping role beyond the NATO borders. In 1998 even the formally pacifist Green Party supported German participation in military action in Kosovo. From 2001, the Chairperson of the Christian Democrats (CDU), Angela Merkel, called for constitutional amendments to allow the German military to deploy inside the country in the case of a serious terrorist threat.

With the renewed crisis over Iraq in 2002, there were major concerns inside Germany about the threat of imminent US military action. As Mary Fulbrook observed, in her *Concise History of Germany*, Chancellor Gerhard Schroeder:

> in part succeeded in winning the 2002 election … because he played to the remarkable levels of pacifism among a German population which had learned only too well the historical lessons of two world wars unleashed from German soil. (Fulbrook 2006, 256–7)

For many German politicians and much of the German populace, the prospect of domestic military deployment recalled the key role of the German military in provoking and overseeing the horrors of the Second World War, in the rise to power of fascism and in the consolidation of the Nazi police-state, built upon violent intimidation, terror and mass murder.

Nevertheless, attempts continued to break down the military/police demarcation. Following an incident in 2003 when a mentally ill man hijacked a small plane and threatened to crash it into the European Central Bank Building, Interior Minister Wolfgang Schauble and others championed a law allowing the air force to shoot down hijacked planes that posed a threat to populated areas. The changes authorised such destruction before any hijacked aircraft could be used to destroy the lives of people in addition to those on the aircraft, if force were the only way to prevent this.

In 2006, however, Germany's highest court declared the law unconstitutional (German Constitutional Court 2006). The Federal Constitutional Court declared that the Aviation Security Act (*Luftsicherheitsgesetz – LuftSiG*), which came into effect in 2005, was 'incompatible with the fundamental right to life' and the opening paragraph of the Constitution, which obliged the state to guarantee 'human dignity to the extent that the use of armed force affects persons on board the aircraft who are not participants in the crime'. The court said: 'By the state's using their killing as a means of saving others, they are treated as mere objects, which denies them the value that is due to a human being' (German Constitutional Court 2006).

In total, the Court agreed that the Act was contrary to four provisions of the Basic Law, including the right to human dignity (in Article 1I) and the right to life (in Article 2II1). However, the Court allowed that aircraft occupied only by terrorists could be shot down without infringing the Basic Law. Hufnagel commented that, 'this is consistent with other German jurisprudence establishing the legality of the 'final life-saving shot'' and, in particular, with a decision allowing terrorists to be killed at any time, as a continued threat to innocent lives (Hufnagel 2008, 108).

The court also ruled that the law invalidly expanded the latitude for using the military within Germany. The judges conceded that the Constitution permitted the armed forces to be deployed within Germany to support the police in extraordinary circumstances – for example, in the case of 'particularly serious accidents', natural disasters and even anticipated terrorist attacks (Hufnagel 2008, 108). However, the court said that in such cases the armed forces would not be allowed to deploy any specifically military means, that is, means that the police are not permitted to use (Hufnagel 2008, 108).

In 2007, Defence Minister Franz Josef Jung publicly stated that hijacked planes would be shot down despite the court's ruling, with such action justified by a 'supra-statutory state of emergency' (Hufnagel 2008, 109–10).

Moreover, even after the court judgment, Interior Minister Schauble and other prominent politicians urged deployment of the German army during the 2006 World Cup football finals, despite the existence of a special police unit capable of dealing with terrorist attacks – the GSG9, established after 11 Israeli athletes were kidnapped during the 1972 Olympic Games in Munich. In January 2006, United Press International reported:

> [Interior Minister] Schauble and most conservative lawmakers are in favor of changing a nearly six decade-old law to have German soldiers boost security

> during the World Cup. But so far, the Bundeswehr, the German armed forces, cannot be deployed domestically. Written in 1949, the German constitution established strict separation between police and military, because the Nazis had blurred that separation leading to a ruthless police state. Conservatives have in the past called for the law to be rewritten in light of Germany's spotless democratic record since World War II. Doing that would require a two-third majority in both houses of parliament. (Nicola 2006; Leicht 2006)

As the reference to the Nazis suggests, the utilisation of an alleged terrorist threat to overturn the separation between police and military functions raises worrying historical experiences. Adolf Hitler cited the 1933 Reichstag Fire, which the Nazis falsely attributed to communists, as the reason for insisting that the parliament agree to rule by decree (Kershaw 1998, 456–60).

In Chancellor Angela Merkel's coalition government, Interior Minister Schauble, Defence Minister Brigitte Zypries and Justice Minister Franz Josef Jung continued to push for domestic military deployment. In 2008, it looked like they might win the day, with support from leading Social Democrats, including parliamentary leader Peter Struck, for constitutional amendments allowing military call-out 'when police resources are insufficient' (Hawley 2008, 2).

However, the Social Democratic Party (SPD) subsequently withdrew its support, saying that the proposed amendment was an 'unacceptable … qualitative shift in German security structure' (Hawley 2008, 1). In this, the SPD was supported by the Greens, the Left Party and the Free Democrats. Although this meant that the CDU could not achieve the three-quarters majority needed in both houses of the German Parliament for constitutional change, the issue is by no means dead, with the CDU continuing to affirm its commitment to such change in the future. Some have argued that no such constitutional change is needed to allow for such domestic deployment (Hawley 2008, 2).

As well as providing a background to this debate, and explaining the high levels of public sensitivity and hostility to increasing military involvement in civilian life in Germany, the history of German militarism provides vivid testimony of the disastrous consequences of such increased involvement.

Germany before the First World War

At the outbreak of the First World War, Germany was a federal empire, or Reich, composed of a number of separate kingdoms, principalities, free states and free cities with their own local political structures and powers, unified under Prussian rule (Fulbrook 2006, 129).

The German imperial state system was not the product of any major political challenge to the landed aristocracy by the rising capitalist class. 'Revolutionary' governments and parliaments were created in the industrial and state capitals of most German principalities in the 1848 uprisings by small traders, artisans and workers, pursuing radical democratic reforms. However, the propertied middle-class citizens handed power in these assemblies were quite unwilling to organise effective opposition to defend such institutions from the old state authorities. The uprisings were crushed by 1849.

Three wars between 1864 and 1870 contributed to the unification of previously independent states under Prussian imperial domination with the proclamation of the German Empire at Versailles in January 1871. A new constitution created a tripartite structure of political power. A parliament or Reichstag, directly elected by universal male suffrage in a secret ballot, had limited veto-powers in relation to legislation initiated in a Federal Council made up of delegates from the separate states. But the Prussian leadership of emperor, chancellor and top ministers and public servants exercised effective executive authority and control of the Federal Council, with the Prussian War Minister and Prussian army leadership operating largely outside parliamentary control (Fulbrook 2006, 128–9). As Fulbrook observes, this lack of effective parliamentary control of the military had profound consequences for German history 'into the First World War and well beyond' (Fulbrook 2006, 129).

At the same time, the democratic institutions of most of the local states had a restricted franchise, with the old landed aristocracy having a majority of the votes. Freedom of speech was highly restricted, with frequent attacks on the left-wing press and arrests of socialists and social democrats. In 1878 Bismarck pushed through the Reichstag a law banning socialist meetings, organisations and associations, including those of the SPD, while still allowing SPD deputies to take their seats in Parliament (Fulbrook 2006, 133). Police and troops were frequently used to attack demonstrations and strikes, 'as in 1912 when cavalry used sabres and bullets against striking miners in the Ruhr' (Harman 1982, 14).

Rapid economic development allowed the state to concede wage increases and social security benefits to workers in the 1880s and 1890s. (Sickness Insurance was instituted in 1883, Accident Insurance in 1884 and Old Age and Disability Insurance in 1889) (Fulbrook 2006, 133). The ban on the SPD ended with Bismarck's departure in 1890. The working day was reduced and unions allowed to organise and influence workplace practices after 1900. The SPD, as the party of the organised working class, was originally committed to socialist revolution, but increasingly focused upon building up its membership, its newspapers, its clubs and trade unions, and seeking representation in parliaments.

The Failed Post-war Revolution

The expansion of German capitalism increasingly involved the takeover and subordination of smaller firms to giant cartels and trusts. These monopoly powers sought government support in expanding their overseas access to cheap labour and raw materials and protected markets. This inevitably brought Germany into conflict with the established imperial powers of Britain and France (Harman 1982, 22). The

First World War was the logical outcome and culmination of these developments, with Germany supporting an Austrian attack on Serbia, while Russia and France backed the Serbs, and Britain joined with the French to fight in Belgium.

Despite vigorous opposition from a minority of socialists within the SPD, the majority leadership supported the war. But conditions for German workers, as well as German soldiers, progressively worsened as the war dragged on, with limited food supplies, and the spread of starvation and epidemic disease in some regions by the winter of 1916–17. Increasing numbers of workers became involved in mass street demonstrations and protest strikes against continued warfare.

For a period in November and December 1918, workers and soldiers' councils 'were the only legal authority in the Reich' (Guerin 1973, 33). However, the Social Democratic leaders were implacably opposed to soviet-style revolutionary councils (Guerin 1973, 33; Fulbrook 2006, 158–60). The party leader, Ebert, moved in the Council of Peoples Representatives to enforce elections for a National Assembly to produce a constitution for a parliamentary system. Significantly, he formed an alliance with the head of the army, General Wilhelm Groener, promising not to move to reform the army command structure if the army supported him in defeating socialist revolution. 'The pair agreed to work together to restore order in the army so that the army could restore order in society as a whole' (Harman 2008, 431–2).

Ebert's use of the military to brutally suppress a Berlin army mutiny in November 1918 was condemned by left wingers. At the end of December, the Spartacist group, which had opposed the SPD-led government, formed the new Communist Party of Germany, the KPD (Fulbrook 2006, 160). In the same month, Social Democratic Minister of the Interior, Noske had agreed with the army generals to set up a special mercenary force, the Freikorps. Drawn from the officers and storm battalions of the old army, it was heavily anti-socialist, nationalist and anti-Semitic.

In January, the Social Democratic leadership 'manoeuvred with the military high command … to provoke a rising in Berlin in order to crush it with troops from outside, blaming the bloodshed on the Communist Party leaders, Liebknecht and Luxemburg' (Harman 2008, 432). These communist leaders were murdered by army officers on the pretext that they were planning violence (Harman 1982, 86). Throughout the first half of 1919, the Freikorps moved through the country attacking organised workers and socialists. It met repeated armed resistance, culminating in the proclamation in April of a short-lived Bavarian Socialist Republic with its own Red Army of 15,000.

To escape from fighting in Berlin, the National Constituent Assembly convened in the city of Weimar. Under the Weimar Constitution, which took effect in August 1919, a president was to be elected by direct popular vote for a period of seven years, and given considerable powers. These included to appoint and dismiss Chancellors, dissolve parliament and call new elections, hold national referenda and rule by emergency decree (Article 48) (Fulbrook 2006, 162–3). The army reported directly to the president, who could thus direct military operations without reference to the parliament.

The post-First World War Versailles Treaty had limited the Reichswehr to 100,000 soldiers and 15,000 sailors. In theory it required replacement of the wartime leadership, but the old German officer class remained in control. The generals moved increasingly to expand the army's operations through the development of 'underground' units, collectively known as the 'Black Reichswehr', made up of nationalist volunteers, financed by wealthy industrialists and trained for operations against left wingers (Harman 1982, 233). These included, not only the Freikorps but also the Baltikum corps, 50,000 strong, which was sent to fight the Soviet army in Lithuania in June 1919 (Campbell 2004, 132).

In 1920 a series of regional civil wars between left and right led to around 20,000 deaths. Suppression of the left was so successful that the army attempted to throw out the Social Democratic leadership and appoint a conservative senior civil servant, Kapp, to take over government in Berlin. In response the head of the main trade union federation called a general strike which received widespread support. People formed new Workers Councils, took up arms and attacked columns of troops known to be sympathetic to the coup. In the Ruhr thousands of workers flocked to form a Red Army which drove the Reichswehr from the country's biggest industrial region. Within days the army coup collapsed. The Social Democratic ministers returned to Berlin but once more united with the Reichswehr to 'restore order' in the Ruhr through repression.

Fascism and the Rise of Hitler

In the summer of 1920, Adolf Hitler first formed a 'shock troops' unit trained to attack and disrupt the public meetings of opponents on the left. Later Hitler would boast of the extreme violence successfully employed by this group with the tacit support of local police, military and government officers. In 1922, he named his force the Storm Troops, the SA, and in 1923 he formed a personal guard, the Hitler Shock Troops, known as the SS.

Hitler modelled the Nazi Party on Mussolini's Italian fascist organisation, initially recruiting war veterans, unemployed young people, peasants seeking work in the towns, desperate small businesspeople, criminals and beggars, as armed gangs, attacking trade unionists and socialists. Initially small bands of armed men launched brutal surprise attacks on crowds of workers, and acted to break strikes and protect scab labour (Guerin 1973, 108).

In the third week of 1923, following the failure of Germany to pay France its full quota of reparations, the French took over two thirds of the Ruhr basin, a major centre of industrial production. These developments contributed to the rapid growth of ultra-nationalist right-wing parties, particularly recruiting from the devastated middle class, and the desperate unemployed.

It was at this time that Hitler first achieved nation-wide recognition, organising right-wing terrorists, anti-Semites and former Freikorps members in a failed coup in Munich. Hitler maintained close links with the German military. 'For the Army High Command, the Nazis and kindred groups were a useful counterweight to the forces of the left', engaging in violent attacks upon any such left wingers in the streets (Harman 1982, 233). The army failed to support the coup, however, and Hitler was imprisoned for six months.

A new right-wing central government presided over the stabilisation of the German mark through a tight credit squeeze, causing large-scale factory closures and higher levels of unemployment and underemployment. The chief of the Reichswehr was given powers of civil intervention. Under the protection of the military, the eight-hour day, achieved through working-class action in late 1918, was scrapped.

In 1926 and 1927 the Nazis successively revived the SS and the SA and Hitler's bands resumed their disruption of working-class public meetings, though by 1927–28 the party was only a marginal electoral force, with only a few thousand members (Guerin 1973, 37). This changed with the onset of the great depression. Along with the US and British economies, the German economy was beginning to turn down before the great crash of October 1929. By the end of 1930 its output was lower than it had been in previous post-First World War recessions, and matters worsened with a third of the workforce jobless and major bank collapses in 1932.

The new crisis contributed to an increase in votes for the Nazi Party, reaching 6 million in 1930 and 12 million, 37 per cent of the vote, in July 1932 (Harman 2008, 483). With the established mainstream parties seemingly unable to save workers from unemployment and their own middle-class supporters from poverty and bankruptcy, increasing numbers of middle-class people, along with some workers, turned to Hitler's movement for salvation. At the same time, despite Hitler's anti-capitalist rhetoric, the Nazis were supported by significant big business leaders, who saw them as a valuable counter-force to left-wing parties, workers and unions, unrestricted by liberal 'legality' (Harman 2008, 486).

The German Social Democrats failed to identify and address the threat posed by the Nazi Party, arguing that it could be defeated and marginalised through liberal democratic legality. But the Nazis were not simply or mainly an electoral party. At the core of their organisation were paramilitary street fighters – the SA or Stormtroopers, numbering 100,000 at the end of 1930, and 400,000 by mid-1932. These armed thugs, recruited from amongst the desperate unemployed, and openly protected by the Reichswehr, were dedicated to battling against those they blamed for the social crisis – attacking supposedly Jewish finance capital on the one side and Jewish Marxist trade unionists on the other (Harman 2008, 483).

The Social Democrats did build their own para-military defence organisations, but they insisted on mobilising these groups for a head-on confrontation with Nazism only if Hitler 'broke the constitution' (Harman 2008, 485). This never happened. Instead, democratic 'legality' allowed President Hindenburg and von Papen to negotiate secretly with Hitler in 1932 to issue a decree overthrowing the Social Democratic government in Prussia, and ultimately to appoint Hitler as Chancellor in January 1933 (Fulbrook 2006, 177). Harman notes:

> within a few days the paramilitary forces of the Nazis were being integrated into the state machine. The SA Stormtroopers and the police worked together to harass the working class parties. Then, on 27 February, the Nazis used a fire in the Reichstag as an excuse to ban the Communist Party, suppress its press and drag off 100,000 of its members to concentration camps. (Harman 2008, 489)

Despite mass intimidation of the electorate, the Nazis still failed to win an absolute majority in elections in March, and even with their Nationalist coalition partners they could not obtain the two-thirds majority required by the constitution to pass an Enabling Law (Fulbrook 2006, 179). But in March, Hitler was able to pass the Enabling Law by preventing communists and Social Democrats from attending the parliament. After this, 'Hitler could pass any "law" he wanted, without regard for parliamentary approval' (Fulbrook 2006, 179).

In the summer of 1933, Hitler moved to dissolve all parties except the Nazis. Having created a one-party state he used terror to destroy the independence of organisations throughout society, with Nazi spies and informers installed at all levels of workplaces, professional associations, clubs and groups. Individuals who even talked of the possibility of resistance were taken away by the Gestapo, the political police, to concentration camps.

The Military and the Post-war Constitution

After the Second World War, the allies divided Germany into zones of occupation, agreeing to policies of denazification, demilitarisation and democratisation, with reparations taken by each power from its own zone, with additional payments to the Soviet Union to compensate for its greater suffering and damage (Fulbrook 2006, 206). With the advent of the Cold War, Germany was split in two. In the west, the Federal Republic formally came into being in May 1949, closely followed by the German Democratic Republic in the east in October.

The Constitution of the Federal Republic, or 'Basic Law', was shaped, in part, by ideas of avoiding the sorts of political developments associated with the Nazis' rise to power. Article 1 established that 'human dignity shall be inviolable'. The Constitution identifies human rights as directly applicable law, and endorses active resistance to any threat to democracy, republicanism and social responsibility. Article 79, paragraph 3, insists that these principles cannot be changed in any future amendment of the Constitution (Basic Law of the Federal Republic of Germany 1949).

The Basic Law has a President as formal head of state, as in the Weimar Constitution. But the President is selected by an electoral college of parliamentarians, rather than a popular vote, and has limited powers, with no emergency powers like those that allowed the Reichsprasident to remove Communist parliamentarians at the time of the Reichstag Fire Decree. When a new West German army, the Bundeswehr, was created in 1955, the amended Basic Law required that it answer to the Secretary of Defence during peacetime and the Chancellor during wartime, with both of them answerable to the parliament (Basic Law of the Federal Republic of Germany 1949).

Following the dissolution of the Wehrmacht at the end of the Second World War, Germany was demilitarised, with the allied powers responsible for security issues. But in West Germany Chancellor Adenauer formed a committee to plan for future re-armament in 1950, responding, in part, to remilitarisation in East Germany. In 1954, following the restoration of sovereignty to the Federal Republic with the London and Paris agreements, the United States, Britain and France agreed to support West Germany's entry into NATO and rearmament, as an ally in the Cold War.

> In the summer of 1955 … the West German Bundestag (lower house of parliament) voted to authorise the recruitment of volunteers for the initial formation of the Bundeswehr (Federal Armed Forces). Later in the year, a cadre of about 100 officers and NCOs were sworn in at a ceremony in Bonn. Most of the initial volunteers were veterans of the World War II Wehrmacht who had been serving in the Federal Border Force since … 1951 …. Training facilities and equipment were made available by the US, and 1500 volunteers reported for the first training cycle, which began in January 1956. The Bundestag soon promulgated compulsory military service. By the end of the Year, the force numbered about 65,000 including 10,000 volunteers from the Border Force, almost all of whom were war veterans. (Nations Encyclopaedia 2008)

The Bundeswehr now has over 200,000 professional soldiers, with 55,000 conscripts, serving for nine months or more, and 2,500 active reservists. Some tens of thousands of civilians are also employed.

After the Second World War, the allied leaders and many in Germany itself saw the failure of the Weimar Constitution to enforce effective parliamentary control of the military as a major factor in Hitler's rise to power. As noted earlier, the Social Democratic leadership played a key role in ensuring that the army reported directly to a President who was effectively outside of parliamentary control. Without any such control, the military went its own way in supporting and participating in terrorism and mass human rights abuses.

When the Constitution was amended to allow the existence of the army, it was clearly established that its role was a purely defensive one (article 87a). Before 1990 its major active role was in disaster relief work. The peacetime commander of the Bundeswehr was the Minister of Defence, with the Chancellor as Commander-in-Chief once a 'state of defence' was declared.

A number of Constitutional Court cases in the 1990s established that a special resolution of the Parliament is required to allow the deployment of the army outside the territory of the NATO member states. Such a resolution is required to spell out full details of the mission and the limits of its term. Recent years have seen a steady expansion of German military activity abroad, however, including in Afghanistan and, most recently, in the Indian Ocean.

Anti-terrorism Powers

During the 1960s, anger toward what was seen as ineffective denazification in West Germany, with many positions in government and the public service occupied by ex-Nazis, along with the outlawing of left-wing parties, contributed to the formation of the Red Army Faction as West Germany's most prominent left-wing terrorist group.

Many on the left saw the 'Grand Coalition' between the two main parties – the SPD and the CDU with Kurt Keisinger, a former Nazi party member as Chancellor – in the late 1960s as a major step towards authoritarianism and intensified political repression. With 95 per cent of the Bundestag controlled by the coalition, the APO or 'Extra-Parliamentary Opposition' was formed with the intent of generating protest and political activity outside of government (Snell 1970).

The Red Army Faction operated from the late 1960s to 1998, committing numerous crimes, especially in the autumn of 1977, which led to a national crisis that became known as the 'German Autumn'. It was responsible for 34 deaths and many injuries in its almost 30 years of existence.

The government's response included measures which have since become familiar internationally since September 2001. While the Basic Law, in Article 1, expressly prioritises the right to human dignity, understood to include the right to a fair trial, along with other basic human rights, ways were found to override such protections in the name of effectively combating terrorism.

One such development was the imposition of 'contact bans' on terrorist suspects and their lawyers, following secret recordings by the German Federal Intelligence Service of meetings in the Stuttgart-Stammheim gaols between Red Army Faction suspects and their lawyers in 1975–76. The state officials responsible justified such secret recording and subsequent contact bans as 'necessary', using a legal concept of necessity that had originally been developed in 1927 in relation to the medical necessity for performing otherwise unlawful abortions. This defence was accepted in a court challenge to such practices (Hufnagel 2008, 102).

To regularise and clarify the legal foundation for such practices, legislation was passed in 1977 which provided that, in circumstances where there is imminent threat to life, physical integrity or liberty of a person, and there is a reasonable suspicion that this threat is made by a terrorist organisation, a contact ban can be ordered. This administrative order may be obtained from the federal state government, a designated high federal state authority or, if more than one federal state is affected by the offence, the Federal Minister of Justice. The Act contains provisions for judicial review of these orders. The order can stipulate that the detained person may be held incommunicado for up to 30 days. This restriction encompasses all contact with other detained persons, the 'outside world' (friends and family) and with lawyers (Hufnagel 2008, 102–3).

Hufnagel argues that there are good grounds for seeing such contact bans as incompatible with the Basic Law, as well as with Article 6(3)9C0 of the European Convention on Human Rights, which gives everyone the right to defend themselves through 'legal assistance of their choosing' and with Article 14(3)(b) of the International Covenant on Civil and Political Rights, which guarantees a right of an accused person to 'communicate with counsel of their choosing' (Hufnagel 2008, 102–3).

The German Constitutional Court considered the constitutional legitimacy of the law in 1978, and concluded that paramount right to life of potential victims of the lawyers' clients overrode the right to a fair trial. Within the order of the Basic Law human life represents the highest value of all. It follows from Article 2II(1) in conjunction with Article 1I(2) that in respect of the high value attached to life, the most serious duty of the state is to protect all human life from the unlawful deprivation by others (German Constitutional Court 1978). However, it is not clear that this law would survive a challenge in the European Court of Human Rights (Hufnagel 2008, 103). Access to a lawyer is of particular importance in relation to preventative detention of alleged terrorists, as a protection against self-incrimination, torture and inhuman treatment.

Another development was the extension of a law allowing police officers to use lethal force as a matter of last resort against a criminal in circumstances where their own lives or the life of a hostage was threatened. The courts held that a terrorist is a 'general, continuous threat' to society, and could therefore legitimately be eliminated even if not at the time immediately threatening a person or a group of people. In effect, because terrorists are a continuous threat to the right to life of innocent people, anyone the authorities consider to be a terrorist can be shot and killed at any time (Hufnagel 2008, 108).

A range of new anti-terrorism laws were introduced following the terrorist attacks of 9/11, with a serious impact on civil and democratic rights. 'Amendments were made to 17 existing laws and five regulations, with consequential changes to more than 100 German laws.' Contact bans with lawyers were extended to where 'there is a risk that the lawyer would conceal evidence from the investigators' (Hufnagel 2008, 102).

The issue of torture during interrogation, supposedly justified by the imminence and extent of terrorist threat, was directly addressed in the Dascher case. A senior police officer raised a defence of necessity to justify assault upon a supposed child kidnapper to try to discover the whereabouts of the victim before the child suffered harm or died. The police also appealed to the 1927 concept of 'supra-statutory emergency' (Hufnagel 2008, 102).

The German District Court held that basic values of the life of the victim as against the dignity and humanity of the prisoner could not be weighed against one another. The judges ruled that torture was never justified and found the officer liable for assault. However, they accepted that 'pressing need' could justify mitigation in sentencing.

As highlighted by Defence Minister Jung's earlier-mentioned defiant response to the similar ruling in the 2005 Constitutional Court case about shooting down hijacked aircraft, such legal judgments are by no means a guarantee against violent domestic use of the armed forces.

Italy

The early years of the twenty-first century witnessed a resurgence of Italian military activity, both overseas and domestically, generating concerns about the potential emergence of parallels to the 1920s and 1930s, when Mussolini's fascist regime combined an internal military-backed dictatorship with aggressive armed expansionism in Libya and Ethiopia (*Economist* 2008; Arens 2008).

Domestically, the Italian government deployed 3,000 troops in 2008, supposedly to crack down on illegal immigrants and combat crime. Following a six-month trial, in 2009 the government moved to implement a second phase of 'Operation Safe Streets', involving up to 30,000 soldiers. The operation began in mid-2008, when Prime Minister Silvio Berlusconi proclaimed a state of emergency due to the inflow of refugees by boat across the Mediterranean Sea, and the Defence Minister signed a decree to permit the use of 3,000 troops for domestic purposes.

One thousand troops were assigned to refugee internment camps, officially called 'identification and classification centres', another 1,000 to sensitive public places (train stations, embassies, St Peter's Cathedral, etc.) and the remainder to patrol streets in Rome and other major cities, alongside police officers. Armed troops, some in body armour and with automatic weapons, appeared on the streets, including some who had previously served in Afghanistan, Iraq or Lebanon (Michaels 2008; Dinmore 2008).

There was widespread criticism, both internationally and domestically, with political commentators accusing the government of seeking to 'militarise' city centres. Others pointed out that crime rates had actually fallen in Italy and the country already had 230,000 police and *carabinieri*. In early 2009, the government decided to extend the operation even though crime statistics for the previous six months had not been compiled (Povoledo 2009).

While the military deployment was not unprecedented in the post-Second World War period – some 20,000 troops were sent to Sicily in 1992 to combat the Mafia, and soldiers were often seen in Italian cities during the Red Brigades attacks in the 1970s and 1980s – the emergency measures revived memories of Mussolini's fascist dictatorship. Just as Jews became scapegoats for fascists in the 1930s, there were signs that gypsies and other immigrants were being targeted as economic and social conditions deteriorated in 2008 and 2009. Prime Minister Berlusconi made his announcement about expanding 'Operation Safe Streets' to 30,000 soldiers against the backdrop of a media campaign against an alleged crime wave involving an influx of Eastern European gypsies (Dinmore and Bianchi 2009).

In January 2009, military units were deployed to make arrests and break up illegally-erected shacks in Rome. After allegations that units of the Folgore parachute brigade were mobilised, an army spokesman said Sardinian grenadiers had been involved in checking the identities of 70 gypsies living in an illegal camp (Dinmore and Bianchi 2009).

To assess the significance of these developments, it is necessary to review briefly the rise of Italian fascism and the essential assistance given to it by the military high command.

As in Germany, the end of the First World War triggered revolutionary activity by industrial and agricultural workers and soldiers, sickened by the massive loss of life in a futile imperial conflict. Proto-fascist movements started out as aggressive 'anti-labour militia, entrusted by capitalist magnates and country landlords with the mission of harassing the organized proletariat and destroying its power of resistance' (Guerin 1973, 102).

A succession of mass strikes and factory occupations forced major concessions, including higher wages, an eight-hour day, 'general recognition of collective contracts and a voice for the working class in the organisation of production through factory committees' (Guerin 1973, 37). Major industrialists and landowners, meeting in Genoa and Milan in 1919 and 1920, formed detailed plans for action against the working class, centred upon the use of armed gangs, including war veterans and unemployed people, under the control of Mussolini, to threaten, harry, attack and terrorise the organised proletariat (Guerin 1973, 38–9).

Mussolini's 'action squadrons' initially operated in the country, with support from local police and the army, launching surprise raids on workers' meetings, killing, wounding and torturing, before rapidly retreating. 'Munitions from the state arsenals came into the hands of the fascist bands, which were trained by officers on leave or even on active service' (Guerin 1973, 105).

Later, Italian capitalists assisted Mussolini to turn his organisation into a political party and increase the sales of his newspaper, the *Populo d'Italia*, campaigning for the destruction of independent labour organisations, an end to democratic rights and an increase in military spending to sustain an expansionary foreign policy.

Disappointed with the post-First World War peace settlement and fearing civilian control, the army generals also sought an alliance with fascism, and allowed Mussolini to seize power in 1922. Over the ensuing years, the armed fascist militia, the 'Blackshirts' or National Security Volunteer Militia (Milizia Volontaria per la Sicurezza Nazionale (MVSN)), which terrorised incipient resistances in the cities and provinces, became integrated into the armed forces. By 1933, Mussolini grew powerful enough to appoint a fascist military leadership over the army. He also created and held the supreme military rank of First Marshal of the Empire, along with the King, giving him supreme control over the military (Gooch 2007; Sullivan 1984).

Written in the aftermath of Italy's defeat in the Second World War, and Mussolini's overthrow, Article 11 of the post-war Italian Constitution states that 'Italy rejects war as a means for settling international controversies and as an instrument of aggression against the freedoms of others peoples'.

Nevertheless, today Italy's military expenditure is the eighth highest in the world, and its total number of military personnel is approximately 308,000. After the 2001 declaration of the 'war on terror', Italy sent troops to join the US-led invasion of Afghanistan and later participated in the occupation of Iraq, with troops patrolling Nasiriyah and surrounding areas in 2003 (Paoletti 2008, 205–15).

Chapter 7
Japan: Undermining the 'Pacifist' Clause

Widespread and deep-going public hostility to military power and to military involvement in civilian life, resulting from Japan's history of militarisation of civil life and imperial aggression, has so far prevented the passing of specific military call-out legislation. At the same time, the continuing influence and re-assertion of some elements of earlier militarisation can be seen in contemporary Japanese politics.

After its defeat in the Second World War, Japan adopted a constitution that renounced war and prohibited the establishment of organised Japanese armed forces. Article 9 of its post-war constitution stated that 'land, sea, and air forces as well as other war potential, will never be maintained'. Today, however, Japan has one of the largest armed forces in the world. The Japanese Self-Defence Forces (SDF) consists of some quarter of a million personnel, including a 160,000-person ground force, a sophisticated air force and a formidable navy. Furthermore, Japan's military establishment designs and builds weaponry and other war equipment that is equal to any in the world (Maeda 1995).

Although known as the pacifist clause, Article 9 has been interpreted, since the establishment of the SDF in 1954, as permitting the SDF to exist, but only to operate strictly in terms of Japan's territorial defence. These limits have been increasingly brushed aside by Japanese governments to allow SDF deployment overseas for so-called peacekeeping, reconstruction, humanitarian and civil emergency missions in Asia and beyond.

In 2004, the Japanese government sent SDF units into an active war zone for the first time since 1945. Despite strong public opposition, 600 SDF personnel were deployed to support the US-led occupation of Iraq. Officially, they fulfilled non-combat roles, such as providing medical treatment, supplying water and reconstructing public facilities. Also in support of the US-led war, another 330 SDF personnel went to the Persian Gulf to transport vehicles and other equipment.

Since then, there has been a continual push by successive governments to expand the activities of the SDF, both at home and overseas. In the face of public disquiet, these operations generally have been presented as counter-terrorist or humanitarian. As one commentator observed, even the participation of the SDF in 'peaceful overseas operations' is a 'sensitive and much debated topic' (Tharp 2008).

In 2005, Japan sent 925 SDF personnel to Indonesia after the earthquake in the Indian Ocean and the tsunami that killed more than 150,000 people. While SDF members participated in disaster relief efforts, it was the largest overseas military deployment since the Second World War. The following year, the Japan Coast Guard (JCG) assisted in the containment of the Guimaras oil spill in the

Philippines. In 2008 Prime Minister Yasuo Fukuda announced that Japan would send SDF officials into Sudan as part of a UN peacekeeping mission.

At the same time, the SDF has begun to be assigned a visible part in domestic security. For the July 2008 G8 summit on Hokkaido, in addition to more than 20,000 police providing ground-based security, military security included four fighter jets, AWACS reconnaissance planes, 12 warships and Patriot surface-to-air-missiles. According to the National Police Agency, the Japanese authorities spent about $US280 million for security at the meeting, which was more than double the $130 million that Germany spent the previous year when it hosted the meeting. Military forces were on hand, even though the police far outnumbered a few thousand anti-capitalist demonstrators. A *New York Times* report described the scene at Date, about 20 kilometres south of Lake Toya, the meeting venue: 'Groups of police officers stopped cars for inspection, and sealed off roads leading to the site. Offshore, armed cruisers were visible, a rare sight in a nation that does not even have a full-fledged military' (Fackler 2008).

In 2005, constitutional revisions were proposed that would create a cabinet-level Defence Ministry and amend, while keeping, the old clauses mandating official pacifism. Under the proposed revisions, the JSDF would also be formally referred to as a military force for the first time since its establishment:

> In order to secure peace and the independence of our country as well as the security of the state and the people, military forces for self-defense shall be maintained with the prime minister of the cabinet as the supreme commander. (International Cooperation Committee Chubu Diocese 2007)

Nonetheless, opinion polls showed that a clear majority opposed Japan's continued military presence in Iraq. In 2006, Prime Minister Koizumi announced the withdrawal of Japanese troops from Iraq. His decision was aimed at ending what had become a major embarrassment for the government, prior to stepping down as Prime Minister.

Koizumi's successor Abe presided over the first ever joint naval exercise of the United States, Japan and India near the Boso Peninsula in central Japan in 2007. In the same year, the inaugural cabinet-level Defence Minister, Fumio Kyuma, outlined a vision of broadening the role of the SDF, including domestically, and gave some statistical indices of the expansion of SDF activities that had already occurred since the Great Hanshin-Awaji earthquake (commonly known as the Kobe earthquake) in 1995:

> In recent years, the missions of the Self Defence Forces have been not only the defence of our nation, but its missions have expanded into response to disasters inside and outside Japan, international peace cooperation and more. And there has also been a dramatic increase in the actual activities performed. Since the Great Hanshin-Awaji Earthquake, a total of approximately 2.73 million Self Defence Forces personnel have been dispatched to engage in disaster relief

> missions. While overseas, roughly 30,000 Self Defence Forces personnel have been engaged in around 20 international peace cooperation activities such as PKO. (Japan Ministry of Defense 2007)

In 2008, Prime Minister Yasuo Fukuda invoked Article 59 of the Constitution to push through legislation restarting Japan's naval refuelling assistance to the NATO-led occupation of Afghanistan, despite continuing widespread popular opposition (Article 59 allows a two-thirds majority of the lower house to override the upper house if it rejects a bill or fails to vote on it within 60 days). Opinion polls had earlier indicated that 55 per cent of voters opposed the extension of the Indian Ocean mission (Symonds 2008).

On both the domestic and international fronts, the growing use of the SDF challenges the post-war restrictions imposed on the military in the light of the pre-war army's central part in imperialist aggression throughout Asia and in the internal police-state regime. To understand the issues involved and their implications it is necessary to briefly review the relevant history.

Japanese Imperialism

Throughout the second half of the nineteenth century the Western powers of Britain, Germany and France established colonies in Asia and divided China into different national 'spheres of influence'. The United States forcibly opened up Japan to Western trade in 1853 and the Western powers thereafter forced Japan into unequal treaties and low tariffs.

Under this pressure, the Meiji Revolution of 1868 paved the way for the subsequent development of Japanese economy and society. A coalition of progressive feudal lords overthrew the Tokugawa Shogun with the aim of modernising the economy so as to be able to effectively resist foreign domination. Those leading the revolution recognised the requirement for capitalist industrialisation in order to maintain national autonomy.

At the same time, this revolution from above meant that there was no mass mobilisation of the population in the name of human and democratic rights to effect a revolutionary transfer of power, as in Britain and France, to pave the way for liberal parliamentary democracy and the rule of law. Initially Meiji-supported deliberative assemblies were appointed by the Emperor, rather than elected. Later parliaments remained 'sharply restricted' in their powers (Pempel 1992, 13).

Members of the former military aristocracy amongst the leaders of the Meiji Revolution pressed strongly for Japan to embark on its own colonial expansion in the early 1870s, starting with strategically significant Korea, to prevent its takeover by Western powers. 'A majority of the country's leaders decided to postpone this military action to concentrate on modernisation and industrialisation, but … did not oppose [such] action in theory' (Gordon 2003, 5). Ultimately, the regime set out to acquire forcefully its own foreign territories between 1894 and 1910. Taiwan was seized in 1895 after the Sino-Japanese War of 1894–95, followed by:

> Korea as a protectorate in 1905 after the Russo-Japanese War of 1904–5, then as a colony when unilaterally annexed by Japan in 1910; and the Kwantung Leased Territories in 1905 in southern Manchuria when Japan succeeded to Russia's leases after the Russo-Japanese War. (Gordon 2003, 5)

Subsequent liberation struggles in the occupied territories were ruthlessly suppressed by the occupying forces. The casualties included 7,000 peaceful protestors killed, 15,000–16,000 wounded and 47,000 arrested in Korea in 1919 (Jansen 2000, 516–17).

Pre-War Militarism

Before the Second World War, Japan remained a highly militarised, stratified and unequal society. Under the Meiji Constitution of 1889 the Emperor exercised all legislative, executive and judicial powers. Theoretically his authority was supreme. In practice he delegated his powers to public servants whom he appointed to carry out his orders. The formal structure of national government laid out in the Constitution consisted of an advisory privy council, a cabinet and a prime minister, a bicameral legislature, a judiciary with limited powers of constitutional review. In addition, a selected body of national civil servants administered the day to day affairs of state. A hereditary aristocracy controlled the upper house of the national legislature, the House of Peers. And after 1900 a body of elder statesmen, the *genro*, played a key role in selecting prime ministers and cabinet members and advising the Emperor (Allinson 2004, 19).

Article 11 of the Constitution gave the Emperor direct command of the army and navy, beyond the authority of the cabinet. From the 1890s, two military chiefs of staff were directly responsible to the Emperor and engaged in operations increasingly divorced from ministerial control (Katzenstein 1996, 53). Only high-ranking military officers on active duty, rather than civilians, could head ministries and military co-operation was necessary to form cabinets. Military officers were appointed to more than a quarter of civilian cabinet posts between 1918 and 1945 (Katzenstein 1996, 54).

As Allinson points out, military officers were subject to special training programmes, apart from the public educational system, where they 'learned a strategic approach that emphasized the distinctive spiritual strength of the Japanese fighting man, exemplified in massed attacks with bayonets' (Allinson 2004, 34). Such education encouraged them to reject democracy and political compromise in favour of military rule.

The militarisation of politics and of public life were carried forward by the introduction of conscription from 1873, seen as a way to build national unity around military values of bravery and self-sacrifice in combat; by the development of a military reserve by the army ministry from 1910, reaching 2.9 million people by 1936; and by the operation of military run youth training centres from 1926. As Katzenstein says, these developments contributed to widespread acceptance of the military as a force for 'unselfish pursuit of national objectives' with only periodic public hostility to military organisation and operations – particularly in the period immediately following the end of the Second World War (Katzenstein 1996, 54).

The original mission of the military in Meiji Japan was maintenance of internal security. In this role they operated in tandem with a highly politicised police system. At first, the 'primary role' of the Metropolitan Police Department (MPD), created on a French and German model in 1871 – at the same time as the military – was 'to suppress traditional elites who had lost power' in the revolution. In 1886 the Ministry of Home Affairs created a special political police unit for covert surveillance and suppression of political activism (Katzenstein 1996, 54).

Violent repression of political dissent led to calls by politicians committed to democracy for the abolition of such political police and to repeated public attacks on police stations. But the Peace Preservation Law of 1925 gave police further quasi-judicial powers – to punish offences without due process. Large numbers of left-wing activists were imprisoned and tortured by police in 1928 (Katzenstein 1996, 54).

The police role included overseas – largely anti-communist – espionage and acts of terrorism (Katzenstein 1996, 54). With increasing Japanese imperial expansion, 22,000 police came to be stationed in Korea, Taiwan and other occupied areas overseas. However, despite mass mobilisation of police forces, the police still relied on the military to contain popular protests, including the attacks on police stations in 1906, and large scale riots in 1912 and 1918 (Katzenstein 1996, 54).

As Katzenstein observes, only after an attempted *coup d'état* in 1932 'did the MPD establish a separate riot squad' and 'the MPD had only 312 security police before 1945, less than 10 percent of the post-war MPD riot police' (Katzenstein 1996, 54). Through a military police force established in 1881, the army retained a foothold on matters of internal security. Although its 1,600 members were for many years no more than a token force, the military police force was charged with planning countermeasures against popular uprisings and organising the reserves for the civilian police (Katzenstein 1996, 54).

At the beginning of the 1930s the aristocracy still continued to exercise power through their control of the House of Peers. The military exercised its influence within the government through two seats on the cabinet and through private audiences with the Emperor conducted by the leaders of its general staff. Big business interests were strongly represented in and through the elected delegates of the House of Representatives. The national civil servants of the bureaucracy exercised the delegated power of the Emperor (Allinson 2004, 19).

Japan was badly affected by the global Great Depression of the 1930s, which initially reduced exports and led to high unemployment. In 1931, Japanese troops moved into Manchuria, and the conquered areas became 'an adjunct to the increasingly militarised Japanese economy' undergoing 'sustained economic expansion on the basis of integrated four year plans' (Harman 1984, 68).

Expanding domestic production spurred the growth of exports, particularly in textiles. But Japan encountered increasing opposition from other producers, especially the United States and Great Britain. 'The world was already dividing itself into a series of autonomous trading blocs and opposition to exports encouraged Japan to carve out its own bloc' focused mainly on its colonies in Korea, Manchuria and Taiwan (Allinson 2004, 30).

Economic revival was accompanied by increasing political instability and conflict. Between 1932 and 1945 13 different cabinets were formed. Most governments served for just a matter of months, with politicians, aristocrats, public servants and the military finding little common ground. Big businessmen, once members, leaders and supporters of the older political parties, moved toward other allies (Allinson 2004, 34). In particular, a deepening alliance arose between business, the military and elements of the state bureaucracy, built around a common interest in crushing left-wing organisations and increasing state contracts for military hardware to defend and extend the empire.

Following the assassination of Prime Minister Inukai in 1932, young officers in the army and navy organised a reign of terror during the 1930s. They conspired to assassinate government officials and business leaders and plotted to seize control of the government. They killed Finance Minister Takahashi Korekiyo when he tried to shift investment away from military spending. In the late 1930s the military-dominated government in Tokyo extended its invasion of China, and subsequently set out to seize control of the pieces of Western empires in Malaya, Borneo and Singapore, along with the French colonies in Indochina and the US-run Philippines. As Allinson points out:

> Japan's military expansion southward into China and Southeast Asia brought insecurity and often wanton death and destruction to millions in nearby Asian nations, while costing the lives of millions of Japanese soldiers, sailors and civilians. (Allinson 2004, 37)

After the War

Japan emerged from the Second World War with half of the areas of its largest cities in ruins and its economy devastated. The occupying allied forces led by the Americans under General MacArthur set about reshaping the Japanese state. A new constitution went into effect in 1947. It gave male and female citizens above the age of 20 voting rights to elect representatives in a bicameral legislature, consisting of a House of Representatives and a House of Councillors. Executive authority rested with a prime minister and cabinet with at least half of all cabinet ministers required to hold seats in the legislature. A supreme court was established, supervising the system of local courts (Allinson 2004, 60).

The drafters of the 1947 Constitution were especially concerned to eliminate the political autonomy and power of the military. They dismantled the aristocratic upper chamber of the previous government, which was seen to have been an instigator and supporter of the war. However, they retained a key role for the Emperor as head of state. The Emperor had been a major landholder in occupied territories overseas and Commander-in-Chief of the armed forces throughout the war. As Robertson argues, there was substantial evidence that Hirohito 'had personally approved all his country's barbaric military ventures and had held out against surrender' until after the bombing of Hiroshima (Robertson 2008, 257). Under US pressure he was exempted from prosecution in allied-administered war crimes trials in Tokyo. (The International Military Tribunal of the Far East, from May 1946 to November 1948, tried 6,000 people and imposed the death penalty on 900 while acquitting over 1,000) (Robertson 2008, 257). These trials provided documentary evidence for 'systematic atrocities' on a par with those dealt with in the Nazi prosecutions at Nuremberg. In Robertson's words:

> the imperial army impaled women on stakes after being raped and cutting their children in half. It dropped bubonic plague germs on Chinese citizens, and boasted of its contempt for the laws of war by executing allied airmen alongside their parachutes and by sending surviving prisoners, at war's end, on death marches. (Robertson 2008, 256)

In the course of his own trial, Prime Minister Tojo admitted that it was 'inconceivable for a high Japanese official to take any action against the wishes of the Emperor' (Robertson 2008, 257). Yet the US stage-managed the trials in such a way as to present the Emperor as innocent of involvement in war crimes. The tribunal also failed to prosecute 'war-mongering industrialists and violent nationalist leaders' seen as bulwarks against communism in post-war Japan, 'overlooked the enslavement of Koreans and Formosans', including 'hundreds of thousands of "comfort women"', and offered immunity to Nazi-style 'scientific' torturers and mass murderers in exchange for their assisting US 'research'. These failures had significant repercussions in subsequent decades.

The Pacifist Constitution

McCormack argues that an assurance that Japan would never again launch military attacks upon its Asian neighbours was a necessary complement to the constitutional restoration of imperial power. Such an assurance is provided in Article 9 of the Constitution:

> Aspiring sincerely to an international peace based on justice and order, the Japanese people forever renounce war as a sovereign right of the nation and the threat or use of force as a means of settling international disputes … In order to

> accomplish the aim of the preceding paragraph land, sea, and air forces, as well as other war potential, will never be maintained. The right of belligerency of the state will not be recognised. (McCormack 2007, 125)

It has been said that Washington regretted the inclusion of the peace clause almost as soon as the Constitution had gone into effect, being more concerned to see a renewed Japanese militarism in the service of US foreign policy, patrolling the Pacific region, than concerned about any future anti-US militarism. There was also the consideration of Japan's export success in the US consumer goods sector being significantly based upon the major differences in levels of military spending between the two countries (McCormack 2007, 125).

Similarly, the Japanese leadership treated Article 9 as 'an inconvenient and troublesome shackle' (McCormack 2007, 126). As McCormack points out, 'no Japanese leader has ever declared with pride to the world its unique constitutional pacifism as something that should be extended to other regions' (McCormack 2007, 126). Instead, 'it has been an embarrassment … and the imperative to normalise the country has preoccupied government after government' (McCormack 2007, 125–6).

On the other hand, there has been widespread and continuing public support for Article 9 and for the three non-nuclear principles forbidding the possession, manufacture or introduction into Japan of nuclear weapons. Remembering the horrors of pre-war militarism and imperialism, and of the war, including the bombing of Hiroshima and Nagasaki, and the subsequent post-war poverty and chaos, large numbers of Japanese people have strongly supported the pacifist Constitution. There were massive street demonstrations against the US-Japan Security Treaty in 1960, during the anti-war movement in the later 1960s, and against the renewal of the US-Japan Treaty in 1970 (Katzenstein 1996, 155).

Revision of the Constitution requires a two-thirds majority in both houses of the Diet and a majority in a special referendum. Given the widespread public support for the pacifist clause, successive governments have failed to win sufficient support for any amendment. However, the government appealed to a universal 'right of self defence' to establish the SDF in 1954 as the minimum military force required to protect the peace and independence of Japan' (Katzenstein 1996, 126). Over the ensuing decades, the SDF played an increasingly prominent role in society. One study notes:

> Article 83 of the Self-Defense Forces Law of 1954, required units to respond to calls for assistance from prefectural governors to aid in fire fighting, earthquake disasters, searches for missing persons, rescues, and reinforcement of embankments and levees in the event of flooding. [And] the SDF … continued to devote much of its time and resources to disaster relief and other civic action. Between 1984 and 1988, at the request of prefectural governors, the SDF assisted in approximately 3,100 disaster relief operations, involving about 138,000 personnel, 16,000 vehicles, 5,300 aircraft, and 120 ships and

> small craft. In addition, the SDF participated in earthquake disaster prevention operations and disposed of a large quantity of World War II explosive ordnance, especially in Okinawa. The forces also participated in public works projects, cooperated in managing athletic events, took part in annual Antarctic expeditions, and conducted aerial surveys to report on ice conditions for fishermen and on geographic formations for construction projects. Especially sensitive to maintaining harmonious relations with communities close to defense bases, the SDF built new roads, irrigation networks, and schools in those areas. Soundproofing was installed in homes and public buildings near airfields. Despite these measures, local resistance to military installations remained strong in some areas. (Maeda 1995)

In the 1950s and 1960s, lower courts declared the existence of the SDF (along with the security treaty with the United States and the presence of US forces in Japan) to be unconstitutional. But the High Court consistently upheld the SDF's legitimacy on grounds of the supremacy of the legislature in political matters and the idea that the Constitution could not have intended to deny such a universal right as self-defence. The Japanese public slowly came to accept the existence of the SDF insofar as it was used only for disaster relief and never as a military force, and the political leadership continued to increase its size and its role.

During the Cold War, prime ministers agreed that it would be impossible for the SDF to function outside Japan and that the duty of the Defence Forces was purely to protect Japan from aggression. There was no conscription and a limit was placed on the defence budget of 1 per cent of GDP (McCormack 2007, 128). Governments also observed the three 'non-nuclear principles', though they turned a blind eye to nuclear-armed US warships 'docking in or passing through Japan' (McCormack 2007, 175).

Nonetheless, as Japan's industrial recovery proceeded, the SDF grew in size and in the sophistication of its weaponry. As McCormack points out, 1 per cent of the current Japanese GDP amounts to $US45 billion, roughly on a par with military spending by the nuclear powers Britain and France, and supports the second largest navy in the world in tonnage terms, and a larger air force than that of Israel. Its armaments include jet fighters, submarines, destroyers and aircraft carriers. It has a prototype intercontinental ballistic missile in the form of its H22A rocket capable of lifting a 5 tonne payload into space, huge stores of plutonium for nuclear warheads and high levels of scientific and technical nuclear expertise (McCormack 2007, 17).

As McCormack observes, Japan is in the process of becoming a 'nuclear superpower' in terms of its investment in nuclear energy, and fuel enrichment and reprocessing facilities (McCormack 2007, 181). Such facilities can provide the foundation for a nuclear weapons programme. Abe Shinzo, as chief cabinet secretary in 2002, argued that 'the constitution would not block Japan's possession of nuclear weapons' (McCormack 2007, 176–7).

Throughout the Cold War, Japanese policy had been to cooperate with both the United States and the United Nations within the general framework of international law and without any direct military support for US policy. The US bases in Japan, particularly Okinawa, played a major role in the US wars in Korea, Vietnam and the Gulf. But the SDF had no direct military role. When Prime Minister Suzuki referred publicly to a treaty relationship between Japan and the United States in 1981, there was a huge public outcry, forcing him to say that his statement had no military implications (McCormack 2007, 57).

In 1990, following Iraq's invasion of Kuwait, the Japanese government refused US requests to send minesweepers to the Gulf. Japan contributed $US13 billion to the prosecution of the first Gulf War, but played no direct military role. SDF ships arrived in the area only after the end of hostilities (Katzenstein 1996, 125). At the time, 'opposition parties, newspaper editorials and citizen protests … maintained that the Japanese government [was] constitutionally precluded from using armed force outside of its own geographic territory' (Katzenstein 1996, 125).

A UN Peace Co-operation Bill introduced by Prime Minister Kaifu in 1990 was defeated in the Diet when it became clear that it aimed to allow a Japanese 'UN Peace Co-operation Corps' to work with multinational forces in the Gulf. A modified version of the Bill was introduced in 1991, restricting SDF participation to UN peacekeeping and humanitarian rescue, 'conditional on the combatants' agreement to a ceasefire, their acceptance of the deployment of a peace-keeping force and the neutrality of the force' (Katzenstein 1996, 126). The Bill was passed in 1992, despite apparently conflicting with UN peacekeeping practice, following which 600 members of the SDF were deployed to the UN peacekeeping operation in Cambodia in 1993 (Katzenstein 1996, 127).

While these troops were an engineering battalion, stationed in a safe region, 75 civilian police who went along with them came under fire. The Japanese government initially objected to arming these police, for self protection, and there were calls from opposition parties and the public for their return home. After a nine month stay, 'the Japanese force was the first to be withdrawn from Cambodia' (Katzenstein 1996, 95).

Guidelines for US-Japan Defence Cooperation legislated in the 1999 Regional Contingency Law committed Japan to 'rear support' of the US military in action in the vicinity of Japan. The second Bush regime, fearful of a possible Japanese accommodation with China, was anxious to see a deepening military bond between Japan and the United States. Shortly after 9/11, Japan adopted an 'Anti-Terrorism Special Measures Law' and sent 24 naval ships to the Indian Ocean to support the Afghan War (McCormack 2007, 63). As McCormack points out, these developments marked 'Japan's entry into the war against terror' (McCormack 2007, 64).

Prime Minister Koizumi cited the need for US military protection in face of the threat of attack by North Korea as grounds for Japanese support of the US-led war, including the involvement of Japanese forces to aid the occupation in 2004. Koizumi's commitment of Japanese forces to support the US occupation of Afghanistan and particularly his dispatch of Japanese troops to Iraq, including units from all three of Japan's Self-Defence Forces, the first to an overseas war zone since the Second World War, provoked widespread opposition from the public (McCormack 2007, 67).

External Security Issues

A comparatively low level of arms spending, compared to the US, seems to have assisted the growth of the Japanese economy in the post-war period. However, successive generations of policy makers have been deeply concerned with Japanese strategic vulnerability, in particular, its dependence on imported raw materials. As Katzenstein points out, with only 15 per cent of its land suitable for farming, Japan is:

> highly dependent on imports of wheat, soy beans, maize, and sorghum … Japan has the lowest level of food self-sufficiency in the industrial world. Japan has few domestic sources of minerals, and in the case of bauxite, nickel ore and uranium it is almost completely dependent on foreign supplies. Japan imports 90 percent of its iron ore, 80 percent of its copper and about 50 percent of its zinc. It relies almost totally on imported petroleum, natural gas, and [other] fossil fuels and has only limited capacities to tap domestic coal, geothermal and hydropower. Japan … imports about 80 percent of its total energy requirements … [Such dependence] has increased greatly since the 1960s. (Katzenstein 1996, 113–14)

In the post-war period, such vulnerability was seen primarily as an economic rather than a military issue, associated with a drive to catch up and surpass the West in terms of technology and productivity, so as to be able to maintain the flow of such necessary imports through the strength of the export economy.

A merger of liberal and democratic parties in 1955 produced a new conservative and pro-US party of big business. The LDP dominated Japanese politics up to 1993, and then again from 2001. At least up until the late 1970s, single-party domination provided a stable political and economic climate of pro-investment macro-economic policy which sustained investors' commitment to long-term projects (Katzenstein 1996, 65). Military interests have historically been 'weakly represented inside the LDP' (Katzenstein 1996, 108).

A Security Treaty with the United States has played a central role in defence policy, with close ties between the Japanese and US military. While Japan has produced an increasing range of military technology, 'most Japanese weapon producers do not depend heavily on military sales. With a few notable exceptions, dependence on weapons contracts is typically lower at bigger companies' (Katzenstein 1996, 110). Nonetheless, Katzenstein acknowledges that 'the defence economy … has been a driving force in Japan's push towards new technologies', with 'virtually all major manufacturing companies ... involved in defence manufacturing' (Katzenstein 1996, 110). While in the past Japan licensed military technology from the United States, putting such technology to civilian commercial use 'as quickly as possible', it has increasingly applied its own civilian innovations in the development of its own military technology (Katzenstein 1996, 110). 'In some Japanese weapons plants defence and civilian production ... run side by side, thereby accelerating the mutual diffusion of defence and civilian technologies' (Katzenstein 1996, 110). Major technological crossovers included transfers from fighter jets to trains, cars and fire trucks. The superiority of Japanese military electronics, compared to that of the United States, led to military exports to the latter from the 1980s.

Revival of Nationalism

The mid-1990s saw the emergence of prominent neo-nationalist, revisionist and reactionary organisations, founded to resist any apologies for past Japanese aggression and colonialism. Particularly important was the Japan Conference, pushing for revision of the Constitution and celebration of Japanese imperialism and the conduct of the Second World War (McCormack 2007, 9).

In 2006, 223 members of the Diet, including the Prime Minister, the Foreign and Finance Ministers and the Chief Cabinet Secretary were members of the League of Shinto Politicians, looking to the establishment of a Shinto spirituality and emperor worship as the foundation of national polity, despite a constitutional ban on state support for religion (McCormack 2007, 9). In 2001, Prime Minister Koizumi started annual formal visits to the Yasukuni Shrine, honouring those who had died in the service of the Emperor. As McCormack points out:

> in pre-War and Wartime Japan it played a central role in generating the ideology of chauvinism and militarism ... After the War ... the state was constitutionally proscribed from any connection with it (by Article 20). (McCormack 2007, 15)

The addition of the spirits of 14 major war criminals to the shrine's 'deities' in 1978 had brought an end to earlier visits in defiance of the Constitution by the Emperor and by Prime Ministers. When Koizumi resumed such visits 'neighbouring countries saw his action as an affront, and as tantamount to an attempted vindication of the war cause' (McCormack 2007, 15).

Koizumi's successor, Abe Shinzo, a core member of the Japan Conference and Shinto Politics groups, had previously been a strong supporter of such visits. He bowed to pressure to delay such visits on his own part, but he pressed ahead to revise the Constitution and the Fundamental Law of Education, and to upgrade the Defence Agency to a Ministry.

Internal Security

Because of the pacifist Constitution, Japan's post-war internal security policy largely evolved around the police forces, including the National Police Agency (NPA) under the control of the national government, and Tokyo's Metropolitan Police Department (MPD). Until recently, the size and power of this apparatus has helped subdue calls for greater SDF involvement in domestic security.

The NPA is organised as a series of bureaus, the second largest, after Criminal Investigation, being the Security Bureau. The NPA's activities are heavily focused on dealing with political unrest and terrorism. Thus, 'under the jurisdiction of its seven regional bureaus, the NPA maintains the Regional Bureau Riot Police, staffed since 1969 by 4,210 prefectural police officers' (Katzenstein 1996, 60–61). In the 1960s and 1970s the NPA established divisions to counter 'extremism' of the left and right. In 1988, it set up a special anti-terrorist division and in 1994, a department dealing with UN peacekeeping operations (Katzenstein 1996, 60–61).

The NPA retains overall control of internal security and operates in and through the MPD, with frequent interchange of personnel between the two. In 1948 the MPD created 2 riot police units, staffed by 1,800 policemen. 'By the late 1960s the riot police had grown to about 5,000' (Katzenstein 1996, 61). By 1988, '13–18 percent of the total police force', between 30,000 and 40,000 men, were in the security police.

The NPA has exercised considerable political influence, with 'high ranking NPA officials, mainly from the security police' gaining senior positions in other government departments and in the Cabinet Secretariat (Katzenstein 1996, 62). A number of NPA bureaucrats have subsequently become career politicians.

Attempts by the LDP from the 1950s to substantially increase police powers met with strong opposition inside and outside parliament, including, in 1958, street demonstrations and strikes involving 4 million people. In practice, however, 'informal extension of the Police Law has substantially enlarged the scope' of police activities (Katzenstein 1996, 62). As Katzenstein says, 'the police rely on Japan's bureaucratic tradition of flexible application of legal provisions' (Katzenstein 1996, 62). He notes that 'an enabling legal environment coupled with the organisational routines of a centralised police', creates 'an aggressive' and indeed, coercive 'investigatory style' on the part of Japanese detectives. The police 'systematically apply minor laws and ordinances to cover the absence of internal security legislation' and they 'interpret broadly what security and police laws do exist, particularly the Police Duties Execution Law' (Katzenstein 1996, 62). Moreover, 'crime and court statistics illustrate a sharp increase in [*de facto*] police powers of investigation' since the early 1970s (Katzenstein 1996, 84).

Individuals identified as political radicals are regularly subjected to round-the-clock surveillance, and police visits to all households and businesses in the country serve to gather information on local political activities. Police also collect information from crime prevention associations run by local business people, from police offices established in schools and from police checkpoints in workplaces. 'Before major public events the police regularly search houses, with or without warrants' (Katzenstein 1996, 85). Tens of thousands of riot police are regularly mobilised on such occasions, controlling roads, buildings, stations and airports. The powers and practices of the police resemble those of the 1930s. In Katzenstein's words:

> Japan's prison system affords the police ample opportunities for isolating political radicals. Japan's pre-trial detention system consists of 1,200 prisons run by the police, compared to the 150 under the jurisdiction of the MOJ. The police can keep suspects incarcerated for up to 23 days. After 3, 10 and 20 days a judge must authorize continued detention for additional questioning … usually a routine formality. Methods of questioning are reminiscent of the 1930s, they aim primarily to break the will of the individual … suspects are kept in police prisons to extract confessions, under conditions that a 1984 report described as shocking …. [A]rrested on minor offenses, suspects … have been questioned around the clock. (Katzenstein 1996, 85)

With the accused detained during lengthy appeals processes, 'judicial procedures permit the police and government to keep political radicals isolated for up to a decade before the final verdict' (Katzenstein 1996, 85).

At the same time, massive public criticism of police brutality in the past, and an unwillingness to create political martyrs, has contributed to relatively low levels of police violence on the streets, compared to other states. In this connection, Katzenstein refers to the comparatively low levels of casualties in the 20-year struggle by farmers and students against the construction, operation and enlargement of the Narita airport. 'The norm of avoiding bloodshed at almost all costs was an important reason why, at the beginning and at the end of the 1960s the police adamantly opposed politicians who demanded that the SDF be used as a back-up force to defend internal security against mass protests' (Katzenstein 1996, 88).

The Japanese police have a long history of collaboration with criminals and right-wing political groups. In 1951, prior to the development of a strong force of state riot police, Justice Minister Tokutaro Kimura, 'a strong nationalist and class D war criminal attempted to form a 200,000-man secret army largely from gangsters and right wingers' to violently suppress left-wing street demonstrations, and up to the early 1960s 'the government turned to private groups to maintain order' (Katzenstein 1996, 73).

The NPA apparently still works closely with both private security agencies and organised crime. Police work with the latter in regulating the 'entertainment' industry – including drugs and prostitution, keeping foreign drugs and prostitutes out of Japan. There is evidence of former police working closely with organised crime in the building industry, banking, insurance and securities (Katzenstein 1996, 60–61).

Japan's recent history of 'domestic terror' has been characterised by the conspicuous failure of security forces to address effectively the violence of religious doomsday cults and right-wing nationalist groups as compared to vigorous clampdowns on left-wing dissent. The activities of 'left wing radicals' in the 1970s and 1980s were a focus of major police activity (Katzenstein 1996, 60–61).

Aum Shinrikyo, by contrast, a religious sect, 'counting some of Japan's best and brightest, including students enrolled in elite universities' and '58 members of the SDF' amongst its membership, did not become a focus of any such major police activity until after the sarin attack on the Tokyo subway in 1995, which killed a dozen people and injured many others (Katzenstein 1996, 71–2). This was despite the fact that in earlier years the sect 'stockpiled … chemical weapons, had plans to attack Tokyo Metropolitan police with laser weapons, and sought to buy nuclear and conventional weapons from Russia … [and] was linked with a number of murders and extortions … an attack on the Head of the National Police Agency, the hijacking of an ANA jet, a letter bomb sent to Tokyo's Governor and an earlier gas attack' (Katzenstein 1996, 72).

On the other side of politics, a Tokyo bookshop worker was held in detention and interrogated by public security police for 44 days in 2003, 'his papers and books ransacked' at the start of the US attack on Iraq, for painting 'Opposition to war' on a lavatory wall in a park in Tokyo. In 2004 a government welfare officer was arrested under the Public Service Law for distributing copies of a Communist Party newspaper. McCormack notes:

> A special taskforce of 200 men was set up to pursue his case, ransacking his files and possessions, trailing him and videotaping him with something approaching fanatical zeal. On 29 June 2006, he became the first person in 32 years to be convicted under a law that … would certainly not have been applied to someone distributing copies of the LDP paper. (McCormack 2007, 22)

Further, three anti-Iraq war activists in Tokyo were held in detention for 75 days and subjected to intense interrogation in 2004 after handing out leaflets in a Defence Agency residential facility calling on SDF officers to 'think' about the leadership's decision to support the war.

Conclusion

In Japan, together with Germany and Italy, there are indications that, just as in the 1930s, when external militarism went hand in hand with internal repression, similar pressures could re-emerge today, under conditions of social stress and great power conflict. Particularly since 2001, successive Japanese governments have sought to weaken, reinterpret, sidestep or remove the pacifist provisions of the post-Second World War Constitution, and moved to expand the role of the armed forces, both domestically and overseas.

Chapter 8
Australia: Legislating Military Powers

In Australia, an attempt has been made to establish a statutory code governing, at least partially, the domestic deployment of the armed forces. In that sense, Australia has gone further than the most comparable countries, the United States, Britain and Canada, in seeking to lay down specific military powers, rather than rely predominantly on the common law or more general legislation.

Legislation was introduced in 2000, and extended in 2006, giving federal governments and the chief of the Australian Defence Force (ADF) explicit peacetime powers to call out the troops if 'domestic violence is occurring or is likely to occur' that 'would be likely to affect Commonwealth interests' or require the protection of a state or territory (*Defence Act 1903* (Cth) ss. 51A–51Y). Both sets of legislation were justified as urgent responses to potential threats of terrorism at key sporting events, first the 2000 Sydney Olympics and then the 2006 Melbourne Commonwealth Games. No acts of terrorism occurred at those events, yet the laws have remained and their wording goes far beyond counter-terrorism.

'Domestic violence' is a vague, anachronistic and seemingly incongruous term, which in contemporary parlance normally refers to violence in the home. Although the expression is taken from s 119 of the Australian Constitution, it is defined neither there nor in the *Defence Act* or regulations. No judicial definition exists either. Likewise, there is nothing in the law about how grave or widespread 'domestic violence' must be before the ADF is mobilised. Enormous discretion has thus been placed in the hands of the government and the ADF itself to intervene against civil unrest.

No call-out has yet occurred under the legislation. Nevertheless, military forces, including elite Special Air Services (SAS) units, have been deployed with increasing regularity for major political and sporting events, and a debate has been opened up on making domestic security a 'core business' of the ADF. These trends have largely emerged under the banner of the indefinite 'war on terror' launched by the United States and its allies following the September 2001 terrorist attacks in America. Yet, the changes underway have been broader and deeper. For example, the ADF has been used on many civilian fronts, including the Northern Territory Aboriginal intervention, the turning back of refugee boats and the patrolling of neighbourhoods in Afghanistan, Iraq, East Timor and Solomon Islands, as well as for counter-terrorism exercises.

Historically, at least since the so-called 'Glorious Revolution' of 1688 established parliamentary sovereignty in England, there has been a political and legal tradition opposing the use of the military against society's citizens. Reflecting that history, the Australian Constitution embodies a basic division of power between domestic law enforcement and the maintenance of armed forces for external defence. At Federation in 1901, the military power was handed to the Commonwealth under s 51(xxxi), the colonial defence forces were transferred to the Commonwealth by s 69, and under s 114, the states were forbidden to raise military or naval forces without the consent of the Commonwealth Parliament. Residual authority over domestic law and order remained in the hands of the states and their police forces. Section 119 provided for the Commonwealth to protect a state against 'domestic violence' – but only on the application of 'the Executive Government of the State'.

Moreover, this principle has become embedded in popular consciousness. Freedom from military rule and intervention in civilian affairs has been seen as a hallmark of liberty. The use of troops as strike-breakers in 1949 and 1953 generated intense hostility (Beddie and Moss 1982, 39–51). Deployment of soldiers against demonstrators at a military intelligence base in central Australia in 1989 caused considerable controversy (Ward 1997, 14–18). On the only occasion since Federation that a Commonwealth government has called out the military in force in an urban situation – following a bomb blast outside a regional Commonwealth Heads of Government meeting at the Sydney Hilton Hotel in 1978 – the sight of armed soldiers patrolling highways and the streets of the New South Wales town of Bowral caused public consternation (Cahill and Cahill 2005; Hocking 2004, 81–100). One local newspaper said the 'virtual siege conditions' were reminiscent of 'Franco's Spain' (*Southern Highland News* 1978).

However, since the terrorist attacks of September 2001, the declaration of a 'war on terror' and the wars in Afghanistan and Iraq, aspects of Australian society have been increasingly militarised. Thousands of soldiers have been mobilised, on alert, for major sporting events such as the Sydney Olympics, the 2003 Rugby World Cup and the Melbourne Commonwealth Games (Bergin and Smith 2006, 10). Naval vessels have been dispatched to repel asylum seekers, with powers to fire on boats or transport their passengers to remote islands (Head 2002, 23–33; Laing 2005, 518–20). Frequent anti-terrorism exercises have been conducted in urban environments, involving heavily-armed troops alongside police and intelligence officers (National Security Australia, National Counter-Terrorism Committee 2003, 95). Deployments have been conducted against civilian populations in Afghanistan, Iraq, Solomon Islands and East Timor (Head 2005, 484–92). The armed forces have been used in highly-publicised shows of strength, including air force jets and helicopters flying overhead during major political events such as the 2002 Commonwealth Heads of Government Meeting at Coolum, Queensland and US President Bush's visit to Australia in 2003 (Bergin and Smith 2006, 10).

By 2006, a report by the Australian Strategic Policy Institute (ASPI) said a new tempo had been established in military involvement in domestic security. It calculated that between the 1956 Melbourne Olympic Games and the 2000 Sydney Olympics, there had been four major special event support operations, an average of one every 11 years. The 2001–2006 period, by contrast, saw four such operations in a much shorter time span, at an average of one per 1.25 years (Bergin and Smith 2006, 10).

There are signs that the extension of the ADF's role will continue. In 2006, the Howard government announced a major expansion in the ADF, citing the need to respond to 'regional challenges' and foreshadowing further military interventions in the South Pacific, including in Papua New Guinea, Fiji and Vanuatu (Howard 2006). To encourage more young people to join the armed forces, a 'Gap Year Program' for school leavers was launched as part of the government's '$3.1 billion commitment to boosting ADF recruitment and retention' (Department of Defence, Australia 2008). During 2007, the Howard government declared a 'national emergency' in order to deploy soldiers to indigenous communities across the Northern Territory, providing active support to police in implementing various polices, including 'quarantining' of welfare benefits and the appointment of business managers to takeover municipal services. The taskforce was headed by an army Major General (Department of Defence, Australia 2008c). In the same year, heavily-armed SAS commandos were deployed, on standby, at the Sydney Asia-Pacific Economic Cooperation (APEC) summit, providing backup for large contingents of state and federal police, Australian Security Intelligence Organisation (ASIO) officers and foreign security personnel, while air force jets patrolled the skies above Sydney (Department of Defence, Australia 2008b).

Apart from occasional minor tactical differences, these operations enjoyed the bipartisan support of the two major parties in Australia, the Liberal–National Coalition and the Labor Party. After the Rudd government took office in late 2007, the trend continued. In 2008, an ADF operation was conducted for the Roman Catholic Church World Youth Day in Sydney. As part of Operation Testament, ADF personnel provided 'personnel and equipment in … specialist and niche capabilities' and hosted 'military pilgrims' from armed forces around the world (Department of Defence, Australia 2008d). This deployment to aid an evangelical exercise by a Christian denomination also raises questions about the separation of church and state, and possible offence to members of other religions, including Islam, not to speak of non-believers.

Following a lead established elsewhere, notably by NATO members (CCOE 2001), the Labor government established an Asia Pacific Centre for Civil-Military Cooperation (APC-CIMIC). Its mission was to 'help avoid continuing instability and revolving door military deployments' in the Asia-Pacific region through 'coordination between security, economic, emergency management, institution-building and non-government organisations' (Australian Labor Party 2007). While said to be seeking to avoid traditional military interventions, the Civil-Military Cooperation (CIMIC) doctrine involves the closer integration of military forces into civilian governance. Among the centre's functions are to 'better coordinate existing resources to act as a focal point for Government agencies in the coordination of stabilisation, reconstruction and peace-building missions' and 'develop doctrine, interagency exchange and training on disaster and crisis management, coordination and preparation' (Australian Labor Party 2007). These functions envisage long-term military engagements within civilian settings in some of Australia's neighbouring countries. These deployments could also set precedents for use at home.

A further step was taken in the militarisation of domestic security in 2008 when Prime Minister Rudd appointed a former military general to the new post of National Security Adviser. For the first time, a military figure became the nation's domestic security head. Ex-Major General Duncan Lewis served for 30 years as an officer in the military, including three tours of overseas duty with the SAS, the elite commando wing of the ADF. Lewis rose to become SAS commanding officer, commander of Australian and New Zealand forces in East Timor during 2000 and then – after leading the SAS again in the 2001–2002 invasion of Afghanistan – the initial chief of the Special Forces Command (SFC). The SFC was established in 2002 as a new 'fourth arm' of the military, together with the army, navy and air force, following the lead of the US and British forces. Having been appointed one of two associate secretaries of the prime ministerial department, Lewis was also to co-chair the National Counter-Terrorism Committee and a host of other security coordinating agencies (Rudd 2008).

Legal and Constitutional Turning Points

The legislative changes, combined with a significant High Court decision, have cleared the way legally and constitutionally for greater domestic use of the ADF. The *Defence Legislation Amendment (Aid to Civilian Authorities) Act 2006* (Cth) considerably enhanced the military call-out powers first enacted in 2000, which themselves expanded previous, unclear, common law powers. After a debate lasting only a total of about six hours in the Senate and House of Representatives, the amendments to the *Defence Act* were passed in 2006 with little public discussion or media coverage, on the basis of essential agreement between the Howard government and the Labor opposition.

As a result, it is now possible for the ADF to be called out whenever a federal government considers that a danger of 'domestic violence' exists that requires the protection of 'Commonwealth interests' or 'critical infrastructure' or a state or territory. The Prime Minister or two other 'authorising ministers' can, in the event of a 'sudden and extraordinary emergency' call out the ADF by a simple telephone call, without a written order. Alternatively, standing orders can be issued for the activation of the ADF whenever the Chief of the Defence Force deems it necessary. Once deployed, military personnel have unprecedented peacetime powers. They will be authorised, among other things, to shoot down aircraft, sink ships, use deadly force, interrogate civilians, issue orders, enter and search premises and seize documents.

In 2007, in *Thomas v Mowbray* ([2007] HCA 33) Australia's supreme court, the High Court, by a five-to-two majority, sanctioned the substantial use of the federal defence power in peacetime and for domestic purposes. The language of the majority judgments was sweeping – both in relation to the potential breadth of the defence power and the lawful capacity of the Commonwealth government to effectively define for itself the limits of the power. In a joint judgment, Gummow and Crennan JJ spoke of the defence power covering 'the defence of the realm against threats posed internally as well as by invasion from abroad by force of arms' (at 140). The judges also effectively expanded the doctrine of 'judicial notice' to accept the many untested assertions about the 'war on terror' made by the federal and state governments and their security agencies, such as the Australian Security Intelligence Organisation (ASIO). Callinan J declared it was 'blindingly obvious' that 'groups of zealots forming part of, or associated with Al Qa'ida' were 'making common cause of hatred against communities posing no threat to them' and 'planned to undertake violent, literally suicidal attacks upon even the institutions and persons of those communities' (543–53).

The immediate effect of the decision was to uphold the constitutionality of the 'control order' imposed on Jack Thomas, an acquitted terrorism suspect, under the provisions of the *Anti-Terrorism Act (No. 2) 2005*. By implication the ruling constitutionally validated most, if not all, of the federal anti-terrorism legislation introduced since 2002. Significantly, it also seems to interpret the defence power widely enough to permit the internal deployment of troops, whether or not under the military call-out legislation, to pursue the 'war on terror' or deal with any other 'threats posed internally'.

By leaving the government and its agencies broad scope to define for themselves the nature of alleged terrorist threats, the decision erodes the 50-year-old principle adopted by the High Court in the *Communist Party Case* of 1951, that the defence power cannot be defined or expanded unilaterally by the executive for domestic political purposes (*Australian Communist Party v The Commonwealth* [1951] HCA 51; 83 CLR 1). In that case, the court rejected the attempt of the Menzies government to ban the Communist Party during the Korean War by inserting recitals in the Communist Party Dissolution Bill that the Bill's measures were required for the 'security and defence of Australia' in the face of a dire threat of violence, insurrection, treason, subversion, espionage and sabotage.

The Expanded Military Call-out Powers

In the brief parliamentary debate when the initial military call-out legislation was introduced in 2000, both the Defence Minister and the opposition shadow minister justified the measures as necessary to deal with 'terrorism'. Yet, clearly 'domestic violence' extends beyond terrorism. In discussing the term in the context of s 119 of the Constitution, Quick and Garran's *Annotated Constitution* refers to 'riots' (Quick and Garran 1901, 964). This reference was cited with approval by Dixon J in the High Court in the 1949 sedition case of *R v Sharkey* ((1949) 79 CLR 121 at 151) and in the 1951 Communist Party dissolution case, where he spoke of 'putting down of all individual or concerted attempts to obstruct or interfere with the discharge of the proper business of government' (*Australian Communist Party v The Commonwealth* (1951) 83 CLR 1 at 188). This language is wide enough to cover many traditional forms of political opposition.

In a joint news release in 2000, the Defence Minister and Attorney-General said the Bill did not change the conditions in which the armed forces could be called out: 'State, Territory and Commonwealth Governments have always had the power to request call out of the Defence Force in Australia in rare situations where police need help to deal with an extreme emergency' (Moore and Williams 2000). During the parliamentary debate, the Labor Party's spokesmen made similar statements. The shadow defence minister condemned those who had opposed the Act 'under the guise of protecting civil liberties', adding that people had been 'fooled by inaccurate and misleading reporting and cheap and populist politics' (House of Representatives, Commonwealth of Australia 2000, 20511). He asserted that the legislation would not, in any way, add to the Government's power to call out the army. Instead, he claimed, the Bill placed new restrictions on the use of the military.

These statements are contradicted by legislation itself. It seeks to add both to the government's call-out powers and to the powers of military personnel once they are called out. It provides that the utilisation and powers of the armed forces under its provisions shall be additional to any other lawful use of the military. The amended s 51Y of the *Defence Act* states that 'this Part does not affect any utilisation of the Defence Force that would be permitted or required, or any powers that the Defence Forces would have, if this Part were disregarded'. (And the Explanatory Memorandum states that s 51Y 'makes it clear that the new process for calling out members of the Defence Force does not in any way detract from the use of the Defence Force that would be permitted or required under any powers that the Defence Force would have if the new Part were not in place'.) Thus, the Act does not place new restrictions on the use of the military, but augments whatever previous call-out powers existed, either under common law or authorised by other parts of the Australian Constitution.

The purpose of the legislation was to overcome definite legal and constitutional limits and restrictions that have, combined with political considerations, provided real constraints on the use of the armed forces in civilian settings. Section 51A of the amended Act goes beyond the previous s 51, which essentially mirrored s 119 of the Constitution. In the first place, the new section allows a military call-out where ministers are satisfied that domestic violence is occurring, 'or is likely to occur'. The latter phrase is an addition to s 119 and is therefore arguably unconstitutional.

Secondly, the section extends the call-out power to the protection of 'Commonwealth interests', regardless of whether there is a request by any state or territory government. It provides that 'the Governor-General may make the order whether or not the Government of the State or the self-governing Territory request the making of the order'. This provision, in so far as it purports to permit a military intervention without the consent of a state, may also contravene s 119, which arguably requires state assent to the use of troops on state soil. Section

51A(3) requires only that an authorising minister 'consult' the state or territory government before the Governor-General makes the order. Plainly, consultation does not mean assent. Moreover, under s 51A(3A), that proviso does not apply if the Governor-General is satisfied that 'for reasons of urgency, it is impracticable' to comply with it. Under s 51A(8A), an authorising minister must notify a state government that an order has been made but 'if this is not done, the validity of the making or revocation of the order is not affected'.

In seeking to bypass s 119, at least for the protection of 'Commonwealth interests', the legislation appears to rest on a combination of other Commonwealth constitutional powers – the defence, external affairs, incidentals, executive and Governor-General's powers – yet the government has not specified upon which of these powers it is relying.

Beyond the constitutional issues, the legislation is an attempt to overcome a variety of serious legal problems. Under existing legislative provisions and the common law, if military personnel kill or maim individuals, damage private property or interfere with people's liberty, they could be charged with criminal offences, including murder or manslaughter, or face civil action. Moreover, soldiers could not necessarily rely on a defence of obeying superior orders (Brett and Waller 1983, 654). In addition, military personnel lacked legislative powers to carry out searches, seizures and arrests. That is why, when troops were called out in 1974 to guard Darwin's petrol depots from looters after the destruction of Cyclone Tracy, General Stretton, the commander of the Natural Disaster Organisation, stipulated that troops not carry arms, that they be accompanied by a police officer and that the soldier's authority would stem from a citizen's duty under common law (Stretton 1976, 82–3).

Widening the Scope of the Powers

The original call-out legislation passed in 2000 limited deployments to where the government alleged that a danger of 'domestic violence' existed which required the protection of 'Commonwealth interests' or the protection of a state or territory where the state or territory could not, or was unlikely to be able to, protect itself (*Defence Act* ss 51A, 51B, 51C).

While 'domestic violence' was nowhere defined legally, it was derived from American usage and meant to relate to intense political, industrial or social crises that imperilled the very existence of the state. In the words of one scholar, s 119 was inserted in the Constitution to allow the military to be mobilised against an 'uncontrollable situation' (Blackshield 1978, 6). The expression 'domestic violence' was borrowed from article IV of the US Constitution, s 4 of which specifies that the United States shall protect each state, on the application of its legislature, against 'domestic violence'. The statutory embodiment of this provision in 10 USC § 331 (1964) uses the more specific term 'insurrection', suggesting that a serious level of rebellion must be involved (Bassiouni 1971,

371–3). Under US law, an insurrection generally means a directed attack against the government with the aim of overthrowing it (Bassiouni 1971, 371). (However, only one recorded instance exists where a US president required a state governor to show that an insurrection existed before sending in troops, and US troops have been used periodically against riots and strikes [Bassiouni 1971, 373–81]).

Whatever doubts remain about the scope of 'domestic violence', the further amendments to the *Defence Act* adopted in 2006 permit the air force and navy, as well as the army, to be mobilised more broadly and routinely to deal with incidents that fall far short of insurrection, including any alleged act or danger of terrorism, and threats to physical property, judged by ministers to be 'critical infrastructure' (Section 51CB(2)). According to the Explanatory Memorandum for the legislation, the amended Act would apply to 'mobile terrorist incidents', allowing for military mobilisations under the broad banner of combating terrorist acts (Parliament of Australia 2005, 2).

The counter-terrorism legislation passed since 2001 defines terrorism widely. A 'terrorist act' includes anything done 'with the intention of advancing a political, religious or ideological cause' and with the intention of 'coercing, or influencing by intimidation' any government (including a foreign government) or 'intimidating the public or a section of the public', if the act causes death, 'serious harm' to a person, 'serious damage to property', 'serious risk to the health or safety' of a section of the public or 'seriously interferes with' an electronic, information, financial or transport system (*Criminal Code 1995* (Cth) 100.1). This definition can cover many traditional forms of political protest, such as mass demonstrations, blockades and picket lines (Head 2002b, 673). While the definition exempts 'advocacy, protest, dissent or industrial action', that exemption is substantially nullified by the proviso that the action must not be intended to cause physical harm to a person or 'create a serious risk to the health or safety of the public or a section of the public'.

The procedures for calling out the ADF have been expedited so that, if satisfied that a 'sudden and extraordinary emergency' exists, the Prime Minister or the two other 'authorising ministers' (the Defence Minister and the Attorney-General) can give the order, which does not need to be in writing (Defence Act s 51CA). Alternatively, one authorising minister, together with the Deputy Prime Minister, Foreign Affairs Minister or Treasurer, can make the order (s 51CA(2)). In addition, standing orders can be issued for the activation of the ADF whenever the chief of the armed forces deems it necessary (s 51AB). Alternatively, authorising ministers can request the Governor-General to make a written call-out order (s 51A).

The Howard government, backed by the Labor opposition, dismissed an amendment to require any ADF call-out be followed by the recall of parliament with the power to disallow the decision (Parliament of Australia 2006, 23–4). As a result, great power has been placed in the hands of the executive, exercisable either by the Governor-General, or the Prime Minister, or two cabinet ministers or the ADF chief. The 2006 amendments also permit the authorising ministers to dispense with a previous requirement to notify both Houses of Parliament (and the general public) within 24 hours of the declaration of a 'general security area'. (Section 51K of the *Defence Act* requires a recall of both Houses of Parliament within six days of a declaration of a 'general security area', but provides that failure to do so 'does not make the declaration ineffective to any extent'. Under the 2006 amendments, s 51K(2AA) permits the authorising ministers to avoid notifying parliament (and the public) of such a declaration, if they are satisfied that it 'would prejudice the exercise of powers'.)

One purpose of the 2006 amendments was to give ADF members specific powers and legal immunities. Once deployed, the military can shoot down aircraft, sink ships, use deadly force, demand answers to questions and require the production of documents. Potentially lethal force can be used where an ADF member considers it necessary 'on reasonable grounds' to protect himself or herself, or another person or any infrastructure that the government designates as 'critical' (Defence Act s 51T(2A). These provisions raise the possibility of soldiers – who are, after all, specifically trained to shoot to kill – killing innocent civilians.

Citizens will have no right to refuse to answer questions or hand over material on the grounds of self-incrimination. Instead, they can be jailed for non-compliance (s 51SO). Similar powers have been given to the intelligence and police agencies where people are detained without trial under the counter-terrorism laws passed since 2002 (for example, *Australian Security Intelligence Organisation Act 1979* (Cth) s 34G) but their extension to the military raises even greater issues, given the lethal weaponry available to the armed forces, which may potentially be used to enforce compliance.

Under the 2006 amendments, all the ADF powers are protected by a defence of 'superior orders', which exempt ADF members from criminal liability, except if the order they obeyed was 'manifestly unlawful' (*Defence Act* s 51WB). They no longer have to wear name tags during operations (s 51S(1)(b)). Furthermore, any criminal prosecutions will be handled by federal authorities under federal law, overriding state laws (s 51WA). The issues and problems raised by these efforts to protect soldiers from legal liability are considered in Chapter 9.

Other Call-out Powers?

The amended provisions of the *Defence Act* have not been invoked since they were introduced in 2000, yet domestic military deployments have occurred with increasing frequency. It has been generally assumed that these operations have been validly conducted under executive power (for example, Moore 2005). It is therefore quite possible that future call-outs could be conducted under a claim of executive power, rather than the *Defence Act*.

Three main possibilities seem to exist. One is the executive power of the Commonwealth, formally vested in the Governor-General by s 61 of the Constitution, possibly augmented by s 68, which nominates the Governor-General as the Commander-in-Chief of the military forces. Another is the residual prerogative power of the Crown, essentially derived from the history of the British monarchy. The third is common law power, perhaps based upon that exercised by English magistrates and ministers during the eighteenth and nineteenth centuries. Beyond that, there is another issue: does legal scope still exist to declare martial law, bypassing both the *Defence Act* and the Regulations?

Section 68 of the Constitution states: 'The command in chief of the naval and military forces of the Commonwealth is vested in the Governor-General as the Queen's representative.' On the face of it, these unambiguous words place the command of the armed forces in the personal hands of the vice-regal representative. As Governor-General Sir Ninian Stephen observed:

> [N]o mention of the Chiefs of Staff, none of the Ministers for Defence, of Cabinet or of Prime Minister. Instead all the panache of a Boulanger, a general on a white horse, at the head of his armies, with a standard unfurled. (Stephen 1984, 563. Note: Georges Ernest Boulanger was a French general who participated in the suppression of the Paris Commune in 1871 and emerged as a potential military dictator in 1888–89, before being charged with treason and fleeing the country.)

Stephen immediately noted that constitutional and legal authorities regard it as a matter of constitutional convention, derived from the nature of representative government, that the Governor-General exercises this power on the advice of the elected government of the day. Nevertheless, a lack of clarity persists, not the least because the drafters of the Constitution decided to leave the words of s 68 untouched, despite some heated debate about amending it to specify that the Governor-General's power could be exercised only on the advice of the Executive Council.

Despite dismissing the notion that the Governor-General could call out troops without ministerial advice, Stephen concluded that a 'quite special relationship' existed between the Governor-General and the armed forces, a 'close relationship of sentiment'. He considered this an expression of a 'democratic society' with 'pride in and respect for its armed forces', on the one hand, and, on the other, 'the willing subordination of the members of those forces to the civil power' (Stephen 1984, 571).

Notwithstanding Stephen's emphasis on its democratic content, the notion of a 'special relationship' is legally and politically problematic. The events of November 1975 demonstrate the potential for a political and constitutional crisis to arise in which a Governor-General seeks to exercise not only 'reserve' powers, but also military authority. Sir John Kerr reportedly held his own meetings, as the titular Commander-in-Chief, with senior defence and intelligence officials before dismissing the Whitlam government (Coxsedge, Caldicutt and Harant 1982, 35, 96). And a former Whitlam government cabinet minister alleged that Kerr secretly placed the armed forces on alert after the dismissal (Watching Brief 1986; Workers News 1976).

Another disturbing feature of that exercise of vice-regal power to dismiss an elected government, despite its clear majority in the House of Representatives, is that, in the words of one scholar, 'constitutionally speaking, nothing prevents a repetition' (Winterton 2003, 251–2). The constitutional crisis highlighted the fact that no legal, judicial or parliamentary authority exists that can check or challenge the exercise of the reserve powers.

A final legal issue is whether the s 119 of the Constitution and the call-out legislation cover the legal field, or can a government or even other official authorities invoke residual common law powers, perhaps derived from that exercised by English magistrates and ministers during the eighteenth and nineteenth centuries? In principle it would seem that the Constitution and the legislation now define and delimit the power of the Commonwealth, particularly given the critical and sensitive character of the powers involved.

However, in the *Tampa* case, the High Court effectively permitted the federal government to deploy military personnel, including SAS troops and sailors, to turn away 433 asylum seekers and forcibly transport them to Nauru, a remote Pacific island, even though the relevant legislation, the *Migration Act 1958* (Cth), required any suspected unlawful entrants to be detained in an Australian immigration facility (Head 2002, 23–33). A panel of three justices refused to consider an appeal from a two-to-one decision of the Full Federal Court upholding the lawfulness of the detention and expulsion of the *Tampa* refugees (Vadarlis 2001). The Federal Court majority held that the government has executive or prerogative power under s 61 of the Constitution to detain and remove 'aliens' and take any other action it considers necessary to protect 'national sovereignty' (*Ruddock v Vadarlis* [2001] FCA 1329).

By analogy, similar reasoning could be applied to a troop deployment to protect 'national sovereignty'. It is doubtful, however, whether the common law power of ministers and local magistrates to use soldiers to put down riots is still intact (Greer 1983, 598).

The Rise of Paramilitary Policing

Alongside the expanding domestic role of the armed forces, militarised forms of policing have emerged and grown since the mid-1970s. Riot and counter-terrorism units have been established in the federal and state police forces, creating a network of paramilitary squads. Units such as the NSW Tactical Response Group (TRG) and Special Weapons Operations Squad (SWOS) and Victoria's Special Operations Group (SOG) have trained with the military, recruited former members of the armed forces, used a range of military weapons and equipment, and engaged in high levels of force. A West Australian coroner, commenting on that state's Tactical Response Group, observed:

> [I]t is apparent that the TRG is a significant police para-military force whose tactics and weaponry are hardly less effective that [*sic*] those of any strictly military force … In terms of their capabilities in weapons and otherwise, the TRG now straddles the line between traditional police resources and the military. (Western Australia State Coroner n.d., 65)

Although the official rationale for these paramilitary units includes combating terrorism, they have been used in a wide and increasing range of police operations, including dealing with political and industrial unrest (McCulloch 2001). One study has documented how 'counter-terrorism' has moved beyond extreme acts of politically motivated violence into the policing of dissent and social and industrial protest and suggested that the police units herald 'an increasingly militarised approach to everyday policing' (Hocking 1993, 27, 160–79; Hocking 2004, 172–9). For instance, in 1984–85 the NSW TRG responded to 1,701 incidents and 'effected 443 arrests' and 'supported general duty and specialist police in operations' (Hocking 2004, 178).

The units are heavily armed and train with the ADF. The Victorian SOG, for example, has trained with the SAS, included former members of the SAS and other army units, and conducted regular joint exercises with the military. The SOG has had a range of military-style weapons, including Heckler and Koch 9mm submachine guns, M16 assault rifles, standard Australian Army issue Styr .223 rifles, 9mm semi-automatic pistols, Remington 870 pump action shotguns, chemical weapons, electric batons or stun guns, stun grenades, electric shields, and armoured and tactical vehicles (McCulloch 2001, 70–71). In 1982, the NSW TRG was equipped with US-made 870-type shotguns, CS and CH gas, riot and ballistic helmets, gas masks and batons, while SWOS members also received military training, including in 'tactical use of weapons' (Hocking 2004, 176).

A 1995 Victoria Police review of the SOG found that 'training is focussed on the option of last resort, that is armed confrontations' (McCulloch 2001, 71). Having been trained and equipped to use military-style levels of force, the units have been responsible for considerable numbers of civilian deaths. McCulloch has documented a pattern of fatal violence in policing in Victoria. In that state, police killed 42 people between 1981 and 1998, with the SOG involved in 30 per cent of the shootings (McCulloch 2001, 118). Having been trained in how to shoot first and survive armed confrontations, rather than avoid such confrontations where possible, the SOG has been involved in a series of violent raids, ambushes and shootings (McCulloch 2001, 116–73). A coronial inquest into one of the deaths concluded:

> The policy of the Victoria Police Force and its SOG accepts … the use of force, forced entry, consequential firearms confrontation, consequential instinctive use of police firearms with legal justification, consequential personal risk to police members exposed to a person with a gun and consequentially and ultimately

> condones shooting by police members with legal justification. (Victoria State Coroner 1989, 258)

The victims have included entirely innocent people, like David Gundy, a young Aboriginal man shot dead in his bed by the NSW SWOS in a mistaken early-morning raid on his home. Commissioner Wootten's Royal Commission report into the shooting found that the police officer who killed Gundy 'had not been trained to cope with an unarmed, near-naked man who reacted angrily when woken from his sleep by armed men bursting into his house' (Wootten 1991, 4). No charges were laid against any member of the police force, however.

The paramilitary units have been deployed frequently over the past two decades to deal with political demonstrations, including anti-war marches, protests against gatherings of government leaders, demonstrations against school closures and Aboriginal rallies (McCulloch 2001, 188–213; Hocking 2004, 177, 179). The paramilitary units work closely with other specialist police squads responsible for 'protective security', 'crowd control' and 'intelligence' (McCulloch 2001, 185–8).

The Pretext: The 'War' on 'Terrorism'

The adoption of the 2000 'aid to civilian authorities' amendments to the *Defence Act* preceded the declaration of the 'war on terror'. This fact points to more underlying factors in the trend toward extending the military call-out powers. Nevertheless, the indefinite 'war' declared by the White House in September 2001 has become the prime justification for the greater domestic mobilisation of the armed forces.

The expanded military call-out legislation introduced in 2006 was among the measures agreed upon by Prime Minister Howard and the state and territory Labor leaders in their joint communiqué from the 27 September 2005 Council of Australian Governments (COAG) 'counter-terrorism' summit. As a result of that bipartisan communiqué, fresh anti-terrorism laws were introduced in the federal, state and territory parliaments in the final months of 2005 (Head 2005b, 1–8). At the Commonwealth level, the *Anti-Terrorism Acts (Nos 1 & 2) 2005* were among more than 30 pieces of counter-terrorism legislation introduced since 2001 (National Security Australia 2005).

The 'anti-terrorist' legislation of 2002 to 2004, introduced in the aftermath of 9/11, established a special category of terrorist crimes and made them punishable by life imprisonment. It allowed secret detention and interrogation by police and ASIO officers for up to a week without charge, the ability to conduct closed-door trials and powers to ban political organisations by executive fiat (Head 2004; Head 2004b).

The legislation introduced in late 2005 went further, notably in allowing the police and intelligence agencies to charge people, or alternatively detain them without trial, without evidence of involvement in specific terrorist activity or planning. The *Anti-Terrorism Act (No. 1) (Cth) 2005* changed the wording of many terrorist offences from 'the' terrorist act to 'a' terrorist act. In effect, it means that people can be convicted of planning or preparing for terrorism without the police producing any evidence of a specific time, date, location or method of the supposed attack. The *Anti-Terrorism Act (No. 2) (Cth) 2005* granted extra powers to intern 'suspects' without any charge or trial, either by way of 'preventative detention' or 'control orders' (Lasry and Eastman 2005).

The new provisions can be exploited to silence many types of political dissent. An organisation that 'advocates' a terrorist act can be outlawed. 'Advocating' includes 'praising' and could mean merely expressing sympathy for, or calling for an understanding of, the social and economic roots of terrorism (Walton 2005, 3). Moreover, the crime of sedition was extended to include urging conduct to assist an 'organisation or country engaged in armed hostilities' against the Australian military, whether or not a state of war has been declared (*Criminal Code Act 1995* (Cth) s 80.2(7) & (8)). These provisions allow for the criminalisation of expressions of support for resistance to Australian military interventions, including the occupations of Afghanistan and Iraq, and operations in the Asia-Pacific region, such as the dispatch of troops to Solomon Islands (Department of the Senate, Senate Legal and Constitutional Affairs Committee 2005, 77; Saul 2005, 873).

This author has argued elsewhere that none of these measures, including the military call-out laws, were necessary to protect ordinary people against terrorism (Head 2005b, 1–9). Every conceivable terrorist act was already a serious crime – from murder to arson and hijacking – and the criminal law amply covered planning, preparing, conspiring, financing, supporting and attempting related to such activities (Hancock 2002b). Moreover, the Australian Security Intelligence Organisation (ASIO) and the state and federal police already possessed powers to infiltrate organisations, tap phones, bug premises, intercept mail, search homes and hack into computers (Head 2002b, 678–9).

By expanding the range of 'terrorist' and related offences, the 2005 anti-terrorism legislative package correspondingly enlarged the sphere of potential military deployment. In 2002, the Commonwealth and the states and territories reached an agreement that the Commonwealth would take charge of 'national terrorist situations', with or without the consent of affected states or territories. While the Commonwealth undertook to consult and seek agreement before declaring a national terrorist situation, the states and territories agreed 'not to withhold unreasonably such agreement' (Laing 2005, 516). A scenario offered by the ADF to a parliamentary committee in 2003 demonstrates the potential for the military to rapidly take control of civilian areas in an alleged terrorist emergency, without prior ministerial authorisation:

> At some point the police officer may come to the view that the incident has deteriorated to such a point that, with his civil resources, he can no longer resolve the incident and will call on the Defence Commander present, who is the commanding officer of the TAG [Tactical Assault Group], to resolve the incident. If that is done in a deliberate and time-allowing way, then approval for

> that employment of the Defence Force will be sought through the minister to government. If, however, time does not allow – if there is a cataclysmic collapse of the situation – then the Military Commander (Forward), in conjunction with the police commander, can launch the Defence Force in an assault on his own call, but needs to satisfy a number of legal requirements, obviously, before that is done. (Department of the House of Representatives, Joint Standing Committee on Foreign Affairs, Defence and Trade 2001–2002, 13)

More generally, the 'war on terror' serves to reinforce a climate of fear and insecurity that can be exploited to justify military measures. Laing's article in the 2005 'Australian Military Law' theme edition of *The University of New South Wales Law Journal* began by recalling the protests against the Vietnam War and President Richard Nixon's invasion of Cambodia, and the use of the Ohio National Guard to shoot down four students at Kent State University in 1970. Laing cited an address to the nation by Nixon just five days earlier, in which the US President accused protesters of producing an 'age of anarchy' by making 'mindless attacks on all the great institutions' (Laing 2005, 507–8). Nixon's stance offers a salutary warning of how military personnel can be mobilised to quell civilian dissenters, with lethal consequences. Laing commented:

> What the world witnessed leading up to that day in Ohio is not that different to the protests we see today in Australia. Australian citizens from all backgrounds have used various city streets, parks and university campuses throughout history, including in recent years, to rally in organised demonstrations; demonstrating and voicing their concerns in relation to, amongst other things, the war on terror, globalisation, university fees and voluntary unionism. (Laing 2005, 508)

This scenario raises the spectre of troops being used against growing social and political unrest. Laing said there was concern in 2000, when the initial military call-out legislation was brought forward, that the ADF would be deployed on Australian streets to disperse such protestors if they caused a serious civil disturbance. However, he argued that this 'fear and paranoia' subsided over the following four years because: 'The current climate of terror has created an overriding and shifting attitude towards the ADF being called out' (Laing 2005, 509). Moreover, Laing concluded by asserting that calling out the ADF was not 'the end of civilisation' because 'the ADF will only ever be deployed for a legitimate purpose' and 'one must have faith in those elected representatives to undertake such a responsibility' (Laing 2005, 521).

Is such faith justified, however, in the light of the now widely-acknowledged false statements made by the US, British and Australian governments to justify the invasion of Iraq as part of the 'war on terror'? As discussed in Chapter 1, the 'war on terror' itself, and its underlying political and geo-strategic purposes, have to be questioned. This suggests that whenever governments and security authorities cite 'national security' threats, especially of indefinite duration, as the reason for suspending or overturning constitutional norms and basic legal rights, the lessons of history – including the traumatic experiences of the United States in 1970–72 – demonstrate a need for distrust and vigilance.

1978: Australia's Most Dramatic Troop Call-out

The only major mobilisation of troops in an urban setting in Australia's history occurred in 1978. At 12.40 am on 13 February 1978, a bomb exploded in a garbage bin outside the Hilton Hotel, the venue for the Commonwealth Heads of Government Regional Meeting (CHOGRM), a gathering of government leaders from former British colonies. The blast killed two garbage collectors, Alex Carter and William Favell, and a police officer, Paul Birmistriw. A number of other people were injured, some seriously, including another police officer, Terry Griffiths, who has continued to raise questions about the bombing and to campaign for a judicial inquiry (Hocking 2004, 82–5).

By any objective measure, the 1978 Sydney Hilton Hotel bombing remains one of Australia's most serious unresolved crimes. Not only were three people killed and several maimed, but the blast was allegedly directed against an international summit of government leaders. Moreover, the event was proclaimed the opening of a new era of terrorism, triggering a significant boosting of the powers and resources of the police and intelligence agencies. Yet, the question of who actually carried out the bombing remains unclear. Twice, the police and intelligence agencies effectively framed-up people, who were convicted and jailed in connection with the explosion, only to have those frame-ups later fall apart ignominiously. Then came a series of judicial and political reviews that failed to provide any answers, or hold anyone to account for the wrongful prosecutions. No genuine inquiry has ever been conducted into the Hilton affair, leaving open the possibility that the security agencies themselves were involved or implicated in the bombing (Head 2008).

Amid blazing media headlines, Prime Minister Fraser and New South Wales Premier Wran mobilised the military. 'Troops Placed on Anti-Terror Alert' was *The Australian*'s headline (*Australian* 1978, 1). 'Terrorism now 'fact of life' – All Australians should mourn: Wran', reported the *Sydney Morning Herald*, which editorialised: 'Australia is not immune from the international disease of terrorism and violence' (*Sydney Morning Herald* 1978, 2, 6; Cahill and Cahill 2005). Without any clear legal or constitutional authorisation (Head 2001, 282–4; Blackshield 1978; *Australian Law Journal* 1978), the federal Liberal government and the state Labor government deployed nearly 2,000 heavily-armed troops, some with bayonets fixed, accompanied by armoured personnel carriers and helicopters. Units took up positions along a major highway on Sydney's outskirts and, for three days, patrolled the Southern Highlands towns of Bowral and Mittagong, near the site of a scheduled CHOGRM leaders' summit (Hocking 2004, 86; Cahill and Cahill 2005).

On the first morning, 14 February, residents of Bowral were awoken at 6.30 am by the sound of helicopters circling overhead, while teams of soldiers scoured garbage bins, drains, hedges and shrubbery. Troops 'camped on the local football field, and patrolled the main street carrying automatic weapons and full magazines in place' (Hocking 2004, 86). It is hardly surprising that the sight of armed soldiers caused public consternation, with rumours that martial law had been imposed (Cahill and Cahill 2005). Journalists from two local newspapers recorded both fear and confusion among residents. One interviewee said: 'Now we have an idea what life in Northern Ireland is like. This is frightening.' Reflecting residents' unease, the Bowral-based *Southern Highlands News* described 'the virtual siege conditions' in Bowral (and to a lesser extent Mittagong) and commented: '[T]hose who remember Franco's Spain could see a parallel in the pairs of uniformed men, all heavily armed, steadily walking their beat, always in sight of each other' (Cahill and Cahill 2005).

The Hilton attack was not the first terrorist incident in contemporary Australia. Previous Liberal governments had largely ignored neo-fascist Croatian Ustashi bombings in the 1960s and early 1970s (Cain 1994, 206–8). Over the ensuing 18 months, however, the Fraser government, with the Labor opposition's essential support, used the Hilton bombing as the pretext to carry through a far-reaching expansion in the powers and resources of the police and security apparatus. The changes included legalised surveillance powers for the Australian Security Intelligence Organisation (ASIO), the formation of the Australian Federal Police (AFP), the establishment of the Office of National Assessments (ONA) in the Prime Minister's Department, the creation of paramilitary SWAT-style units in state police forces and domestic SAS units in the ADF (Hocking 2004, 101–19; Head 2008). The aftermath also revealed the establishment of Crisis Policy Centres with the authority to take control over parts of the country in times of alleged emergency (Hocking 2004, 180–92).

It is now known that, following the precedent established by the post-Hilton call-out, the Cabinet Intelligence and Security Committee formally decided in September 1978 to adopt a policy of deploying the ADF whenever 'appropriate' in response to alleged terrorist acts. The partial release in 2009, by the National Archives of Australia, of the 1978 cabinet documents revealed that the committee agreed that:

> Australia adopt a 'hard line' policy in dealing with terrorist incidents, that is:- (i) the police and, where it is appropriate to authorize their employment, elements of the Defence Force, be instructed to take firm action against the terrorists and obtain their surrender; (ii) if tactical negotiations aimed at surrender fail and in particular if violent action by the terrorists (for example, killing or injuring hostages or major property damage) is anticipated, action be taken to subdue the terrorists by force .... (National Archives of Australia 1978, 138)

The timing, force and tactics applied were to be 'in the final balance, subject to the principle of minimising the risk of the loss of innocent life' (National Archives of

Australia 1978, 139). Who would make those critical judgments and decisions was not specified, however. It seems that intimate involvement of the Prime Minister and other ministers was intended. The cabinet minute stated that only if options (i) and (ii) above were considered unacceptable, 'would the possibility of concessions (other than minor concessions such as food and medical supplies) be considered by Ministers in consultation with the Prime Minister' (National Archives of Australia 1978, 139).

Considerable secrecy surrounded this policy. It was not to be published, but statements were to be made on behalf of the government emphasising the government's intention to 'take all appropriate action' to counter terrorism (National Archives of Australia 1978, 139). In other words, the crucial decision that the ADF would be authorised to use force on domestic soil was not communicated to the public, nor was any public debate conducted on the issue. Many of the security decisions made during 1978 remain classified to this day. The National Archives of Australia noted that material had been withheld from the released documents to 'protect Australia's defence, security or international relations' (National Archives of Australia 2009, 2). A total of 30 cabinet submissions and decisions were censored before release, and two decisions and their accompanying submissions were considered so sensitive that their titles, as well as their contents, remained secret (Solomon 2009).

Many questions remain about why, and by what legal authority, the unprecedented decision was made to call out the troops in immediate response to the Hilton blast. Official media statements were 'positively evasive' as to the legal basis for the military action (Blackshield 1978, 6). On the evening of 13 February 1978, after consultations between Prime Minister Fraser and Premier Wran, Governor-General Sir Zelman Cowan signed an Order to call out the ADF (a) 'for the purpose of safeguarding the national and international interests of the Commonwealth of Australia' and (b) 'for giving effect to the obligations of the Commonwealth of Australia in relation to the protection of internationally protected persons' because of 'terrorist activities and related violence that have occurred in the State of New South Wales' (Andrews 1995, 153). The Order was to remain 'in force until revoked' (Hocking 2004, 255). No limits were placed on the numbers of troops, the geographical area of the deployment, or the powers of the ADF personnel. Subsequently, it was learned that the Rules of Engagement specifically authorised military personnel to open fire against civilians and vehicles in various circumstances, including if a person was carrying a lethal object and 'was about to use it for offensive purposes' (Beddie and Moss 1982, 81–2). The legal protection provided for soldiers by these rules of engagement, however, was unclear. One scholar accused the government of 'cavalier disregard for the legal position of army personnel' (Blackshield 1978, 10).

This official response raised significant legal questions. Two inter-related issues arose:

1. Were such interventions constitutional and, if so, what was their precise constitutional basis?
2. What were the powers of the military personnel and the rights of civilians in relation to the military?

Neither question was addressed directly in the two formal documents ordering the military intervention, namely the joint statement by the Prime Minister and the New South Wales Premier, and the Order issued by the Governor-General. The wording of the Order suggested a reliance on the defence and foreign affairs powers. Presumably for the purposes of the latter, the Foreign Affairs Minister also signed a 'Requisition of the Civil Authority' requiring the call-out (Hope 1979, 279). The Governor-General revoked the Order on 20 February 1978, when the last of the foreign leaders had left Australia (Moore 2005, 526).

In his statement to parliament, Prime Minister Fraser stated that the New South Wales Premier had concurred with the call-out but had not requested it. He did not specifically refer to s 119 of the Constitution, or explain the precise legal basis for the call-out, instead stating:

> The mechanism for the legal approach to the call-out was discussed with the Premier in two terms: In terms of a strict request from the State, and therefore in terms of aid to the civil power; or, secondly, in terms of the use of the Commonwealth's own authority and responsibility to protect people against possible acts of terrorism. For various reasons as I explained to the House I think yesterday, the second course was chosen, but the Premier had made it perfectly clear to me that if it was thought best to pursue it through the first mechanism, the Premier would certainly act in full cooperation. (House of Representatives, Commonwealth of Australia 1978, 159)

Three months later, after some speculation as to the legal basis for the Government's action, the Attorney-General Peter Durack confirmed that no recourse had been made to s 119 of the Constitution. Instead, he pointed to a 'second possible basis, namely a call-out on the initiative of the Commonwealth':

> [T]he view of the government's legal advisers is that, where domestic violence is of such a character that the operations of the Commonwealth government are affected, the Commonwealth government may, without request from a State, intervene with all the force at its disposal, not to protect the State but to protect itself. (Hope 1979, 273)

For this proposition, Durack cited a passage from Quick and Garran's *Annotated Constitution of the Australian Commonwealth*, which was approved by Dixon J in the 1949 sedition case, *R v Sharkey* ((1949) 79 CLR 121 at 151). Remarkably, the Attorney-General also relied upon the authority of Regulation 415 of the *Australian Military Regulations*, which specifically recognised that the military forces could be employed by the Commonwealth on its own initiative. It goes without saying that a regulation cannot provide a constitutional foundation for federal power.

Several other possibilities were canvassed. One, asserted by Justice Hope in his 1979 *Protective Security Review*, commissioned by the Fraser Government, was that the Governor-General acted under s 68 of the Constitution, which states, without qualification: 'The commander-in-chief of the naval and military forces of the Commonwealth is vested in the Governor-General as the Queen's representative.' Another possibility, advanced by academic commentators, was that the federal government exercised its executive power, also formally exercisable by the Governor-General, under s 61 of the Constitution to ensure the 'execution and maintenance of this Constitution, and of the laws of the Commonwealth'. References were also made to the Commonwealth's defence power (s 51(vi) of the Constitution), combined with the external affairs power (s 51(xxix)), and the incidental powers (s 51(xxxix)). Other possibilities mentioned were an 'inherent self-protecting' power of the Commonwealth, 'inherent law and order powers' and the Crown's prerogative power over defence and military matters (*Australian Law Journal* 1978; Lane 1974, 77).

Blackshield concluded that the call-out was valid as an exercise of the Commonwealth's executive power, which 'includes an amorphous and unexplored bundle of attributes of sovereignty, "inherent in the fact of nationhood and of international personality"' (Blackshield 1978, 7). Reliance on such a vague and uncharted 'bundle' of concepts hardly seems a wise or safe manner to proceed when the issue at stake is the mobilisation of potentially lethal force by the ADF for the purposes of internal security. A 1978 note in the *Australian Law Journal* observed that the Hilton bombing call-out had 'exposed gaps, inadequacies, and uncertainties in the legal and constitutional powers of Commonwealth and State enforcement agencies' (*Australian Law Journal* 1978, 296).

Despite this lack of constitutional clarity, no legislation was introduced to provide clear authority for military deployment. Quoting the eighteenth-century conservative Edmund Burke, Justice Hope called for legislation, observing:

> Use of the military other than for external defence, is a critical and controversial issue in the political life of a country and the civil liberties of its citizens. 'An armed disciplined body is in its essence dangerous to Liberty; undisciplined, it is ruinous to Society'. Given that there must be a permanent Defence Force, it is critical that it be employed only for proper purposes and that it be subject to proper control. (Hope 1979, 142)

Aware of the political sensitivity of the issue, the Fraser Government did not legislate. Instead, the only relevant legislative instruments remained the *Australian Military Regulations* and internal Defence Instructions, not all of which have been made public. Part 5 of the Regulations, 'Duties in Aid of the Civil Power During Domestic Violence', provided that a magistrate must accompany the defence forces into an area and 'read the Riot Act' before the troops moved in. 'The

Defence Instructions (General) on Defence Force Aid to the Civil Power' remain a classified document (Ward 1997), a highly unsatisfactory situation when the implications for civil liberties are great. Of equal concern is the fact that under the Defence Act, the Instructions may be changed at any time without parliamentary or public scrutiny (Bayne 1991).

Two precedents were set by the 1978 call-out: the open-ended use of executive power, and the utilisation of 'terrorism' as the justification for domestic military intervention (Hocking 2004, 94–7). Despite the lack of proof that the Hilton bombing was actually a terrorist act (Head 2008), the terrorism label was employed to elevate the incident into an issue of 'national security', a doctrine notorious for its vagueness and elasticity. In the words of the *Australian Law Journal*, a 'paradoxical aspect of the importance commanded by the concept is its nebulousness' (*Australian Law Journal* 1984, 67). In 1984, the editors of that journal warned presciently:

> The concept of 'national security' in peacetime has in the past three decades attained a degree of significance and a measure of political and judicial recognition at the highest level that are without precedent in the past history of Australia. Already, it has had a far-reaching impact upon the law of civil liberties, and who can now say to what extent it may reach into other corners of our legal system? (*Australian Law Journal* 1984, 67)

Two decades after the 1978 call-out, and taking advantage of the 2000 Sydney Olympics, the Howard Government brought forward legislation that sought to expand the military call-out power, again in the name of 'counter-terrorism' and 'national security', without addressing the constitutional doubts or the civil liberties concerns. Just as the 1978 Hilton bombing became the occasion for claims that Australia had entered the 'age of terrorism', police and military authorities claimed that the Olympics would be a 'magnet' for terrorists. Six years later, similar unsubstantiated claims were made about the 2006 Melbourne Commonwealth Games to justify a broadening of the powers adopted in 2000.

For many reasons, from the collapse of its police frame-ups to the security measures adopted in its wake, the Hilton affair underscores the need to challenge constantly the claims being made by governments about the 'war on terror' and to oppose every erosion of civil liberties and basic legal rights being carried out in its name (Head 2008).

Chapter 9
Legal Immunities and Uncertainties

The Australian legislation, considered in the previous chapter, provides called-out soldiers with explicit powers to use lethal force, combined with a defence of acting in obedience to superior orders. This provides a case study for considering the legal and policy issues, as well as the problems and uncertainties, raised by official measures intended to clothe the armed forces with immunities to protect their personnel from criminal and civil liability for their actions, which may lead to losses of lives, serious injuries, damage to property and other infringements of legal and civil rights. The issues include:

- What degrees of violence and violation of legal rights are permissible during domestic military operations? In particular, what is the scope of 'reasonable and necessary force'?
- In the event of the unlawful killing or injuring of civilians, can members of the armed forces rely upon the defence of superior orders?
- What is the legal effect of any relevant manuals, rules of engagement or guidelines issued to govern the conduct of military personnel?
- Can government ministers or military officers be held liable criminally or civilly for any loss or damage?

Lethal Force

As a result of the amendments passed in 2000 and 2006, Australia's *Defence Act 1903* grants Australian Defence Force (ADF) personnel extraordinary powers in various circumstances. They include to use 'reasonable and necessary' lethal force (s 51T(2A)), shoot down planes (s 51ST), board, search or sink ships (s 51SE), interrogate people and command the handing over of documents (s 51SO), search people and premises (s 51SK) and seize things (s 51SG).

Many of these powers exceed those held by police officers, notwithstanding the expansion of police powers by the anti-terrorism legislation adopted by the Australian federal, state and territory parliaments in late 2005. The common prerequisite for their use – that ADF personnel consider them 'reasonable and necessary in the circumstances' – provides little real safeguard against misuse or overuse. Some of the powers require written ministerial authorisation, unless the ADF member believes on reasonable grounds that there is insufficient time to obtain authorisation because of 'a sudden and extraordinary emergency' (for example, s 51SE(4),(5)). But how is the existence of such an emergency to be gauged? The phrase leaves considerable leeway for unilateral military decisions.

The military's lethal force powers have been extended beyond reasonable force to protect people from death or injury, to the protection of any physical assets designated as 'critical infrastructure'. The relevant parts of s 51T of the Act provide as follows:

> *Use of reasonable and necessary force*
>
> (1) A member of the Defence Force may, in exercising any power under Division 2 or 3 or this Division, use such force against persons and things as is reasonable and necessary in the circumstances.
>
> *Further restrictions on use of force*
>
> (2) However, a member of the Defence Force must not, in using force against a person:
>
> (a) do anything that is likely to cause the death of, or grievous bodily harm to, the person unless the member believes on reasonable grounds that doing that thing is necessary to protect the life of, or to prevent serious injury to, another person (including the member); or
>
> (b) subject the person to greater indignity than is reasonable and necessary in the circumstances.
>
> (3) In addition, if a person is attempting to escape being detained by fleeing, a member of the Defence Force must not do anything that is likely to cause the death of, or grievous bodily harm to, the person unless the person has, if practicable, been called on to surrender and the member believes on reasonable grounds that the person cannot be apprehended in any other manner.

While, on the face it, subsections (2) and (3) limit the breadth of subsection (1), the scope that remains for the use of grievous or deadly force is substantial. Moreover, subsections (2) and (3) may have the effect of specifically authorising, or at least legitimising, such force in certain circumstances.

This opens up the possibility of military personnel justifying the infliction of fatal or serious injuries on the basis that soldiers felt threatened by the actions of their victims or others associated with them. The cases reviewed below highlight the difficulties of challenging such claims, particularly where courts are loath to second guess judgments made in the heat of conflict or in the context of 'national security'.

Moreover, a person 'attempting to escape being detained by fleeing' may be killed or caused grievous bodily harm if they have been called on to surrender and a soldier believes on reasonable grounds that the person cannot be apprehended in any other way. This establishes the danger of killings or woundings being justified by equally difficult-to-assess allegations that the victims attempted to escape.

One of the key parts of s 51T reads:

> (2A) Despite subsection (1), in exercising powers under Division 2A, a member of the Defence Force must not, in using force against a person:
> (a) do anything that is likely to cause the death of, or grievous bodily harm to, the person unless the member believes on reasonable grounds that doing that thing is necessary to:
> (i) protect the life of, or to prevent serious injury to, another person (including the member); or
> (ii) protect, against the threat concerned, the designated critical infrastructure in respect of which the powers are being exercised; or
> (b) subject the person to greater indignity than is reasonable and necessary in the circumstances.

Subsection (2A)(a)(ii) could justify shooting people to stop a threatened disruption of any facility, without any alleged direct danger to human life. Property, no matter how 'critical', should not outweigh the right to live. In submissions on the legislation, the Australian Muslim Civil Rights Advocacy Network and the NSW Council for Civil Liberties objected that the provision deviates from the long-held legal principle that killing or causing serious injury to protect property is not permissible (Department of the Senate, Senate Legal and Constitutional Affairs Committee 2006, 25). In fact, intentional use of lethal or grievous force to protect property is expressly forbidden by the self-defence provisions of the Australian *Criminal Code Act 1995* (s 10.4(3)). The Human Rights and Equal Opportunity Commission (HREOC) called for the provision to be excised from the Bill because it potentially placed Australia in breach of article 6 of the International Covenant on Civil and Political Rights (Department of the Senate, Senate Legal and Constitutional Affairs Committee 2006, 25). The ICCPR article 6(1) provides: 'Every human being has the inherent right to life. This right shall be protected by law. No one shall be arbitrarily deprived of his life.'

These objections were rejected by a Senate Committee on the grounds that the power would be used only in 'the most extreme circumstances' and that an attack on any critical infrastructure has 'the potential to threaten life indirectly as well as compromise the ability of the country to defend itself' (Department of the Senate, Senate Legal and Constitutional Affairs Committee 2006, 26). Such vague formulations add to the concern that lethal force can now be used to protect facilities on the basis of political or military judgments about their importance to national defence.

Similar objections can be made regarding the power to use force against an aircraft 'up to and including destroying the aircraft ... whether or not [it] is airborne' (Defence Act s 51ST). Although such action requires ministerial authorisation, the Defence Minister may 'authorise the taking of measures against an aircraft in specified circumstances' (s 51ST(6)). That is, rather than authorise the shooting down of a specific plane, the Minister can issue an ongoing authorisation. One caveat is that the Minister must have regard to Australia's international obligations, which include the Convention on International Civil Aviation (Chicago Convention) that instructs member states not to endanger the lives of passengers on civil aircraft (s 51ST(8); Bronitt and Stephens 2007, 272–3).

Another section that raises particular concerns is s 51SO, which empowers a called-out ADF member to 'require a person to answer a question put by the member or to produce a particular document to the member' (ss(1)). The only qualification is that the ADF member must believe on reasonable grounds that it is necessary for preserving the life or safety of other persons or 'to protect Commonwealth interests against the threat concerned' (ss(2)). This latter phrase is especially susceptible to wide application because 'Commonwealth interests' are not defined by the Act, while the nature of the requisite 'threat' is also unspecified. A person who fails to comply faces a penalty of 30 units (ss(3)), and is not excused on the ground of possible self-incrimination (ss(4)), although any answer given or document produced is not admissible in most criminal proceedings. These provisions open the prospect of interrogation of civilians by heavily-armed military personnel, something normally associated with military regimes.

Significantly, the authority to use force under s 51T exceeds that given to Australian Federal Police (AFP) officers, whose powers relate to arrests made for offences, whereas the ADF powers are more sweeping once general security and designated areas have been declared. With the exception of the power to detain people, none of the far-reaching powers, such as to capture premises, issue directions, evacuate people and search and seize, are limited to any belief by the officer that an offence has been committed. Moreover, the risk of ADF members using lethal force in the exercise of policing functions is considerably greater, given that they are armed only with high-powered weaponry, designed to kill, and that soldiers are trained to kill, or be killed (McCulloch 2001, 17–31).

These issues can be illustrated by two British House of Lords decisions arising out of fatal shootings by soldiers of unarmed men during the course of British military operations in Northern Ireland.

In *Attorney-General for Northern Ireland's Reference (No. 1 of 1975)* ([1977] AC 105), a soldier on patrol in Northern Ireland shot and killed an unarmed man, who ran away when challenged. The trial judge found that the prosecution had failed to prove that the soldier intended to kill or cause serious bodily harm, and further found that the homicide was justifiable under s 3 of the *Criminal Law Act (Northern Ireland) 1967 (UK)*. That section provided:

> A person may use such force as is reasonable in the circumstances in the prevention of crime, or in effecting or assisting in the lawful arrest of offenders or suspected offenders or of persons unlawfully at large.

The House of Lords decided that the judge's ruling was purely one of fact, and therefore declined to answer the question of law referred to it, as to whether the soldier had committed a crime. However, Lord Diplock made the following remarks, which point to the uncertainties and high risks associated with military mobilisations in civilian areas:

> There is little authority in English law concerning the rights and duties of a member of the armed forces of the Crown when acting in aid of the civil power; and what little authority there is relates almost entirely to the duties of soldiers when troops are called upon to assist in controlling a riotous assembly. Where used for such temporary purposes it may not be inaccurate to describe the rights and duties of a soldier as being no more than those of an ordinary citizen in uniform. But such a description is in my view misleading in the circumstances in which the army is currently employed in aid of the civil power in Northern Ireland … In theory it may be the duty of every citizen when an arrestable offence is about to be committed in his presence to take whatever reasonable measures are available to him to prevent the commission of the crime; but the duty is one of imperfect obligation and it does not place him under any obligation to do anything by which he would expose himself to risk of personal injury, nor is he under any duty to search for criminals or seek out crime. In contrast to this a soldier who is employed in aid of the civil power in Northern Ireland is under a duty, enforceable under military law, to search for criminals if so ordered by his superior officer and to risk his own life should this be necessary in preventing terrorist acts. For the performance of this duty he is armed with a firearm, a self-loading rifle, from which a bullet, if it hits the human body, is almost certain to cause serious injury if not death. ([1977] AC 136–7)

Lord Lloyd of Berwick cited these comments in the second pertinent case, *R v Clegg* ([1995] 1 AC 482), where he emphasised the last sentence in the quotation and added:

> In the case of a soldier in Northern Ireland, in the circumstances in which Private Clegg found himself, there is no scope for graduated force. The only choice lay between firing a high-velocity rifle which, if aimed accurately, was almost certain to kill or injure, and doing nothing at all. ([1995] 1 AC 497–8)

The implication, it seems, is that when a government deploys highly-armed soldiers, equipped and trained to kill, in a civilian area, it is precisely because of that circumstance that the law must give the armed forces greater leeway to kill or maim than would be permitted for any other person (including, presumably, a less lethally-equipped police officer).

Private Clegg was convicted by a trial judge of murder. While on a patrol to catch 'joyriders' Clegg fired three shots at the windscreen of a car as it approached at speed. He fired a fourth shot, killing a passenger, after the car had passed him and was already more than 50 feet along the road. The judge accepted that the initial three shots were fired in self-defence or in defence of a colleague, but that the fourth shot could not have been fired in self-defence because the danger to the soldiers no longer existed. The House of Lords upheld the conviction, ruling that where a person used a greater degree of force than necessary for self-defence, the charge could not be reduced to manslaughter, even if the accused was a soldier or police officer acting in the course of his duty. Yet, the court expressed regret that, under existing law, the judge had no choice but to convict Clegg of murder, and urged the parliament to change the law relating to murder and manslaughter.

In an interesting insight into the lengths that military personnel may go in conspiring together to obscure their criminal liability, Clegg argued that he had fired the fourth shot to stop the driver of the car in the belief that it had struck another member of the patrol. The judge found that bruising on the other soldier's leg had not been caused by the car but by another soldier stamping on it to give the misleading appearance that he had been struck by the car.

The House of Lords observed that an army 'yellow card' entitled 'Instructions for opening fire in Northern Ireland' could, on a literal reading, justify firing on a car where a person had been injured by it, irrespective of the seriousness of the injury. Significantly, however, the court said the card had no legal force ([1995] 1 AC 491). (This finding relates to the issue of the legal effect of any military manual or rules of engagement – see below.)

Clegg's conviction caused a considerable political backlash. The British government released him on licence, a series of re-trials ensued, evidence was found to be unreliable and he was ultimately acquitted (Watt 2000). This outcome points to the political and legal difficulties involved in finding members of the armed forces guilty of offences committed during operations.

After reviewing the earlier cases on self-defence and excessive force, Lee drew the conclusion that 'the courts have shown a disinclination to insist on a strict standard in measuring the reasonableness of the force applied' (Lee 1984, 241). All these considerations suggest that the 'reasonable and necessary force' test is likely to be interpreted generously toward the military in circumstances where ADF members act under lawful orders.

Superior Orders

Under the Australian legislation, the potential for misuse of the call-out powers has been increased by overturning the common law's rejection of a general defence of superior orders (reaffirmed in *R v Clegg*, discussed above) and also by providing expanded legal immunities from prosecution for ADF personnel. Before the 2006 amendments, legal doubts remained about aspects of the criminal and civil liability of military personnel in some circumstances, particularly if a state government or its police force had differences with the military call-out, leading to a lack of cooperation. Despite the wide powers that the Act granted to military personnel, it was not clear that the Act covered every instance in which an officer or soldier might otherwise be exposed to criminal liability or civil actions for assault, battery or false imprisonment. The Act did not specifically provide a blanket legal protection, nor did it follow a previous recommendation that military personnel on call-out be granted the legal status of police officers.

The traditional canons of statutory interpretation provide that a court should presume that an Act is not intended to deprive members of the public of their civil liberties. The dilemma identified by Brett and Waller could still therefore arise:

> The hardship upon soldiers is, that if a soldier kills a man in obedience to his officer's orders, the question whether what was done was more than was reasonably necessary to quell civil disturbance has to be decided by a jury, probably on a trial of murder. Whereas, if he disobeys his officer's orders to fire because he regards them as unlawful, the question where they were unlawful as having commanded something not reasonably necessary would have to be decided by a court-martial upon the trial of a soldier for disobeying orders, and for obvious reasons the jury and the court-martial are likely to take different views as to the reasonable necessity and therefore as to the lawfulness of such an order. (Brett and Waller 1983, 654)

Since the Australian case of *Re Tracey; Ex parte Ryan* ((1989) 166 CLR 518) it has been reasonably clear that the defence power of the Australian Constitution cannot be used to exempt military personnel from the general criminal and civil law for conduct for which they have already been tried for a 'service offence' under military law. Five members of the High Court in that case held invalid provisions of the *Defence Force Discipline Act 1982* (Cth) (DFDA) that sought to do so, insisting that, after reviewing the history, a soldier remains a citizen and liable to the ordinary criminal law.

Section 51WB of the *Defence Act*, inserted by the 2006 amendments, states:

> *Defence of superior orders in certain circumstances*
>
> (1) Subject to subsection (2), the fact that a criminal act was done, or purported to be done, by a member of the Defence Force under this Part under an order of a superior does not relieve the member of criminal responsibility.
>
> (2) It is a defence to a criminal act done, or purported to be done, by a member of the Defence Force under this Part that:
>
> (a) the criminal act was done by the member under an order of a superior; and
>
> (b) the member was under a legal obligation to obey the order; and
>
> (c) the order was not manifestly unlawful; and
>
> (d) the member had no reason to believe that circumstances had changed in a material respect since the order was given; and
>
> (e) the member had no reason to believe that the order was based on a mistake as to a material fact; and
>
> (f) the action taken was reasonable and necessary to give effect to the order.
>
> (3) Subsection (2) does not limit the defences that may be available to the person.

The Explanatory Memorandum states that on occasion, military service 'will require unhesitating compliance with orders' (Parliament of Australia 2005, 25). It also states: 'As matters currently stand, an ADF member prosecuted for a crime will have a defence if they can show they acted under lawful authority' (Parliament of Australia 2005, 26). In other words, the key proviso is intended to extend the defence to cover unlawful superior orders that were not 'manifestly unlawful'.

Superior orders defences have traditionally been confined to armed conflicts, and none currently exist for Australian police officers (Department of the Senate, Senate Legal and Constitutional Affairs Committee 2006, 21). Even in combat situations, the DFDA and explanatory *Australian Defence Force Discipline Act 1982 Manual* provide that only lawful commands need to be obeyed (DFDA s 27; Manual 4-33). It is a defence to any offence under the DFDA that an act or omission was performed in obedience to 'an unlawful order that the person did not know, and could not reasonably be expected to have known, was unlawful' (DFDA s 14).

The new 'manifestly unlawful' defence is arguably wider than the DFDA defence. This shift in the law opens up dangers that military personnel can kill, maim or seriously violate the rights of civilians with impunity. It may be argued that the new formulation is similar to that in Article 33 of the 1998 Rome Statute of the International Criminal Court. The adoption of the 'manifestly unlawful' test in the Rome Statute remains controversial, however, because it is arguably a retreat from the standard applied at the post-Second World War Nuremburg tribunals (Garraway 1999, 785–94; Osiel 1999).

At Nuremberg, Article 8 of the Charter of the International Military Tribunal stated:

> The fact that the Defendant acted pursuant to order of his Government or of a superior shall not free him from responsibility, but may be considered in mitigation of punishment if the Tribunal determines that justice so requires.

This principle was adopted to prevent Nazi officials and officers from escaping liability for the violence and denial of basic human rights they committed against civilians, notably Jews. The experience of fascist totalitarianism was so horrific that people around the world demanded that such conduct never be permitted again.

Doubts still exist that the 'superior orders' defence fully protects ADF personnel. Military personnel ordered to use force against civilians may face a dilemma. Under military law, if they disobey orders, they could face dire consequences, including imprisonment. However, under civilian law, if they execute orders that are subsequently ruled unlawful, they may have no defence of obeying superior orders.

While the DFDA and Manual provide that only lawful commands need to be obeyed, these instruments are heavily tilted toward obedience. Thus, 'a person given an order requiring the performance of a military duty may infer it to be lawful and disobeys it at peril' (Manual 4-33). Disobedience of a lawful command is punishable by up to two years' imprisonment (DFDA s 27; Manual 4-33). It is a defence to any offence under the DFDA that an act or omission was performed in obedience to 'an unlawful order that the person did not know, and could not reasonably be expected to have known, was unlawful' (DFDA s 14). For officers, the duty of obedience is reinforced by their officer's commission:

> I (name of Governor-General) … Charge and Command you faithfully to discharge your duty as an officer and observe and execute all such orders as you may receive from your superior officers …. (Wheate and Wheate 2003, 21)

Under the DFDA, there is no doubt that ADF members are under a legal obligation to obey the orders of superiors. Much less clear is what is meant by 'manifestly unlawful', 'no reason to believe that circumstances had changed in a material respect', 'no reason to believe that the order was based on a mistake as to a material fact' and 'reasonable and necessary to give effect to the order'. The tests are couched in objective, not subjective, terms, so the question is not whether the ADF member believed these things to be true; the question is whether these requirements were actually met. How is a soldier to know what is 'manifestly unlawful' or what is 'reasonable and necessary'?

Two scholars, one an ADF officer, have expressed the view that the provisions, while offering some degree of legal protection to ADF members, may be 'a trap for the unwary', particularly in 'morally controversial' decisions to kill people pre-emptively in order to protect property ('critical infrastructure'). Bronitt and Stephens note:

> [U]nlike the criminal and civil immunities conferred on law enforcement officials by controlled operations legislation, there is no similar protection conferred on ADF members acting under Part IIIAAA. Indeed, the legislation states that the fact that a member of the ADF has acted in accordance with Part IIIAAA, thus attracting the superior orders defence, does not otherwise relieve that member of criminal responsibility. (Bronitt and Stephens 2007, 275)

Bronitt and Stephens describe reliance on Rules of Engagement (ROE) as another 'trap for the unwary' because ROE do not provide a source of legal authority for action, despite being a 'lawful general order' under the DFDA (Bronitt and Stephens 2007, 275).

These questions are crucial given that the common law provides no 'superior orders' defence. In *R v Clegg*, discussed above, it was said that no general defence of superior orders was known to English law. Lord Lloyd of Berwick cited ancient authority as well as the Australian High Court in *A v Hayden (No 2)* ((1984) 156 CLR 532), followed by the Privy Council in *Yip Chiu-Cheung v The Queen* ([1995] 1 AC 111). In *Hayden*, Murphy J stated:

> In Australia it is no defence to the commission of a criminal act or omission that it was done in obedience to the orders of a superior or the government. Military and civilians have a duty to obey lawful orders, and a duty to disobey unlawful orders. ((1984) 156 CLR 532 at [5])

It must be noted, however, that the effect of this rule in *Hayden* was to permit the superior officers and other higher authorities (including the relevant minister) to disown the individual officers who had violated the criminal law. In addition, a closer examination of the case reveals that, in the end, the officers involved also escaped prosecution.

Hayden arose out of a 1983 Australian Secret Intelligence Service (ASIS) training operation at Melbourne's Sheraton Hotel, in which the masked and heavily-armed participants smashed open a door, engaged in a fight in an elevator and terrified guests and staff as they ran through a lobby to a waiting car. The incident attracted media headlines and an inquiry conducted by Justice Hope concluded that the participants had possibly committed 21 serious criminal offences. However, the minister responsible for ASIS, Foreign Minister Bill Hayden, was absolved of responsibility for the agent's misconduct. Hope concluded that Hayden had no duty to inquire into specific details of ASIS training programmes, and the Acting Director-General had no duty to inform him (Royal Commission Sheraton Hotel Report 1984, 18).

Alleged participants in the incident sought an injunction prohibiting the Commonwealth from disclosing their identities to the Victorian chief police commissioner for the purpose of investigating whether they had committed criminal offences. The plaintiffs argued that, as they worked with ASIS, their identification would endanger national security and breach confidentiality agreements in their contracts of employment with the Commonwealth.

Members of the High Court made apparently strong statements to the effect that ASIS and other security agencies must operate within the law. Mason J, for example, declared: 'For the future, the point needs to be made loudly and clearly that if counter-espionage activities involve breaches of the law they are liable to attract the consequences that ordinarily follow from breaches of the law' ((1984) 156 CLR 532, [2]). Other justices described the incapacity of the executive to dispense its servants from obedience to legislation as 'the cornerstone of parliamentary democracy' ((1984) 156 CLR 532, [6]) and essential to the 'rule of law' ((1984) 156 CLR 532, [3]).

Yet, the case was unusual because the federal government opposed the plaintiffs, denying that national security would be threatened. (An agreement had been reached with the Victorian government and specific state legislation introduced to prevent public disclosure of the plaintiffs' identities and provide for *in camera* trials of any criminal charges.) Thus, the court did not have to decide whether a government claim of national security would have protected the ASIS officers ((1984) 156 CLR 532, [18]).

In addition, the judges accepted that the Commonwealth itself was immune from criminal prosecution, even though senior officials had initiated the training exercise ((1984) 156 CLR 532, [21]). In other words, individual intelligence operatives might be criminally liable, but not their superior officers or members of the government. Finally, Brennan J opined that, at least during wartime, legislation could be passed exempting ASIS officers from other laws. He stated: 'The Commonwealth Parliament has made no law granting to ASIS officers exemption from any law; it is unnecessary to consider whether its constitutional powers could support such a law in times of peace' ((1984) 156 CLR 532, [8]). This suggestion could take on new meaning in the light of the 'war on terror'.

Finally, it must be noted that no prosecutions resulted. Public and private requests by the Commonwealth government not to proceed prevailed. Officially, the Victorian Commissioner of Police, on the advice of the State Director of Public Prosecutions, announced that matters would not proceed. It was maintained that as the suspects had worn masks, it was not possible to determine who had done precisely what, and that lack of evidence precluded the laying of specific charges. Instead, the hotel management received $259,000 in exemplary damages from the government, while employees received undisclosed payments (Grabosky 1989, Ch. 8).

Thus, the *Hayden* case also highlights the discretion in the hands of prosecutors not to lay charges against ADF members. This discretion, moreover, is legally unreviewable, just like an Attorney-General's decision not to intervene in a case. It is for the Commonwealth Director of Public Prosecutions to decide whether to prosecute under Part IIIAAA, and according to the Explanatory Memorandum for the 2006 amendments, prosecutors are expected to exercise 'common sense' in that decision-making, and give consideration to the applicable Rules of Engagement (ROE). That is so, even though ROE are simply instruments of executive action, not a source of legal authority.

Bronitt and Stephens opine that 'prosecutorial discretion does not provide sufficient protection for the military exercising these powers', and if innocent lives are taken there may be political and public pressure to prosecute (Bronitt and Stephens 2007, 275). This prospect can never be discounted. Nevertheless, it appears that despite 'traps for the unwary', prosecutions are unlikely to be launched, or convictions obtained, where ADF personnel rely on the superior orders defence, at least where the order was authorised by the applicable ROE. This likely result is highly problematic, not least because of the secrecy surrounding ROE. Members of the public subjected to military intervention have no means of knowing the precise orders that ADF members have been given, and hence may unknowingly conduct themselves in ways that could lead to the use of lethal force.

Rules of Engagement (ROE)

During the passage of the Australian call-out legislation in 2000, the government rejected an amendment that would have required the tabling in parliament of the manuals and protocols that will apply to military interventions. This proposal was raised after a senator read out extracts from the then current Australian Army *Manual of Land Warfare*.

This secret manual, produced in 1983, had been leaked to the media in 1993 (McCulloch 2001, 177). It asserted an extremely wide and highly-political role for the ADF, with an Introduction that stated: 'Civil disobedience, mass violence and terrorism have become common methods of dissent throughout the world in recent years' (McCulloch 2001, 178). It said the ADF may be involved in countering the threat posed by the activities of dissidents, including riots, mass demonstrations, and industrial, political and social disturbances (McCulloch 2001, 178). It referred to establishing detention centres and to opening fire on 'unlawful assemblies' (McCulloch 2001, 182–3). The further stated:

> As a last resort troops may be required to open fire on the crowd to disperse it. The principles of minimum force must be kept in mind by the commanders. Therefore, initially, only selected individuals should be nominated to fire upon selected agitators in the crowd. (McCulloch 2001, 183)

Section 543 of the manual instructed military personnel in how to then cover up the killing or wounding of 'dissidents':

> Dead and wounded dissidents, if identifiable, must be removed immediately by the police … When being reported, dissident and own casualties are categorised merely as dead or wounded. To inhibit propaganda exploitation by the dissidents the cause of the casualties (for example, 'shot') is not reported. A follow-up operation should be carried out to maintain the momentum of the dispersing crowd. (Brown 2000, 17398)

A government minister said the Army manual was 'under revision' and would be replaced with a new version once the Act was passed. He refused, however, to give any assurance that a similar clause would not appear in the rewritten document. The current rules have been withheld from the public. In 2005, the author put this question in writing to Defence Minister Robert Hill, who replied as follows:

> I am informed that there is a manual to provide guidance to ADF members for the conduct of operations under Part IIIAA of the Defence Act 1903, but this manual is not available for release to the public.
>
> If the ADF was called out under Part IIIAA of the Defence Act, the Chief of the Defence Force would issue situation-specific rules of engagement (ROE) to regulate the use of force. The Force Commander would translate these ROE into situation-specific orders for the use of force. These orders would be issued to all ADF members before they were deployed. ADF members would have those orders explained to them and would be trained in their application so they were

> clear as to the level of force which is authorised in a particular situation, as well as the way in which force may be used.
>
> Rules of engagement are, by necessity, highly classified. Precise knowledge by an adversary of the limitations that have been placed on the use of force by ADF members could endanger their [i.e. ADF members'] lives. For reasons of operational security, it is not appropriate to release ROE into the public domain. (Hill 2005)

The Minister's reply raised a number of questions. No reason was given for withholding the manual from public scrutiny. Presumably, the reasons given for not releasing the ROE were meant to apply. Vague and uncertain concepts, 'necessity' and 'operational security' were used to justify denying members of the public the right to know what levels of potentially lethal force have been, or could be, authorised for use against them. How such knowledge could endanger the lives of ADF members was not substantiated. The use of the term 'adversary' underscored the fact that anyone against whom the armed forces will be deployed will be regarded as an enemy, akin to a wartime target, not as a civilian member of society. Moreover, the secrecy makes more difficult the necessary task of determining the legality of any call-out and the powers given to called-out ADF members.

Further questions arise about the extraordinary powers placed in the hands of military commanders – the Chief of the Defence Force and Force Commanders – to issue 'situation-specific' ROE and orders. These powers in themselves challenge the framework of civilian control over the armed forces. How can anyone be assured that the ROE and orders, presumably to be issued with great urgency in the context of a military call-out to respond to imminent 'domestic violence' or threats to Commonwealth interests, will not exceed the parameters set by the legislation? The secrecy may hinder any attempt to establish whether any orders were 'manifestly unlawful'.

Finally, the Minister's letter failed to explain how soldiers could be trained in the application of their orders, so they were clear about the levels of force they were authorised to use, if 'situation-specific' orders were given under conditions of urgency or emergency.

It must be noted that there is strong pressure on armed forces members to abide by ROE, regardless of any doubts they may have about their lawfulness. As Bronitt and Stephens comment, 'there is a strong culture for compliance around ROE in the military, which is underscored by the legal duty to obey lawful orders, with failure to do so constituting a disciplinary offence' (Bronitt and Stephens 2007, 275).

In sum, a lack of clarity exists about the interplay between the superior orders defence and ROE. It is by no means guaranteed that soldiers who kill civilians while acting under orders and in line with the relevant ROE will be shielded from criminal prosecution. There is also no guarantee that a soldier who defies an unlawful order in order to refrain from causing fatalities will be protected from military disciplinary measures. Overall, it must be said, however, that wide legal scope has been created for the use of lethal force, with an apparent legislative intention to make criminal prosecutions unlikely.

How to Challenge the Legality of Any Call-out?

To what extent is it possible legally to challenge decisions made under the Australian *Defence Act*, including those made by the 'authorising ministers' (or the Governor-General) to issue a call-out order, specify a 'general security area' or declare a 'designated area'?

There is no provision for legal review in the Act. Instead, s 51X provides for limited scrutiny, after the event, by parliament. Within seven days of a call-out order ending, the Defence Minister must present both houses with a copy of the order and a report on the utilisation of the ADF under the order. Section 51W provides:

> If, before, during or after exercising power under Division 2 or 3 or this Division, a member of the Defence Force fails to comply with any obligation imposed under any of those Divisions that relates to the exercise of the power, the member is not, or is taken not to have been, entitled to exercise the power.

The effect of this section is not clear. It relates only to the legality of actions taken by individual ADF members under a call-out order, not to the lawfulness of the government's proclamations.

Australia, like Britain and Canada, has no strict US-style 'political questions' doctrine forbidding the courts from reviewing sensitive political questions. But the courts will not review the exercise of certain prerogative powers, and may decide not to intervene in sensitive political or national security decisions. Decisions made under the 'prerogative powers', such as appointment and dismissals of prime ministers, and decisions relating to foreign policy, declarations of war, national security and such matters as the award of royal honours have traditionally been regarded as 'non-justiciable', that is, lying outside the purview of the courts. In Britain, the House of Lords accepted in *Council of Civil Service Unions v Minister for the Civil Service* ([1985] AC 374) that these exclusions still exist.

However, the law of 'justiciability' has become somewhat fluid in recent years, arguably reflecting popular concerns about the growth of executive power, including in the conduct of foreign affairs, involving violations of human rights. The English Court of Appeal has been prepared to consider an application for relief by an English citizen detained in the US detention camp at Guantánamo Bay (*Abbasi v Secretary of State* [2002] EWCA Civ 1598). Their Lordships said the 'forbidden area' of foreign policy identified by the House of Lords could be impinged upon where 'a clear breach of a fundamental human right' occurred (*Abbasi v Secretary of State* [2002] EWCA Civ 1598 at [66] and [107]).

This approach was followed by Tamberlin J of the Australian Federal Court when lawyers for David Hicks, an Australian citizen incarcerated at Guantánamo Bay, sought a writ of habeas corpus instructing the Australian government to ask the US authorities to release him (*Hicks v Ruddock* [2007] FCA 299). The application also sought an order that the government acted on 'irrelevant considerations' and for 'improper purposes' in refusing to request Hicks's release. Tamberlin J rejected a government application to have the case summarily dismissed on the grounds that courts should not interfere in negotiations between two countries. The judge stated: 'The concept of a "forbidden area" arguably states the position far too generally to be applied at face value' (*Hicks v Ruddock* [2007] FCA 299, [85]).

Where issues of national security are involved, Australian courts are willing to inquire into the legality of executive decisions and actions, but they have interpreted the law in ways that make it almost impossible for litigants to demonstrate that the behaviour at issue is legally flawed. One prominent example is *Church of Scientology Inc v Woodward* ((1982) 154 CLR 25). The High Court considered whether it would review decisions by ASIO to collect information about the church as a possible security risk. While the majority insisted that no exercise of Commonwealth power could be excluded from judicial review, all the judges considered that applicants would face almost insuperable difficulties in introducing evidence and convincing a court that ASIO's judgments on national security were legally flawed.

The High Court dismissed the notion that ASIO could act lawfully beyond the limits set by the *Australian Security Intelligence Organisation Act 1979* (Cth), in purported exercise of the Commonwealth's executive power. But, in practice, the judges threw doubt on any judicial review of ASIO's security assessment decisions.

Mason J, who concurred with Gibbs CJ in ruling in favour of ASIO, forming a statutory majority, said s 17(1) of the ASIO Act contained an exclusive and comprehensive list of the activities ASIO was authorised, and *un*authorised, to engage in ((1982) 154 CLR 25, 57). Yet, in so far as those functions were required to be relevant to 'security', it would be difficult for a plaintiff to challenge ASIO's decision-making. Mason J described security as a 'fluctuating concept, relying on circumstances as they exist from time to time – not unlike the issue of defence' ((1982) 154 CLR 25, 60). The onus was on the plaintiff to establish that there was '*no* reasonable basis to conclude that the actions in question have a real connection with security' ((1982) 154 CLR 25, 61). While not, in theory, ruling out judicial review of ASIO operations, Mason J described the satisfaction of the test as a 'formidable task'. This was in part due to the severe challenges facing an applicant in satisfying a court that ASIO erred in its decisions as to national security. One such obstacle was the exclusion of material relied upon by the plaintiff by virtue of Crown privilege ((1982) 154 CLR 25, 61).

Murphy and Brennan JJ, who dissented, also maintained that, in theory, no exercise of Commonwealth power could be excluded from judicial review, at least not without clear and express words. But in practice, they too considered that applicants would face almost insuperable difficulties in introducing evidence and convincing a court that ASIO's judgments on national security were erroneous. Brennan J, for example, asked: 'How can the gravity of a security risk be evaluated by a court?' A plaintiff would not be able to force the disclosure of ASIO documents as evidence for a challenge. 'Discovery would not be given against the Director-General save in a most exceptional case', he stated. 'The public interest in national security will seldom yield to the public interest in the administration of civil justice' ((1982) 154 CLR 25, 76). Brennan J concluded: 'There are thus large obstacles in the path of a plaintiff who seeks to restrain an alleged activity of the Organization on the ground that it does not lie within the functions assigned to it by s. 17' ((1982) 154 CLR 25, 76).

Likewise, the majority of the court in *A v Hayden* refused to rule out the possibility that, under certain circumstances, the interests of 'national security' could override those of 'the administration of justice'. Wilson and Dawson JJ stated: 'The administration of justice, important though it is, may on occasions have to give way to an even more compelling public interest. In a proper case, national security may well satisfy that description' ((1984) 156 CLR 532, [16]). They indicated that the government's view of national security would always 'carry great weight'. 'The consequence of a decision of a court on a matter of national security which is contrary to the considered view of the government could be very serious indeed' ((1984) 156 CLR 532, [19]).

Claims of public interest immunity may be invoked to prevent access to documents said to relate to defence or national security. In *Alister v R* ((1984) 154 CLR 412), by a three-to-two majority, the High Court held that, for the purpose of an appeal by Alister, a civilian, against a conviction for conspiracy to murder, it should inspect ASIO documents subpoenaed by the defence, despite a ministerial certificate claiming public interest immunity on national security grounds. The documents concerned the activities of an ASIO agent, Richard Seary, who was involved in the alleged conspiracy. The majority said a higher standard of 'public interest' was required where the information requested related to a criminal conviction. Strong statements of principle were made. Brennan J, for example, said:

> It is of the essence of a free society that a balance is struck between the security that is desirable to protect society as a whole and the safeguards that are necessary to ensure individual liberty. But in the long run the safety of a democracy rests upon the common commitment of its citizens to the safeguarding of each man's liberty, and the balance must tilt that way. ((1984) 154 CLR 412, 456)

Upon inspection of the documents, however, a differently-constituted majority (with only Murphy J dissenting) held that, since none of the documents was relevant to the issues at the trial, the public interest in their non-production outweighed any contrary public interest. Given that the court's examination of the documents was conducted in secret, it is difficult to assess this conclusion. It remains of concern, however, that the Attorney-General can readily claim public interest immunity and that the 'balance' to be struck with civil liberties remains substantially hidden from public scrutiny.

In another example, an applicant sought to challenge the cancellation of his passport by the Australian Foreign Affairs Minister on security grounds (*Traljesic v Attorney-General (Cth)* (2006) 150 FCR 199). In the Federal Court, Rares J dismissed an appeal against an Attorney-General's national interest certificate under ss 36, 39A and 39B of the *Administrative Appeals Act*, which barred both the applicant and his lawyer from hearing or having access to the evidence presented by ASIO, because of a 'potential but unsubstantiated risk' that the lawyer might inadvertently divulge confidential material. The judge ruled this was a relevant and not unreasonable consideration, even though the certificate effectively prevented the applicant from refuting the secret allegations made against him. Such decisions open the door to virtually unchallengeable executive power.

A similar result was achieved in another case in which two members of the High Court rejected an application for leave to appeal against a decision denying an applicant the right to even know why he had been assessed as a security risk *Leghaei v Director-General of Security & Anor* ([2007] HCATrans 655). The judges insisted that procedural fairness had to give way to 'the protection of the public interest in national security'. Their decision upheld two decisions in the Federal Court, both featuring the giving of partly confidential reasons by judges. Such decisions produce the Kafkaesque outcome that people can be deprived of passports or visas without any right to know the evidence or the legal case against them.

How these approaches might play out in the highly-charged context of a military call-out to put down 'domestic violence' can perhaps be seen from the House of Lords decision in *Chandler v Director of Public Prosecutions* ([1964] AC 763), which involved a prosecution for breach of the *Officials Secrets Act 1911* (UK). Lord Reid stated that he did not 'subscribe to the view that the government or a minister must always or even as a general rule have the last word' about the safety or interests of the state. But he agreed, together with the other lords, that cross-examination was not permissible to challenge the evidence of a senior Air Force officer that a proposed obstruction of an airfield was contrary to the 'safety or interests of the state', which were the relevant words of the statute. Lord Reid went on to refer to the proposition that decisions about military deployments are not justiciable:

> The defence of the State from external enemies is a matter of real concern, in time of peace as in days of war. The disposition, armament and direction of the defence forces of the State are matters decided upon by the Crown and are within its jurisdiction as the executive power of the State. So are treaties and alliances with other states for mutual defence …. ([1964] AC 763, 796)

The law lords invoked a passage in *The Zamora*, where the Privy Council declared:

> Those who are responsible for the national security must be the sole judges of what the national security requires. It would be obviously undesirable that such matters should be made the subject of evidence in a court of law or otherwise discussed in public. ([1916] 2 AC 77, 107)

This statement, which amounts to placing the executive above the law when it comes to decisions made in the name of national security, cannot be dismissed as out-of-date. It was cited by approval by members of the House of Lords in *Council of Civil Service Unions v Minister for the Civil Service*, discussed above, in ruling that the requirements of national security outweighed those of procedural fairness. That decision permitted the Thatcher government to ban trade union membership in the Government Communications Headquarters without consulting the unions.

Can a Minister or Military Commander be Held Liable?

Can an authorising minister or senior armed forces commander be held liable for abuses or excesses that occur during a military call-out? In principle, a minister or officer who issued an illegal order should be held to account. In his *Protective Security Review* report, presented to the Australian government in 1979, Justice Hope said it was undoubted that an officer 'would be liable in civil, criminal and military courts for the consequences of any illegal orders he may give' (Hope 1979, 169).

Unfortunately, the true legal picture is not so clear. In terms of civil liability, it is extremely difficult to sue successfully for damages, because plaintiffs must generally prove a specific tort, and therefore show malice, intention to cause them harm, negligence, trespass, assault or false imprisonment on the part of the decision-maker, not simply that an unlawful decision was taken.

In 1989, for example, the Australian High Court confirmed that even where South Korean businessmen had been wrongly detained, and were entitled to declaratory orders to that effect, they could not obtain damages, unless they sued separately for false imprisonment (*Park Oh Ho v Minister for Immigration and Ethnic Affairs* (1989) 167 CLR 637). An added difficulty in tort suits could be establishing that the defendants owed any duty of care to the plaintiff, rather than a duty to carry out their lawful responsibilities (*Rush v Commissioner of Police* [2006] FCA 12). In *Northern Territory v Mengel* ((1995) 185 CLR 307) the High Court rejected an attempt to establish an administrative tort based on damages simply for an 'unlawful act'.

The common law tort of misfeasance in public office offers very limited prospects for obtaining damages. It applies only where a person suffered economic loss because the defendant knowingly, whether or not maliciously, committed an intentional and wrongful act amounting to an abuse of his or her public office. The plaintiff must be a member of the public to whom the defendant owed a duty not to commit the particular abuse complained, and has to show that the act was knowingly or recklessly performed without power (*Northern Territory v Mengel* (1995) 185 CLR 307).

There is authority for the proposition that officials will be liable for 'wanton or cruel acts' that were not justified by the necessities of the situation. In *Wright v Fitzgerald* ((1799) 27 St. Tr. 759), the High Sheriff of County Tipperary was held liable for a public flogging, despite an Indemnity Act (one of seven passed in Ireland between 1796 and 1800) that protected the authorities from actions brought against them as a result of their unlawful activities in suppressing rebellion.

However, unless deliberate abuses of power or malicious purposes can be proved, the overall picture is that civilians who suffer damage or loss as the result of 'military aid to the civil power' are likely to face considerable legal problems in mounting damages actions against armed forces personnel and their military and political commanders.

The culpability or responsibility might lie at a number of levels, from the authorising ministers and Chief of Defence Forces, through the military hierarchy down to individual officers and non-commissioned personnel. If the responsibility properly rests with the government that authorised the call-out, political redress may be possible through parliament, except that governments will normally have parliamentary majorities to shield them. Ultimately, governments arguably can be held accountable by the population as a whole through elections, but this sanction will carry little weight if the military intervention enjoys bipartisan support.

In terms of legal redress, the prospect of government ministers or senior military officials being held culpable or liable is also dim. Not only have courts been traditionally reluctant to second-guess, or call into question, official decisions made in the realm of national security, but it is also difficult to obtain damages for a breach of exercise of a discretionary power, let alone find the decision-maker criminally liable.

If serious atrocities occurred during a domestic military intervention, some avenues of complaint or redress could be found in international law or via United Nations institutions. Government ministers could even be prosecuted before the International Criminal Court (and a brief was sent to the ICC in 2008 to request charges against former Prime Minister John Howard for deploying Australian troops to Iraq in violation of international law [Frueh 2008]), but delving into these possibilities is beyond the scope of this book.

Both politically and legally, it is more likely that efforts will be made to blame individual members of the armed forces for any excesses and abuses that occur. In the words of Bronitt and Stephens, 'if mistakes are made and innocent lives are taken, the political and public pressure to scapegoat the military may be intense' (Bronitt and Stephens 2007, 275). Arguably, this was the case with the 1983 episode involving heavily armed ASIS operatives at Melbourne's Sheraton Hotel. As noted earlier, a subsequent inquiry found that 21 serious criminal offences had been committed but absolved the minister of responsibility (and ultimately no prosecutions resulted against the ASIS operatives either).

One well-known American experience concerns the shooting of students by National Guard troops at Kent State University in 1970. A presidential commission concluded that the shootings were unjustified, but only individual guardsmen were prosecuted, and they were acquitted on grounds of self-defence (see the case study at the end of this chapter). As another example, when revelations appeared of torture and abuse of prisoners inside Iraq's Abu Ghraib jail, mostly low-ranking soldiers were placed on trial, despite evidence of a chain of command from the White House (Hersh 2004; Mestrovic 2006; Morris and Gourevitch 2008).

Obvious conflicts of interest can arise in these kinds of circumstances. Governments and senior officers may have an interest in arguing that any excesses were the product of 'bad apples' in the ranks, rather than the result of policies or orders adopted at higher levels. Politicians and military personnel alike may seek to cover-up, obscure or minimise the extent of the abuses.

Criminal Prosecutions: The Historical Record

No Australian cases have been recorded in which a member of the armed forces has been prosecuted for killing or injuring a civilian during the course of a military operation. History suggests, however, that even if soldiers are prosecuted in civil courts, the prospects of conviction are not strong.

As noted in Chapter 2, a test case was conducted against four members of the armed forces involved in the 1819 Peterloo Massacre, in which soldiers killed 15 people and wounded between 400 and 700. The case ended in acquittal, with the court ruling that the soldiers' actions had been justified to disperse an illegal gathering (Reid 1989, 203–4). Likewise, in the Bristol riots of 1831, an officer who had fatally shot a boy was acquitted of manslaughter. Lord Tindal instructed the Grand Jury that if the shot was 'discharged in the fair and honest execution of his duty, in endeavouring to disperse the mob', the killing was justified and amounted to accidental death only (*R v Pinney* (1832) 170 ER 962, 969). By contrast, two officers who had refused to order the troops to fire without a magistrate's sanction were found guilty of neglect of duty, causing one to commit suicide. Lord Tindal insisted that soldiers had a duty, as citizens, on their own authority to do their utmost to 'put down riot and tumult'.

A similar result followed the Featherstone Colliery Riots of 1893. Four people, including two bystanders, were killed when an infantry captain ordered soldiers to fire on striking coal miners and their supporters after a local magistrate had read the Riot Act proclamation. The 1893 *Report of the Select Committee on the Featherstone Riots* exonerated the captain and his troops, saying 'The necessary prevention of such outrage on person and property justifies the guardians of the peace in the employment against a riotous crowd of even deadly weapons' (Whelan 1985, 272).

Between 1970 and 1979, the army killed 186 people in Northern Ireland, but between 1972 and 1976, only 28 soldiers were prosecuted for offences involving shooting, of whom 13 were convicted. Only one soldier was convicted of manslaughter, and his conviction was quashed on appeal (Rowe 1985, 201). After one solder was acquitted of murder, the House of Lords was asked to provide an advisory opinion. The Law Lords said the 'reasonableness' of force was a question of fact for a jury, although Lord Diplock stated that a jury ought to take into account that a soldier may have to make a split-second decision to open fire or not (*Reference under s 48A of the Criminal Appeal (Northern Ireland) Act 1968 (No. 1 of 1975)* [1976] 2 All ER 937). During the 1990s, as discussed earlier, one private was convicted of murder, when he fired a fatal shot into the back of a passing car. However, the British government released him on licence and he was ultimately acquitted of all offences after a series of re-trials.

This record indicates that in criminal cases, as in civil matters, courts are reluctant to hold members of the armed forces liable, even where they have killed civilians, at least where their actions occurred in the course of authorised military operations. Judging by history, the test of 'reasonable and necessary force' is likely to be interpreted favourably toward armed forces members acting under orders.

A Brief Case Study: The Kent State Shootings

The American Kent State University shootings of 1970, at the height of the movement against the Vietnam War, provide a cautionary example of the difficulties involved in legally holding to account those responsible for shooting down protestors. On 4 May 1970, members of the Ohio National Guard killed four students and wounded nine others, one of whom suffered permanent paralysis. Ohio Governor James A. Rhodes sent the troops to the campus, in the city of Kent, Ohio, at the request of the local mayor. The only instruments the Guardsmen had to dispel demonstrators were bayonets, CS gas grenades, and .30-06 ball ammunition (Bills 1988; Caputo 2005).

Some of the students who were shot were protesting against the American invasion of Cambodia, which President Richard Nixon had announced in a television address on 30 April. Other students who were shot were merely walking nearby or observing the protest at a distance. The shootings led to protests on college campuses throughout the United States and a student strike, causing more than 450 campuses across the country to close. Five days after the shootings, 100,000 people demonstrated in Washington against the war and the killing of unarmed student protesters.

A month after the shootings, President Nixon established the President's Commission on Campus Unrest, known as the Scranton Commission, which he charged to study the dissent, disorder and violence breaking out on college and university campuses across the nation. The Commission issued its findings in a September 1970 report that concluded that the Ohio National Guard shootings were unjustified (US President's Commission 1970). The report said:

> Even if the guardsmen faced danger, it was not a danger that called for lethal force. The 61 shots by 28 guardsmen certainly cannot be justified. Apparently, no order to fire was given, and there was inadequate fire control discipline on Blanket Hill. The Kent State tragedy must mark the last time that, as a matter of course, loaded rifles are issued to guardsmen confronting student demonstrators.

Eight of the guardsmen were indicted by a grand jury. The guardsmen claimed to have fired in self-defence. In 1974, US District Judge Frank Battisti dismissed charges against all eight on the basis that the prosecution's case was too weak to warrant a trial. Between 1970 and 1979 lawsuits were filed by families of the victims against the State of Ohio, in hope of placing blame on Governor Rhodes and the Ohio National Guard. Trials were held at both the federal and state level but all ended in acquittals or were dismissed, except one.

One civil trial for wrongful death and injury against Rhodes and the National Guardsmen was originally dismissed but eventually the dismissal was overturned due to the judge excluding evidence. The students' families were awarded approximately $63,000 per victim and the defendants agreed to state for the record that they regretted their actions.

Chapter 10
Wider Legal, Political and Democratic Implications

It is impossible for the historic shifts of the magnitude analysed in this book not to have significant legal and political implications. Moves toward greater reliance on the military for domestic security indicate that serious societal threats are anticipated, not just to public safety but also to political stability. At the same time, recourse to the armed forces to deal with these threats raises serious questions about basic democratic rights, and the state of democracy itself. This is particularly so in light of the longstanding public antipathy toward internal military intervention, and the legal and constitutional traditions against such mobilisations. It can be anticipated that attempts to use the armed forces against protests, industrial action or other forms of civil unrest could be resisted, possibly triggering serious conflicts.

A number of underlying trends has emerged in the countries we have studied. They include:

- an historic pattern of governments or regimes resorting to military force whenever they have felt threatened by social unrest, particularly during periods of economic breakdown or intense class conflict;
- a contemporary shift in governmental and military doctrine to make 'domestic security' a core function or central mission of the armed forces, alongside the traditional role of external defence;
- growing use of the military in civilian settings, both in overseas operations and at home, including for major political and sporting events;
- the introduction of new legislation or constitutional provisions designed to break down the military/police demarcation, enhance the powers of governments to deploy the armed forces internally, and boost the powers of military personnel, notably to use lethal force against civilians;
- expanding official claims to emergency or executive powers – often vague – to mobilise or command the defence forces, both at home and abroad;
- the maintenance or extension of measures that restrict legal and political accountability for the use of the armed forces, and provide military personnel with legal immunities.

Variations in the legal mechanisms adopted to facilitate domestic deployments have developed in the various jurisdictions. In some of the Anglo-American countries, notably the United States, Britain and Canada, no attempt has been made to codify completely the relevant procedures and powers. Instead, more piecemeal legislative changes have been made, leaving much in the hands of uncertain executive and common law powers. By contrast, the Australian legislation of 2000 and 2006 was designed to establish a clearer and more sweeping statutory framework, although one that did not detract from other common law and prerogative powers.

Arguably, the expansion of the scope for domestic military intervention has been the most marked in the United States, which also spends by far the most in the world on its armed forces, and deploys the greatest number of personnel internationally. The creation of the Northern Command, in particular, marks an historic shift. For the first time since the American Revolution, which inscribed on its banners opposition to a standing army and to any internal use of troops, a specific command has been established for the purpose of dealing with perceived security threats on home soil.

It is in the United States that the 'war on terror' declared in September 2001 has most undermined protections against domestic deployment of the armed forces. The *Posse Comitatus Act*, a longstanding congressional prohibition on law enforcement by the military has been substantially eroded. The Northern Command has developed plans for military deployments during political crises, and conducted exercises based on such scenarios. The increasingly visible role of the military in domestic political events was illustrated when Northern Command forces were on high alert during President Barack Obama's 2009 inauguration.

Striking developments have also taken place in the three former fascist or military dictatorships, Italy, Germany and Japan. In Italy, thousands of troops were placed on the streets of major cities in 2008–2009 in the name of combating crime and illegal immigration. Their operations included evicting gypsies, who are living legally in Italy under European Union rules, from unauthorised settlements, raising concerns about the echoes to Mussolini's mobilisation of the fascist Black Shirts and military units against perceived opponents, including Jews.

In Germany, government ministers have made a series of moves since 2001 to repeal, erode or undermine Article 35 of the post-war 1949 Constitution that specifically prohibits the German military from being deployed domestically except in cases of natural disaster. Ministers have called for the use of the army for major sporting events, such as the 2006 World Cup soccer finals, and championed a law allowing the air force to shoot down hijacked planes that posed a threat to populated areas. At least one minister has publicly stated that hijacked planes would be shot down despite the Federal Constitutional Court declaring the law unconstitutional, with the minister seeking to justify such action by 'supra-statutory state of emergency'. During the same period, German troops have been sent abroad to war zones for the first time since the Second World War.

In Japan too, there has been a continual push by successive governments to expand the activities of the Self Defence Forces (SDF), both at home and overseas, despite the so-called 'pacifist clause' – Article 9 of the post-war constitution, which states that 'land, sea, and air forces as well as other war potential, will never be maintained'. Article 9 has been interpreted, at least since the establishment of the SDF in 1954, as permitting the SDF to exist, but only to operate strictly in terms of Japan's territorial defence. These limits have been increasingly brushed aside by Japanese governments to allow SDF deployment overseas for so-called peacekeeping, reconstruction, humanitarian and civil emergency missions in Asia and beyond. At the same time, the SDF has been assigned an increasingly prominent part in domestic life, with nearly three million SDF personnel sent to engage in disaster relief missions since the Hanshin-Awaji (Kobe) earthquake of 1995. This role has begun to spill over into domestic security, as witnessed by the SDF involvement in the large-scale security operation mounted for the July 2008 G8 summit on Hokkaido.

However, it may be that the most significant development lies in the three other countries examined. The fact that moves have been made to enhance the power of governments to call out the troops in countries commonly thought to be among the most stable and peaceful democracies in the world – Britain, Canada and Australia – highlights the general character of the tendency.

In Britain, the political climate created by the 'war on terror' and the introduction of extraordinary emergency powers in the *Civil Contingencies Act 2004* suggest that preparations are being made for greater dependence on internal military operations. As in Japan and Germany, but even more so, these developments have been accompanied by the dispatch of troops to overseas wars. After the United States itself, Britain, which has been an active participant in US-led military interventions since 2001, has sent the second largest contingents of troops to Afghanistan and Iraq.

Moreover, Ministry of Defence policies are based on vague and sweeping common law, executive and prerogative powers that purportedly can authorise the use of troops against a wide range of challenges to 'public order'. Secretive preparations have been made for Military Aid to Civil Power and the 2012 London Olympics will involve a substantial military deployment, alongside an unprecedented police mobilisation.

Canada's entire civilian national security apparatus has been transformed since 2001, and a remarkable array of legal mechanisms exists for mobilising Canadian Forces personnel and capacities, including intelligence resources, to deal with civil unrest. In 2006, the Canada Command was established to focus on domestic operations, and in 2008 the Canada Command and its US counterpart, the Northern Command, signed a Civil Assistance Plan (CAP) that allows the military of each nation to support the other during 'civil emergencies', including terrorist incidents and 'criminal activity'.

In Australia, comprehensive legislation was introduced in 2000, and extended in 2006, giving federal governments and the chief of the Australian Defence Force (ADF) explicit peacetime powers to call out the troops if 'domestic violence is occurring or is likely to occur' that 'would be likely to affect Commonwealth interests' or require the protection of a state or territory. Although the legislation has not yet been invoked, military forces, including elite SAS units, have been deployed with increasing regularity for major political and sporting events. Moreover a debate has been opened up on making domestic security a 'core business' of the ADF. While these trends have largely emerged under the banner of the 'war on terror', the ADF has been used on many other civilian fronts, including the Northern Territory Aboriginal intervention, the turning back of refugee boats and the patrolling of neighbourhoods in Afghanistan, Iraq, East Timor and Solomon Islands.

A related development, the study of which is beyond the parameters of this book, is the development of civil-military cooperation doctrines that provide for lengthy military 'peacekeeping' and 'stabilising' interventions in civilian settings. In Europe, the NATO-related Civil-Military Co-operation Centre of Excellence (CCOE) was established in 2001, in the light of the ongoing NATO intervention in the former Yugoslavia. Likewise, the Australian government has established an Asia Pacific Centre for Civil-Military Cooperation (APC-CIMIC). These doctrines, which envisage long-term military engagements overseas, including policing civilian populations and suppressing dissident or insurgent threats to the established order, could set precedents for domestic use, and train military personnel for similar internal purposes.

Domestic Security as a 'Core Business'

Calls have been made within the political and military establishments for a deeper restructuring of the armed forces and a fundamental re-definition of their role to make domestic security one of their core functions. Indeed, this is the logic of the establishment of NorthCom in the United States and its cross-border partner, the Canada Command.

One of the most explicit and public proposals for a basic shift in the function of the armed forces has come from Australia. In 2006, the government-funded Australian Strategic Policy Institute (ASPI) published a 'Strategic Insight' report suggesting that while 'impressive' progress had been made already in integrating the military into internal security, 10 'next steps' needed to be taken to establish domestic security as a 'core business' of the Australian Defence Force (ADF) (Bergin and Smith 2006, 16–22).

The 10 steps included developing a 'defence domestic security strategy', strengthening 'special event security', re-orienting military education, conducting 'no-warning' exercises involving 'whole-city terrorism' and upgrading links and shared training with police and emergency services. Above all, the document called for a shift in 'defence culture', complaining that it had not yet 'embraced domestic security as core business':

> This reflects Australia's constitutional arrangements, but may not recognise the reality that, when the Australian people perceive themselves to be under attack, they will demand that governments bend every resource to their protection. Defence is a significant and highly visible government resource that will be expected to play its role in a domestic security crisis, not just trying to prevent an

attack but also helping to restore some degree of normalcy after a major terrorist strike. (Bergin and Smith 2006, 21)

Hence, the report specified that the ADF's role should extend beyond a purely military function. The reference to 'restoring some degree of normalcy' envisaged a longer-term policing role, directed against any signs of political instability or popular unrest, perhaps in something akin to a martial law situation.

Moreover, the 'Strategic Insight' suggested ignoring or sweeping aside Australia's 'constitutional arrangements', which partly embody the centuries-old objection to using the military on home soil. In effect, ASPI, an officially-funded military and strategic think-tank, cast doubt on the constitutional framework. The Australian Constitution contains only one mechanism for amendment – it requires a referendum, that is, a majority vote by citizens carried in a majority of states (s 128). The importance of that safeguard was underlined in 1951 when Prime Minister Robert Menzies called a referendum to override the decision in the *Communist Party* case and was defeated, despite his efforts to whip up a red-baiting anti-communist campaign in the context of the Cold War (Winterton 1992, 133–78). As discussed in Chapter 8, Menzies' proposal would have effectively permitted Australian governments to set their own limits for the use of the defence power of the Australian Constitution for political purposes during peacetime. Historically, then, the Australian people have proven resistant to expanding the power of the government and its security agencies to override basic legal and democratic rights.

The ASPI document suggested that, for political as well as technical reasons, the High Readiness Reserve (HRR), which covers the six Reserve Response Forces (RRFs), could be of assistance in establishing this new role, and in gaining public acceptance of it:

> [A]s the likelihood of ADF personnel being used to assist public order in a domestic crisis appears to increase, people who are themselves 'members of the public' most of the time, would provide a more empathetic ADF presence than members of the permanent forces. Reservists are effectively 'pre-deployed' in communities and bring a set of skills and life experience that may suit them better to domestic security roles. (Bergin and Smith 2006, 8–9)

The ASPI report canvassed overtly political calculations in advocating a further expansion and entrenchment of the ADF's internal role. It contended that the events of September 2001 and the ensuing declaration of a 'war on terror' by the Bush administration and its allies have created a political climate in which the public will support – indeed demand – the ADF's mobilisation for domestic purposes.

> Government is attracted to using the ADF because it projects strength. There is a high degree of public respect for the ADF. This image supports a public view that with Defence involved, security on the homefront is in capable hands. Decisions

> on the employment of the ADF in domestic security post-9/11 have therefore been influenced by the political necessity of demonstrating effectiveness in the face of national security threats (Bergin and Smith 2006, 15).

Presumably, the APSI report reflects a significant body of opinion among senior figures in political and military circles, where the report is likely to carry considerable weight. One author, Anthony Bergin, was the institute's research director, while co-author Brigadier Andrew Smith commanded the army's 7th Brigade. Smith served in the Iraq war and headed military task forces at the Sydney 2000 Olympics and the Melbourne 2006 Commonwealth Games. Although ASPI report stated it represented the personal views of the authors, and did not in any way express or reflect the views of the Australian government or represent the formal position of APSI, such 'Strategic Insight' reports are intended to help shape official policy.

Bergin and Smith dismissed concerns for civil liberties as 'an elite debate':

> Unlike in other countries ... history has provided little reason for the Australian population to develop an aversion to the use of Defence in the homeland. Although civil liberty watchdogs have at times raised concerns about the dangers of excessive involvement by the armed forces in domestic security, especially where it involves the use of force, this appears to be an elite debate that does not resonate with the general public. (Bergin and Smith 2006, 21)

Similar views have been expressed by others associated with the military. In a 2005 law journal article, Norman Laing, a barrister and former member of the parachute battalion 3 Royal Australian Regiment, depicted public concerns that troops could be deployed to disperse a serious civil disturbance as 'fear and paranoia' produced by 'scare-mongering' or 'misunderstanding'. Referring to the terrorist acts of September 2001 in the United States and October 2002 in Bali, he asserted:

> The attacks on both the United States and Bali provided the catalyst for the government to reshape the modern ADF. Australia now has a defence force capability that can, and will, be utilised both inwardly on Australian soil and outwardly internationally in relation to Australia's security and defence. (Laing 2005, 515)

Referring to the military call-out legislation, Laing wrote:

> With these crucial new provisions firmly in place, and given the current political climate, Australians should no longer fear the sight, or possibility, of Australian troops being deployed onto our streets – protecting our civil liberties is important, but protecting these liberties should not be used as an excuse to prevent soldiers from detaining, apprehending or even killing those who seek to undermine these freedoms we all take for granted. (Laing 2005, 522)

Both the ASPI report and Laing's article illustrate the use of the 'war on terror' as a justification for overturning long-standing limits on the internal deployment of the armed forces. They also focus on utilising fear of terrorism as a means of conditioning public opinion to accept that process. As discussed in Chapter 2, history demonstrates the readiness of governments to exploit vague and elastic phrases such as 'emergency', 'essential' and 'security', or to act without clear legal authority and, if necessary, obtain retrospective indemnity.

Civil Liberties and Human Rights

Some of the most basic civil liberties and human rights are threatened by the domestic deployment of the armed forces. Such fundamental principles as freedom of speech, association, assembly and movement, no detention without trial and freedom from arbitrary rule can be violated, pushed aside or made difficult to exercise under conditions where troops can be called out to suppress social, political or industrial discontent, or where citizens live under the intimidating shadow of possible military intervention. Genuine democracy is impossible unless all members of society are free, and feel free, to express their views, organise against the government and even seek to overturn the established order, without the fear of armed reprisal.

As reviewed in earlier chapters, it must be a matter of concern that essential doctrines established in centuries of struggle against absolutism in Britain and the United States, including civic freedom from military interference, the abolition of standing armies and civilian supremacy over any armed forces, have been substantially eroded. These historical principles were among the 'natural', 'self-evident' and 'inalienable' rights inscribed upon the banners of the English, American and French revolutions of the seventeenth and eighteenth centuries ('Life, liberty and property' in the case of England – at least as defined by John Locke; 'Life, liberty and the pursuit of happiness' in the 1776 American Declaration of Independence; 'Equality, liberty, property, security and resistance to oppression' in the 1789 French Declaration of the Rights of Man and the Citizen).

However, contemporary international human rights law provides little reliable protection against the violation of basic legal and democratic rights, including by the military. In the first place, its provisions provide numerous exemptions for alleged emergencies or dire challenges to the stability of the national state. In the Universal Declaration of Human Rights, the International Covenant on Civil and Political Rights (ICCPR), and other related instruments, such as the European Convention on Human Rights and Fundamental Freedoms and the UK *Human Rights Act 1998*, the listed civil and legal rights are mostly subject to far-reaching exemptions, including 'national security' and 'public safety' – leaving considerable leeway for draconian measures, such as the forms of detention without trial and other provisions imposed in the name of fighting the 'war on terror'.

Thus, Article 4 of the ICCPR states:

> 1. In time of public emergency which threatens the life of the nation and the existence of which is officially proclaimed, the States Parties to the present Covenant may take measures derogating from their obligations under the present Covenant to the extent strictly required by the exigencies of the situation, provided that such measures are not inconsistent with their other obligations under international law and do not involve discrimination solely on the ground of race, colour, sex, language, religion or social origin.
>
> 2. No derogation from articles 6, 7, 8 (paragraphs I and 2), 11, 15, 16 and 18 may be made under this provision.

These exceptions to derogation relate to killing, torture, slavery, trial by law and freedom of religion. Neither they, nor the prohibition against discrimination, offer any guarantee of protection against the trampling over of a broader range of human rights, or against the mobilisation of the military itself.

Under the European Convention on Human Rights and Fundamental Freedoms even the right to life is carefully circumscribed to permit killing by state forces in order to make arrests, prevent escapes from detention and quell riots and insurrections (Article 2). The rights of non-citizens (so-called 'aliens') are treated with particular contempt – they can be detained without trial, denied political rights and forcibly deported (Articles 5 and 16). Governments can derogate from most obligations under the European Convention 'in time of war or other public emergency threatening the life of the nation' (Article 15).

Particularly since the declaration of the 'war on terror', courts have tended to give executive governments considerable scope to use these provisions. In 2004, the English House of Lords, with Lord Hoffman dissenting, accepted that indefinite detention without trial of foreign national terrorist suspects, unable to be prosecuted or deported, could be permissible under the 'public emergency' clause in the context of the 9/11 attacks in the United States (*A and others v Secretary of State for the Home Department* [2004] UKHL 56). However, the majority ultimately declared the provisions to be discriminatory and disproportionate to the exigencies of the public emergency.

In his controversial dissent on the threshold issue of whether the threat of terrorism constituted a 'public emergency threatening the life of the nation', Lord Hoffman stated:

> The real threat to the life of the nation, in the sense of a people living in accordance with its traditional laws and political values, comes not from terrorism but from laws such as these. ([2004] UKHL 56, [94–7])

Nonetheless, the eight-to-one majority view was that the courts had to defer heavily to the views of the executive government. In the words of Baroness Hale:

> Assessing the strength of a general threat to the life of the nation is, or should be, within the expertise of the Government and its advisers … If a Government were to declare a public emergency where patently there was no such thing, it would be the duty of the court to say so. But here we are considering the immediate aftermath of the unforgettable events of 11 September 2001. The attacks launched on the United States on that date were clearly intended to threaten the life of the nation. ([2004] UKHL 56, [226])

Because the nation-state system still prevails globally, international law is not normally legally binding domestically unless it is incorporated into national legislation. Moreover, with some notable exceptions, such as the US Constitution's Bill of Rights, domestic human rights measures are not constitutionally entrenched, and can therefore be abridged, amended or repealed by legislatures. Generally, the provisions merely require courts to interpret all legislation, where possible, consistently with enumerated human rights, generally drawn from the International Covenant on Civil and Political Rights. If the legislation under consideration cannot be interpreted consistently with a human right, the court may only declare that an incompatibility exists, and report the issue to the legislature. Such a declaration does not affect the validity of the legislation in question.

Furthermore, under provisions like the UK *Human Rights Act*, the courts are instructed to permit reasonable limits to human rights if the limit is 'demonstrably justified in a free and democratic society'. This proviso, which English House of Lords judges have described as one of proportionality, leaves considerable scope for governments to brush aside or whittle down human rights. For example, in *Spinks v SSHD* ([2005] EWCA Civ 275), the English Court of Appeal rejected a claim by a prisoner with terminal cancer that his detention involved inhuman and degrading treatment. The court said the issue depended on the degree of danger posed by the prisoner.

Threats to Civilian Rule?

In a parliamentary democracy it is generally assumed that the final authority rests with civilian rule, secured by parliamentary control over the military budget. However, if a government calls out the military for support, the balance of power can begin to shift, particularly if the civil authorities become to any degree dependent upon, or politically indebted to, the armed forces. As noted by Jeffery:

> [W]hen the army is called in actively to support the government, both the responsibility and, perhaps more significantly, the initiative for action may shift from civilians to soldiers themselves. Between the extremes of, for example, troops assisting the police on a 'once and for all basis', meeting just one disturbance, and the full introduction of martial law and military rule, there are

> a number of stages during which the precise distribution of civil and military power is not at all clear. (Jeffery 1985, 57)

Even within the British-derived custom that the civilian government decides when and where military forces are to be deployed, and may give political direction to the armed forces, but has no right to issue operational directives, there is potential for disagreements and conflicts over the use of force. Jeffery pointed out that, although rare, the issue of the military disobeying civilian orders has arisen on occasions in Britain. One was the 1914 Curragh incident, when a number of officers resigned rather than accept orders that they thought sought to coerce Ulster Unionists into a united Ireland. Another was the 1918–22 breakdown in relations between Prime Minister Lloyd George and army chief, Sir Henry Wilson, who was outraged by the government's reluctance to take coercive measures against striking workers and Irish nationalists. And in 1919, the Army Council objected to cabinet plans to dismiss General Dyer after the Amritsar massacre (Jeffery 1985, 57–9).

Moreover, as Jeffery also observed, the use of troops to break strikes or keep order during industrial disputes 'raises the possibility that the army might be employed explicitly as an instrument of class conflict' (Jeffery 1985, 59). One could go further and suggest that, in the final analysis, the armed forces constitute the ultimate instrument of force for protecting the property and interests of the present ruling class and bolstering its power against threats posed by the industrial and political struggles that erupt in the working class. In so-called 'normal' times, that instrument is not required, or is kept in reserve, but in periods of turmoil, such as those ignited by economic catastrophe or war, the military may be called into the frontline. In those periods, civilian and democratic forms of rule can come under acute strain, and may even be dispensed with.

Furthermore, as mentioned in Chapter 3, in the United States, the pre-eminent economic power and supposed contemporary model of democracy, the 'military-industrial complex' has grown massively in size and economic influence since President Eisenhower warned of its emergence in 1961. Kohn, a military historian, and Bacevich, a former officer, have demonstrated that, while the United States may not have experienced a *coup d'état*, the military has grown in influence to the point of being able to impose its own perspective on many policies and decisions.

These developments have not ended with the Clinton and Bush administrations of 1993 to 2009. President Obama appointed three recently retired four-star military officers to top government positions – as National Security Adviser, Secretary for Veterans Affairs and Director of National Intelligence – believed to be the strongest representation of former military commanders in a Democratic Party administration. Shortly after the Obama administration was sworn in, the US commander in Iraq dismissed the President's campaign pledge to withdraw all US combat troops within 16 months, announcing that the speed and level of troop withdrawals would be determined by the military according to its assessment of the security situation on the ground in Iraq (Grey 2009).

Canada and Australia, traditionally regarded as less militarist and more stable societies, are not exempt from these factors. In 1975, when the Governor-General dismissed the elected Whitlam government in Australia, the vice-regal representative conducted his own meetings with defence officials and may have been prepared to invoke his formal constitutional authority as Commander-in-Chief of the armed forces to deal with resistance by the ousted government or large-scale protests and strikes against the dismissal. And during 2008 there was a reminder of the 'reserve powers' of the vice-regal post in Canada when the Governor-General granted Prime Minster Stephen Harper his request to suspend parliament for more than a month to avoid almost certain defeat in a parliamentary vote of no-confidence over the government's reaction to the economic crisis (Gillies 2008).

Finally, the lessons of what happened in Italy, Germany and Japan in the inter-war years must be recalled. In all three countries, albeit in somewhat different forms, a combination of economic tensions and acute political conflicts produced a turn by the old establishment and authorities to rely upon military and para-military methods of rule. The integration of the armed forces and their generals into the civilian government apparatuses was central to the establishment of dictatorial forms of rule.

Social, Economic and Political Tensions

Today's utilisation of alleged terrorist threats to erode traditional civil liberties and argue for greater domestic use of the military raises disturbing historical experiences. Adolf Hitler cited the 1933 Reichstag Fire, which the Nazis falsely attributed to communists, as the reason for insisting that the parliament agree to rule by decree (Kershaw 1998, 456–60). The morning after the fire, Hitler's cabinet adopted the emergency decree, 'For the Protection of the People and State'. In the words of historian Ian Kershaw:

> With one brief paragraph, the personal liberties enshrined in the Weimar Constitution – including freedom of speech, of association and of the press, and privacy of postal and telephone communications – were suspended indefinitely … The hastily constructed emergency decree amounted to the charter of the Third Reich. (Kershaw 1998, 459)

A month later, on 23 March 1933 the Nazi-controlled Reichstag passed 'enabling' legislation declaring that the executive had the power to make laws. 'The Act to Relieve the Distress of the People and the Reich' cemented dictatorial power in Germany under Hitler. It essentially transformed into legislation legal opinions previously prepared by the leading Nazi jurist Carl Schmitt. These authorised executive rule because of the 'state of exception' in Germany, namely its economic and political crisis and the alleged threat of revolution. Schmitt set out a 'legal defence' of the enabling legislation in the *Deutsche Juristen Zeitung*, in which he opined that the executive prerogative was unlimited at a time of national crisis (Neumann 1942; Meier 1988; Muller 2003).

This is not to say that contemporary Western societies face the imminent danger of fascist dictatorship. Nevertheless, the very fact that governments and security authorities are citing 'national security' threats, especially of indefinite duration, as the justification for suspending or overturning constitutional norms and basic legal rights, and that calls are being made for the military to embrace a 'core' function of domestic security, are causes for grave concern. Any attempt to explain this trend as a temporary aberration in order to defeat 'terrorism' also fails to address the issue as to why terrorism has become such an allegedly all-pervasive threat. Although exploring the roots of disaffected movements engaged in violent attacks is beyond the scope of this book, it is suggested that they lie, ultimately, in deepening global inequality and the increasingly aggressive military activities of the major powers themselves, notably the United States (Zinn 2002).

Moreover, the potential for widespread social unrest in the years ahead has been demonstrated by the meltdown of the global financial and share markets that began with the sub-prime crisis in the United States in mid-2007. The fallout quickly triggered the collapse of some of the world's largest banks and financial institutions, and then spread to the 'real' economy, causing rising unemployment, house repossessions and cuts to living standards in many countries. As a result, by the end of 2008, substantial political turmoil had already erupted in a number of countries, including Iceland, Greece and Canada.

By early 2009, concerns were being widely expressed about the depth and seriousness of the economic crisis and its implications for social and political stability. In its 2009 Global Employment Trends report, the International Labour Organization (ILO) stated:

> In 2008, global financial markets experienced their worst crisis since the 1930s. The crisis was triggered by the collapse of the housing bubble in the United States, although the actual causes go deeper. In the United States and other developed countries there were credit excesses in residential mortgages, commercial mortgages, credit cards, auto loans and student loans. And there were excesses in the securitized products that converted these debts into toxic financial derivatives; in financing for leveraged buyouts and in the dangerous credit default swap market. During the last ten years large global imbalances between deficit and surplus countries have emerged. The high commodity and energy prices, the sub-prime crisis, contraction of the real estate market in many developed countries, and the severe global financial services shock, which has triggered a massive tightening in lending have had a significant impact on most sectors of the economy and on employment. This was evident through an unusually sharp increase in layoffs. Investment, production and consumption all declined through diminishing investor and consumer confidence as credit markets froze and millions of people have been losing their jobs. The decline of

> many economies has raised growing concern that social tensions may begin to rise. (International Labour Organization 2009, 6)

The ILO forecast that as many as 51 million workers could be laid off during 2009, potentially pushing the global unemployment rate to 7.1 per cent (up from 5.7 per cent in 2007). According to this projection, unemployment in the developed economies would average 7.9 per cent, while the ILO concluded that 'in some of the developing economies the unemployment rate would reach unprecedented levels'. The ILO forecast that the number of 'working poor' (earning less than $US2 a day) could rise to 1.4 billion, or 45 per cent of the world's employed. Up to 20 per cent of those living marginally above the poverty line could fall back into extreme poverty. And the proportion of people in 'vulnerable employment' – either contributing family workers or own-account workers who are less likely to benefit from safety nets that guard against loss of incomes during economic hardship – 'could rise considerably in the worst case scenario to reach a level of 53 per cent of the employed population' (International Labour Organization 2009, 15–20).

Unemployment was not the only source of likely social discontent. The collapse of home prices and retirement funds destroyed the net wealth of millions of heavily-indebted families who had come to rely on home equity to finance basic necessities like food, health care and education. By early 2009, the housing price decline in the United States since its peak was already more than twice that registered during the Great Depression. A December 2008 report by J.P. Morgan gave one indication of the impact of this crash on the conditions of the American people:

> The balance sheet of the American household has recently experienced a record destruction of wealth … A huge drop in equity prices (including 401(k) retirement savings), combined with the ongoing decline in house prices has undone most of the gains in wealth that had accumulated over the previous few years. In the third quarter alone household wealth declined $2.8 trillion, or 4.7 percent. Since peaking in the third quarter of last year, $7.1 trillion of wealth has been destroyed, off 11.1 percent from its peak. (US Federal Reserve 2009)

The post-2007 crash also undermined faith in the market, raising political and ideological issues. Politicians, businessmen, professional economists and media commentators who had insisted that all economic problems were best left to the market, pleaded, amid the backdrop of failing banks, for gargantuan government bailouts to prop up their institutions. It was widely noted in the media that the US and other governments offered 'socialism for the rich', while insisting on capitalism for everyone else. In reality, government policy had nothing to do with socialism. All of the measures taken were aimed at securing the interests of the financial and corporate elites. But the massive state intervention in the economy dealt blows to the intellectual legitimacy and prestige of the private profit system.

The economic breakdown came on top of several decades in which, around the world, the jobs, wages, conditions and welfare entitlements of working people were driven down in order to satisfy the demands of global corporations and wealthy investors for lower tax rates, cheaper labour and greater profits. Through downsizing, outsourcing and privatisation, full-time, permanent jobs were replaced increasingly by insecure, temporary and part-time employment. Driven by global competition for markets and profits, transnational corporations had demanded, as the price for their investment, continual cutbacks to working-class wages and basic rights (United Nations 2005).

Among the results was a wide gulf between the rich and the poor. In the United States, the 'free-market' model, as an example, there was a stark concentration of wealth from the late 1970s. In 1960, the average CEO salary at a Fortune 100 company was 41 times that of an average factory worker. Such a disparity was already at odds with the rationale of democracy, which is said to provide each member of society with equal political power. But by 1990, CEO pay had risen to 85 times that of an average worker. By 1996, it was 209 times, and by 2000 it was 531 times (North 2004, 83–4).

Results for other countries are not so marked but they are heading in the same direction, even in the countries traditionally regarded as relatively egalitarian. A paper released in 2006 by the Australian National University's Centre for Economic Policy Research, *The Distribution of Top Incomes in Australia*, concluded that in 1992, a typical CEO in Australia received 27 times the wage of an average worker. By 2002, this had risen to 98 times. The income share of the top 1 per cent of the population had increased from under 5 per cent in 1980 to 9 per cent in 2002 (Atkinson and Leigh 2006, 7–9).

These inequalities, exacerbated by the post-2007 global economic meltdown, are highly likely to generate deep disaffection and unrest, which could see resort to armed force by the political establishment. As noted in the Introduction, police and intelligence officials have identified economic and political instability as a primary threat to 'national security'.

Marxist Insights

It can be argued that these developments confirm the Marxist view of the state (Head 2007). Marx and Engels famously characterised the capitalist state as a 'committee for managing the common affairs of the whole bourgeoisie' (Marx and Engels 1973, 110–11). Engels described the emergence, at the heart of the state, of bodies of 'armed men' alongside 'material adjuncts, prisons and institutions of coercion' (Engels 1977, 167). He warned that this apparatus of force grew stronger as class antagonisms within the state became more acute and as tensions grew between rival international powers. Another Marxist, Lenin, observed that behind the democratic façade of modern capitalist states, with their formal undertakings to uphold freedom of assembly, freedom of the press and 'equality of all citizens before the law', there existed provisions allowing for all these guarantees to be swept aside to suppress threats from below during periods of crisis:

> There is not a single state, however democratic, which has no loopholes or reservations in its constitution guaranteeing the bourgeois the possibility of dispatching troops against the workers, of proclaiming martial law, and so forth, in case of a 'violation of public order,' and actually in case the exploited class 'violates' its position of slavery and tries to behave in a non-slavish manner. (Tucker 1975, 468)

It can be argued also that Marxist theory offers important insights into the processes and tendencies, at work in periods of economic crisis. Perhaps the best-known early Soviet jurist, Evgeny Pashukanis, contended that the capitalist state was bound up with the principle of commodity exchange, and hence the protection of dominant private interests. These interests required, as far as possible, limits on the power of the state, and an avoidance of dictatorial methods that could threaten personal and property rights (Pashukanis 1978, 149). However, in times of crisis, particularly when capitalist interests as a whole were threatened from below, the ideal of the constitutional state would be dispensed with:

> For the bourgeoisie has never, in favour of purity of theory, lost sight of the fact that class society is not only a market where autonomous owners of commodities meet, but is at the same time the battlefield of a bitter class war, where the machinery of state represents a very powerful weapon … The more the hegemony of the bourgeoisie was shattered, the more compromising these corrections became, the more quickly the 'constitutional state' was transformed into a disembodied shadow, until finally the extraordinary sharpening of the class struggle forced the bourgeoisie to discard the mask of the constitutional state altogether, revealing the nature of state power as the organised power of one class over the other. (Pashukanis 1978, 149–50)

Pashukanis noted that in the face of exceptional revolutionary upheaval, the impersonal nature of public power could give way to the private or semi-private wielding of power, via the mobilisation of fascist and other violent militias.

> In our times of heightened revolutionary struggle, we can observe how the official machinery of the bourgeois state retires into the background as compared with the volunteer corps of the fascists and others. This further substantiates the fact that, when the balance of society is upset, it seeks salvation not in the creation of a power standing above society, but in the maximal harnessing of all forces of the classes in conflict (Pashukanis 1978, 139, fn 10).

These observations were highly pertinent in the 1920s and 1930s, when fascist thugs, and later stormtroopers, were let loose in Italy and Germany, and totalitarian forms of rule emerged in other major countries, such as Spain and Japan. But the analysis seems to remain relevant today (Head 2007, 231–52).

Conclusion

There are many reasons to be concerned about the expansion of military powers. In most cases, the legislative provisions or other instruments have a wide, ill-defined scope, leaving broad discretions in the hands of government ministers and military officers. In Australia, where the most complete codification of domestic military powers has been attempted, the enlarged scope of the military call-out power, covering 'critical infrastructure' and 'acts of violence', could allow domestic military deployments to become much more common. Military personnel will have unprecedented powers, such as to shoot down passenger aircraft, use lethal force, interrogate civilians and seize documents. The exercise of these powers will be protected by legal immunities, including a 'superior orders' defence. Secrecy surrounds the Rules of Engagement that will apply. At the same time, vague common law or prerogative powers remain in the hands of the executive.

Moreover, in most jurisdictions, these measures accompany the growth of paramilitary policing. They are part of a more general challenge to civil liberties and human rights in the context of the 'war on terror' and the historical record demonstrates that such anti-terrorism powers can be misused for political and industrial purposes. Finally, the provisions have been advanced amid a broader, creeping militarisation of official policy, designed to accustom ordinary people to the sight of troops on the streets. The global dimensions of this trend further suggests that preparations are being made to deal with domestic unrest as social and international tensions rise. Hopefully, this book will contribute to the development of an informed and vigilant response to these tendencies.

Bibliography

ACLU (2008), 'ACLU Demands Information on Military Deployment within US Borders', media release, 21 October 2008, http://www.aclu.org/safefree/general/37274prs20081021.html (accessed 12 May 2009).

Adelaide, D. (2002), 'G-8 Security Operation: The Stifling and Criminalizing of Dissent', *World Socialist Web Site*, 27 June 2002, http://www.wsws.org/articles/2002/jun2002/g8-j27.shtml (accessed 12 May 2009).

Agamben, G. (2005), *State of Exception* (Chicago, IL: University of Chicago Press).

Allinson, G. (2004), *Japan's Postwar History* (Ithaca, NY: Cornell University Press).

Amnesty International (2002), 'Amnesty International's Concerns Regarding Post September 11 Detentions in the USA', March 2002.

Andrews, E. (1995), 'Civil Power, Aid to the (ACP)', in Dennis et al.

Arens, M. (2008), 'Italian Government Imposes National State of Emergency', *World Socialist Web Site*, 6 August 2008, http://www.wsws.org/articles/2008/aug2008/ital-a06.shtml (accessed 8 August 2008).

Atkinson, A. and Leigh, A. (2006), *The Distribution of Top Incomes in Australia* (Canberra: Australian National University, Centre for Economic Police Research).

Australian (1978), 14 February 1978, 1.

Australian Labor Party (2007), media statement, 13 November 2007, http://www.alp.org.au/media/1107/msdeffahsida130.php (accessed 20 March 2008).

Australian Law Journal (1978), 'Current Topics: Legal and Constitutional Problems of Protective Security Arrangements in Australia', 52 *Australian Law Journal* 296.

Australian Law Journal (1984), 'Current Topics: Scope and Content of Concept of "National Security"', 58 *Australian Law Journal* 67.

Babington, A. (1990), *Military Intervention in Britain: From the Gordon Riots to the Gibraltar Incident* (London: Routledge).

Bacevich, A. (2002), *American Empire: The Realities and Consequences of US Diplomacy* (Cambridge, MA: Harvard University Press).

Bacevich, A. et al. (2006), 'American Coup d'Etat: Military Thinkers Discuss the Unthinkable', *Harper's Magazine*, April 2006.

Banks, W. (2005), 'Mold, Mildew and the Military Role in Disaster Response', *Jurist*, 17 October 2005.

Barnes, J. (2008), 'Military To Be on High Alert for Inauguration', *Los Angeles Times*, 18 December 2008.

Bartlett, T. and Jeffrey, K. (eds) (1996), *A Military History of Ireland* (Cambridge: Cambridge University Press).

Basic Law of the Federal Republic of Germany (1949), http://www.iuscomp.org/gla/statutes/GG.htm (accessed 17 December 2008).

Bassiouni, M. (ed.) (1971), *The Law of Dissent and Riots* (Springfield, IL: Charles C. Thomas).

Bayne, P. (1991), 'Policy Guidelines and the Law: Some Intersections', 65 *Australian Law Journal* 607.

Beddie, B. and Moss, S. (1982), *Some Aspects of Aid to the Civil Power in Australia*, Occasional Monograph No. 2 (Sydney: University of New South Wales, Department of Government).

Bell, J.B. (1993), *The Irish Troubles: A Generation of Violence 1967–1992* (New York: St. Martin's Press).

Bergin, A. and Smith, A. (2006), *Australian Domestic Security: The Role of Defence* (Canberra: Australian Strategic Policy Institute).

Bills, S. (1988), *Kent State/May 4: Echoes through a Decade* (Kent, OH: Kent State University Press).

Blackshield, A. (1978), 'The Siege of Bowral: The Legal Issues', 4 *Pacific Defence Reporter*.

Blackstone, W. (2001), *Commentaries on the Laws of England*, ed. W. Morrison (London: Routledge-Cavendish).

Bloody Sunday Inquiry (n.d), http://www.bloody-sunday-inquiry.org.uk/ (accessed 17 June 2008).

Blum, W. (2002), *Rogue State: A Guide to the World's Only Superpower* (Monroe, ME: Common Courage Press).

Bramall, E. (1985), 'The Place of the British Army in Public Order', in Rowe and Whelan (eds).

Brett, P. and Waller, P. (1983), *Brett and Waller's Criminal Law: Text and Cases* (Sydney: Butterworths).

Brinkerhoff, J. (2002), 'The Posse Comitatus Act and Homeland Security', *Journal of Homeland Security*, February 2002.

Bronitt, S. and Stephens, D. (2007), '"Flying under the Radar": The Use of Lethal Force against Hijacked Aircraft: Recent Australian Developments', 7 *Oxford University Commonwealth Law Journal* 265.

Brown, B. (2000), Commonwealth of Australia, *Parliamentary Debates*, Senate, 6 September 2000.

Burghardt, T. (ed.) (2002), *Police State America: US Military 'Civil Disturbance' Planning* (Toronto: Arm The Spirit).

Cahill, D. and Cahill, R. (2005), 'Civilian Responses to Peace-Time Military Occupation: The 1978 Bowral Call-out and its Implications for the "War on Terrorism"', History Cooperative, Australian Society for the Study of Labour History Conference Proceedings (Sydney: Australian Society for the Study of Labour History), http://www.historycooperative.org/proceedings/asslh/cahill.html (accessed 18 February 2008).

Cain, F. (1994), *ASIO: An Unofficial History* (Melbourne: Spectrum).
CAIN Web Service (n.d), 'Background Information on Northern Ireland Society: Security', http://cain.ulst.ac.uk/ni/security.htm#06 (accessed 23 July 2008).
Calder, G. (2008), 'Routing a Rebellion or Crushing a Crime Wave? Proclaiming Martial Law and a Call-to-Arms in Van Diemen's Land, 1828–1830', 12 *Legal History* 127.
Campbell, B. (2002), *The SA Generals and the Rise of Nazism* (Lexington, KY: University of Kentucky Press).
Canada Command and US Northern Command (2008), Canada-US Civil Assistance Plan (CAP) (Ottawa: Canada Command and United States Northern Command), http://www.northcom.mil/News/2008/CAP%20-%20For%20Public%20Posting%20-%2028%20May%2008.pdf (accessed 12 May 2009).
Capua, J.V. (1977), 'The Early History of Martial Law in England from the Fourteenth Century to the Petition of Right', [1977] *Cambridge Law Journal* 152.
Caputo, P. (2005), *13 Seconds: A Look Back at the Kent State Shootings* (New York: Chamberlain Bros).
Cavallaro, G. (2008), 'Brigade Homeland Tours Start Oct. 1', *Army Times*, 8 September 2008.
CBC and Gillmor, D. (2001), *Canada: A People's History* (Toronto: McClelland & Stewart).
CCOE (2001), Civil-Military Co-operation Centre of Excellence, http://www.cimic-coe.org/ (accessed 20 March 2008).
Chalmers, J. (2004), *The Sorrows of Empire: Militarism, Secrecy, and the End of the Republic* (New York: Metropolitan Books).
Clark, D. (2007), *Principles of Australian Public Law*, 2nd edition (Sydney: LexisNexis Butterworths).
Cobbett, W. (ed.) (1814), *The Parliamentary History of England* (London: Bagshaw), 688–98.
Commission of Inquiry into the Deployment of Canadian Forces to Somalia (1997), *Dishonoured Legacy: The Lessons of the Somalia Affair* (Ottawa: Public Works and Government Services).
Coxsedge, J., Caldicutt, K. and Harant, G. (1982), *Rooted in Secrecy: The Clandestine Involvement in Australian Politics* (Melbourne: Committee for the Abolition of Political Police).
De Smith, S.A. (1981), *Constitutional and Administrative Law*, 4th edition (London: Penguin/Longmans).
Dennis, P. (1981), 'The Territorial Army in Aid of the Civil Power in Britain, 1919–1926', *Journal of Contemporary History* 16, 705–24.
Dennis, P., Grey, J., Morris, E. and Prior, R. (1995), *The Oxford Companion to Australian Military History* (Melbourne: Oxford University Press).
Department of Defence, Australia (2004), 'Aid to the Civil Power', http://www.defence.gov.au/army/AHU/HISTORY/aid_to_the_civil_power.htm (accessed 8 March 2008).

Department of Defence, Australia (2008), 'Gap Year Marches On', Defence media release, 28 March 2008, http://www.defence.gov.au/media/DepartmentalTpl.cfm?CurrentId=7532 (accessed 31 March 2008).

Department of Defence, Australia (2008b), 'Operation Deluge', http://defence.gov.au/opdeluge/facts.htm (accessed 31 March 2008).

Department of Defence, Australia (2008c), 'Operation Outreach', http://www.defence.gov.au/opoutreach/default.htm (accessed 31 March 2008).

Department of Defence, Australia (2008d), 'Operation Testament', http://www.defence.gov.au/optestament/index.htm (accessed 20 March 2008).

Department of National Defence, Canada (2006) Defence Policy Statement, http://www.forces.gc.ca/site/reports/dps/index_e.asp (accessed 20 June 2008).

Department of National Defence, Canada (2008), Canada First Defence Strategy 2008.

Department of National Defence, Canada (n.d.) Joint Task Force Two, http://www.jtf2.forces.gc.ca/index-eng.asp (accessed 18 August 2008).

Department of National Defence, Canada, Defence Planning and Management (2004), 'Scenario 7: Aid of the Civil Power', http://www.vcds.forces.gc.ca/dgsp/pubs/rep-pub/dda/scen/scen-7_e.asp (accessed 15 August 2008).

Department of the House of Representatives, Joint Standing Committee on Foreign Affairs, Defence and Trade (2001–2002), *Review of the Defence Annual Report 2001–2002* (Canberra: Joint Standing Committee on Foreign Affairs, Defence and Trade), http://www.aph.gov.au/House/committee/jfadt/defence_report2001-2002/d_annualreport/chapter2.pdf (accessed 28 March 2008).

Department of the Senate, Senate Legal and Constitutional Affairs Committee (2005), *Provisions of the Anti-Terrorism Bill (No. 2) 2005* (Canberra: Department of the Senate, Parliament House), http://www.aph.gov.au/senate/committee/legcon_ctte/terrorism/report/index.htm (accessed 1 December 2005).

Department of the Senate, Senate Legal and Constitutional Affairs Committee (2006), *Defence Legislation Amendment (Aid to Civilian Authorities) Bill 2005* (Canberra: Department of the Senate, Parliament House).

Dewar, M. (1997), *The British Army in Northern Ireland* (London: Arms and Armour Press).

Dicey, A. (2005), *Introduction to the Study of the Law of the Constitution* (Boston, MA: Adamant Media Corporation).

Dinmore, G. (2008), 'Italy Deploys Troops to Fight Urban Crime', *Financial Times*, 4 August 2008, http://www.ft.com/cms/s/0/4141be22-6238-11dd-9ff9-000077b07658.html (accessed 8 August 2008).

Dinmore, G. and Bianchi, B. (2009), 'Tensions Rise over Italy's Gypsy Migrants', *Financial Times*, 27 January 2009.

Dorrill, S. and Ramsay, R. (1992), *Smear! Wilson and the Secret State* (London: Harper Collins).

Doyle, C. (2000), *The Posse Comitatus Act and Related Matters: The Use of the Military to Execute Civilian Law*, CRS Report for Congress, 1 June 2000 (Washington, DC: Congressional Research Service).

Economist (2008), 'The Thin Green Line, *The Economist*, 7 August 2008, http://www.economist.com/world/europe/displaystory.cfm?story_id=11893683 (accessed at 8 August 2008).

Ehling, M. (2008), 'US Military Will Have Role in RNC Security', *Twin Cities Daily Planet*, 29 June 2008.

Emergencies Act, R.S., 1985, c. 22.

Engdahl, D. (1971), 'Soldiers, Riots and Revolution: The Law and History of Military Troops in Civil Disorders', 57 *Iowa Law Review* 1.

Engdahl, D. (1985), 'Foundations for Military Intervention in the United States', in Rowe and Whelan (eds).

Engels, F. (1977), *The Origin of the Family, Private Property and the State* (Moscow: Progress Publishers).

Fackler, M. (2008), 'A Lockdown on Hokkaido as Police Outnumber Summit Protesters', *New York Times*, 9 July 2008, http://www.highbeam.com/doc/1P1-154066586.html (accessed 13 May 2009).

Farrer, W. and Brownbill, J. (2003), 'The City and Parish of Manchester: Introduction', *The Victoria History of the County of Lancaster: Lancashire, Vol. 4* (University of London and History of Parliament Trust, 2003–2006 [1911]).

Forcese, C. (2008), *National Security Law: Canadian Practice in International Perspective* (Toronto: Irwin Law).

Fox News (2008), 'Italy to Deploy Troops after Slaying of Immigrants', Foxnews.com, 23 September 2008, http://www.foxnews.com/story/0,2933,426343,00.html (accessed 12 May 2009).

Freier, N. (2008), *Known Unknowns: Unconventional 'Strategic Shocks' in Defense Strategy Development* (Washington, DC: US War College Strategic Studies Institute), http://www.strategicstudiesinstitute.army.mil/pdffiles/PUB890.pdf (accessed 16 February 2009).

Frueh, D. (2008), 'Australia Group Seeks ICC War Crimes Charges against Ex-PM for Iraq Deployment', *Jurist*, 2 June 2008, http://jurist.law.pitt.edu/paperchase/2008/06/australia-group-seeks-icc-war-crimes.php (accessed 31 August 2008).

Fudge, J. and Tucker, E. (2004), *Labour Before the Law: The Regulation of Workers' Collective Action in Canada, 1900–1948* (Toronto: University of Toronto Press).

Fulbrook, M. (2006), *A Concise History of Germany* (Cambridge: Cambridge University Press).

Garraway, C. (1999), 'Superior Orders and the International Criminal Court: Justice Delivered or Justice Denied', *International Review of the Red Cross* 836, 785–94.

Geraghty, T. (1998), *The Irish War* (London: HarperCollins).

German Constitutional Court (1978), Decision B VerfGE 49, 24 (53).

German Constitutional Court (2006), Decision 1 BvR 357/05. (See the Federal Constitutional Court press release, 'Authorisation to Shoot Down

Aircraft in the Aviation Security Act Void', 15 February 2006, http://www.bundesverfassungsgericht.de/en/press/bvg06-011en.html [accessed 18 May 2006]. No English language translation of the entire judgment is available. The German original can be read at http://www.bundesverfassungsgericht.de/entscheidungen/rs20060215_1bvr035705 [accessed 18 May 2006].)

Gillies, R. (2008), 'Analysis: Quiet Canada Mired in Unexpected Chaos', Associated Press, 8 December 2008.

Gooch, J. (2007), *Mussolini and His Generals: The Armed Forces and Fascist Foreign Policy, 1922–1940* (Cambridge: Cambridge University Press).

Goodman, A. (2008), 'Invasion of the Sea-Smurfs', *Democracy Now!*, 2 October 2008.

Gordon, B. (2003), 'Explanations of Japan's Imperialistic Expansion, 1894–1910', http://wgordon.web.wesleyan.edu/papers/imperialism.htm (accessed 22 August 2008).

Grabosky, P. (1989), *Wayward Governance: Illegality and its Control in the Public Sector* (Canberra: Australian Institute of Criminology).

Graham, B. (2005), 'War Plans Drafted to Counter Terror Attacks in US: Domestic Effort is Big Shift for Military', *Washington Post*, 8 August 2005.

Greer, S. (1983), 'Military Intervention in Civil Disturbances: The Legal Basis Reconsidered', [1983] *Public Law* 573.

Grey, B. (2001), '*New York Times* Documents Military Role in Theft of 2000 Election', *World Socialist Web Site*, 19 July 2001, http://www.wsws.org/articles/2001/jul2001/vote-j19.shtml (accessed 12 May 2009).

Grey, B. (2009), 'Obama Names Third Republican to Cabinet: A Further Bow to the Right', *World Socialist Web Site*, 4 February 2009, http://www.wsws.org/articles/2009/feb2009/obam-f04.shtml (accessed 9 February 2009).

Guardian (2005), 'Pentagon Prepares for Homeland Security Role', *The Guardian*, 8 August 2005, http://www.guardian.co.uk/usa/story/0,12271,1545109,00.html (accessed 12 January 2006).

Guerin, D. (1973), *Fascism and Big Business* (New York: Monad Press).

Hague, W. (2007), 'The Seal of Approval', *Guardian*, 15 May 2007, http://www.guardian.co.uk/commentisfree/2007/may/15/thesealofapproval (accessed 14 January 2008).

Hailsham, Lord (ed.) (1973), *Halsbury's Laws of England*, 4th edition (London: LexisNexis Butterworths).

Hale, M. (2000), *The History and Analysis of the Common Law of England* (Union, NJ: Law Book Exchange).

Hamill, D. (1986), *Pig in the Middle: The Army in Northern Ireland 1969–1985* (London: Methuen).

Hammond, M. (1997), 'The Posse Comitatus Act: A Principle in Need of Renewal', 75 *Washington University Law Quarterly* 953.

Hancock, N. (2002), *Terrorism and the Law in Australia: Supporting Materials*, Research Paper No. 13, 2001–2002 (Canberra: Department of Parliamentary Library).

Hancock, N. (2002b), *Terrorism and the Law in Australia: Legislation, Commentary and Constraints*, Research Paper No. 12, 2001–2002 (Canberra: Department of Parliamentary Library).

Harman, C. (1982), *The Lost Revolution: Germany 1918 to 1923* (London: Bookmarks).

Harman, C. (1984), *Explaining The Crisis* (London: Bookmarks).

Harman, C. (2008), *A People's History of the World* (London: Verso).

Haslip, S. (2002), 'A Critical Consideration of the Use of the Aid to Civil Power Provision against Aboriginal Peoples in the Light of the Promises of Protection Made to Aboriginal Peoples in Canada', CDA-CDAI Symposium, 2002, http://www.cda-cdai.ca/symposia/2002/haslip.htm (accessed 15 August 2008).

Hawley, C. (2008), 'Domestic Military Deployment Remains Taboo in Germany', *Spiegel OnLine*, 20 October 2008, http://www.spiegel.de/international/germany/0,1518,druck-585276,00.html (accessed 12 November 2008).

Head, M. (2001), 'The Military Call-Out Legislation: Some Legal and Constitutional Questions', 29 *Federal Law Review* 273–94.

Head, M. (2002), 'The High Court and the *Tampa* Refugees', 11 *Griffith Law Review* 23–33.

Head, M. (2002b), 'Counter-Terrorism Laws: A Threat to Political Freedom, Civil Liberties and Constitutional Rights', 26 *Melbourne University Law Review* 666–89.

Head, M. (2004), 'Another Threat to Democratic Rights: ASIO Detentions Cloaked in Secrecy', 29 *Alternative Law Journa*l 127.

Head, M. (2004b), 'ASIO, Secrecy and Lack of Accountability', 11 *Murdoch University Electronic Journal of Law*.

Head, M. (2005), 'Calling Out the Troops: Disturbing Trends and Unanswered Questions', 28 *University of New South Wales Law Journal*, 484–92.

Head, M. (2005b), Editorial: 'Detention and the Anti-Terrorism Legislation', 9 *University of Western Sydney Law Review* 1.

Head, M. (2007), *Evgeny Pashukanis: A Critical Reappraisal* (London: Routledge-Cavendish).

Head, M. (2008), 'Thirty Years since Sydney's Hilton Hotel Bombing: Unanswered Questions', 12 *Legal History* 241–58.

Hennessy, P. (1985), 'Whitehall Contingency Planning for Industrial Disputes', in Rowe and Whelan (eds).

Herald (2008), 'RAF Drones To Be Used for 2012 Olympics Security', *The Herald*, 9 January 2008.

Heron, C. (1998), *The Workers' Revolt in Canada, 1917–1925* (Toronto: University of Toronto Press).

Hersh, S. (2004), *Chain of Command: The Road from 9/11 to Abu Ghraib* (New York: HarperCollins).

Heuston, R. (1964), *Essays in Constitutional Law*, 2nd edition (London: Stevens).

Hickley, M. (2008), 'Military Told to Wear Uniform in Public as Often as Possible to Improve National Recognition of the Armed Forces', *Daily Mail*, 29 October 2008, http://www.dailymail.co.uk/news/article-1081608/Military-told-wear-uniform-public-possible-improve-national-recognition-armed-forces.html (accessed 14 January 2009).

Hill, R. (2005), Minister of Defence, letter, 4 August 2005, on author's personal file.

Hocking, J. (1993), *Beyond Terrorism: The Development of the Australian Security State* (Sydney: Allen & Unwin).

Hocking, J. (2004), *Terror Laws: ASIO, Counter-Terrorism and the Threat to Democracy* (Sydney: University of New South Wales Press).

Holdsworth, W.S. (1902), 'Martial Law Historically Considered', 18 *Law Quarterly Review* 117.

Hope, R. (1977), *The Royal Commission on Intelligence and Security*, Reports I, II, III, IV (Canberra: Australian Government Publishing Service).

Hope, R. (1979), *Protective Security Review Report* (Canberra: Australian Government Publishing Service).

House of Representatives, Commonwealth of Australia (1978), *Parliamentary Debates*, House of Representatives, 23 February 1978.

House of Representatives, Commonwealth of Australia (2000), *Parliamentary Debates*, House of Representatives, 7 September 2000.

Howard, J. (2006), 'A Stronger AFP: Responding to Regional Challenges', Prime Minister of Australia media release, 25 August 2006, http://www.pm.gov.au/news/media_releases/media_Release2096.html (accessed 25 August 2006).

Hsu, S. and Tyson, A. (2008), 'Pentagon to Detail Troops to Bolster Domestic Security', *Washington Post*, 1 December 2008, http://www.washingtonpost.com/wp-dyn/content/article/2008/11/30/AR2008113002217.html?hpid=topnews (accessed 12 May 2009).

Hufnagel, S. (2008), 'German Perspectives on the Right to Life and Human Dignity in the "War on Terror"', 32 *Criminal Law Journal* 100.

Ignatieff, M. (2004), *The Lesser Evil: Political Ethics in an Age of Terror* (Toronto: Penguin Canada).

International Cooperation Committee Chubu Diocese (2007), 'Changing Japan's Constitution: A Giant Step Backwards for World Peace', *Peace Talk Newsletter* (Peace Action Maine), Autumn 2007, http://www.peaceactionme.org/changing-japans-constitution-giant-step-backwards-world-peace (accessed 13 May 2009).

International Labour Organization (2009), *Global Employment Trends 2009* (Geneva: ILO), http://www.ilo.org/wcmsp5/groups/public/---dgreports/---dcomm/documents/publication/wcms_101461.pdf (accessed 2 February 2009).

International Monetary Fund (2009), *World Economic Update 2009* (Washington, DC: IMF), http://topforeignstocks.com/wp/wp-content/uploads/2009/01/imf-world-economic-outlook-2009.pdf (accessed 2 February 2009).

Jacobs, J. (1985), 'The Role of Military Forces in Public Sector Labor Relations', in Rowe and Whelan (eds).

Jansen, M. (2000), *The Making of Modern Japan* (Cambridge, MA: Harvard University Press).

Japan Ministry of Defense (2007), Speech by Defense Minister Fumio Kyuma, 9 January 2007, http://www.mod.go.jp/e/publ/lastest/press01.html (accessed 21 June 2008).

Jeffery, K. (1985), 'Military Aid to the Civil Power in the United Kingdom: An Historical Perspective', in Rowe and Whelan (eds).

Jeffery, K. (1996), 'The British Army and Ireland since 1922', in Bartlett and Jeffery (eds).

Katzenstein, P. (1996), *Cultural Norms and National Security: Police and Military in Postwar Japan* (Ithaca, NY: Cornell University Press).

Keelty, M. (2009), 'Law Enforcement Contribution to National Security', National Security Australia 2009 speech, 23 March 2009, Sydney, http://www.afp.gov.au/media/national_media/national_speeches/2009/law_enforcement_contribution_to_national_security (accessed 3 April 2009).

Kershaw, I. (1998), *Hitler, 1889–1936: Hubris* (London: Allen Lane).

Kitson, F. (1971), *Low Intensity Operations: Subversion, Insurgency, Peacekeeping* (London: Faber & Faber).

Kohn, R. (2002), 'The Erosion of Civilian Control of the Military in the United States Today', *Naval War College Review*, Summer 2002.

Laing, N. (2005), 'Call-Out the Guards: Why Australia Should No Longer Fear the Deployment of Australian Troops on Home Soil', 28 *University of New South Wales Law Journal* 507.

Lane, P. (1974), *An Introduction to the Australian Constitution* (Sydney: Law Book Company).

Lasry, L. and Eastman, K. (2005), 'Memorandum of Advice: Anti-Terrorism Bill 2005 (Cth) and the Human Rights Act 2004 (ACT)', 9 *University of Western Sydney Law Review* 111.

Laybourn, K. (1993), *The General Strike of 1926* (Manchester: Manchester University Press).

Leahy, P. (2008), 'Bush Signs Bill Enacting Leahy's National Guard Empowerment Reforms, and Leahy's Repeal of the "Insurrection Act Rider"', Office of Senator Leahy, press release, 30 January 2008, http://leahy.senate.gov/press/200801/013008b.html (accessed at 8 August 2008).

Lee, H. (1984), *Emergency Powers* (Sydney: Law Book Company).

Lee, H. and Winterton, G. (eds) (2003), *Australian Constitutional Landmarks* (Cambridge: Cambridge University Press).

Legras, F. (1998), 'Quebec's Winter Storm: The Social Issues', *World Socialist Web Site*, 24 February 1998, http://www.wsws.org/articles/1998/feb1998/queb-f24.shtml (accessed 12 May 2009).

Legras, F. (2001), 'Rubber Bullets, Tear Gas and Mass Arrests at the Summit of the Americas in Quebec City', *World Socialist Web Site*, 2 May 2001, http://www.wsws.org/articles/2001/may2001/queb-m02.shtml (accessed 12 May 2009).

Leicht, J. (2006), 'Germany: Politicians Urge Army's Deployment for World Cup', *World Socialist Web Site*, 11 January 2006, http://www.wsws.org/articles/2006/jan2006/wcup-j11.shtml (accessed 12 January 2006).

Leigh, D. (1998), *The Wilson Plot* (London: Heinemann).

Lendrum, S. (1977), 'The "Corrong Massacre": Martial Law and the Aborigines at First Settlement', 6 *Adelaide Law Review* 26.

Lerhe, E. (2004), 'Civil Military Relations and Aid to the Civil Power in Canada: Implications for the War on Terror', CDAI-CDFAI 7th Annual Graduate Students Symposium, RMC, 29–30 October 2004, http://www.cda-cdai.ca/symposia/2004/Lerhe,%20Eric-%20Paper.pdf (accessed 15 August 2008).

Louis, L. (1992), '"Operation Alien" and the Cold War in Australia, 1950–1953', 62 *Labour History* 1–18.

McCluskey, S. (2004), 'USNORTHCOM and Canadian Domestic Operations: An Opportunity for Positive Change', School of Advanced Military Studies, United States Army Command and General Staff College, Fort Leavenworth, KS.

McCormack, G. (2007), *Client State: Japan in the American Embrace* (London: Verso).

McCulloch, J. (2001), *Blue Army: Paramilitary Policing in Australia* (Melbourne: Melbourne University Press).

McKinlay, B. (1979), *A Documentary History of the Australian Labor Movement, 1850–1975* (Melbourne: Drummond).

Madsen, S. (1993), 'The Japanese Constitution and Self-Defence Forces: Prospects for a New Japanese Military Role', 3 *Transnational Law and Contemporary Problems* 549–79.

Maeda, T. (1995), *The Hidden Army: The Untold Story of Japan's Military Forces* (Chicago, IL: Edition Q).

Maloney, S. (1997), 'Domestic Operations: The Canadian Approach', *Parameters* (US Army War College Quarterly), Autumn 1997, 135–52.

Mark, R. (1978), *Report to the Minister for Administrative Services on the Organisation of Police Resources in the Commonwealth Area and Other Related Matters* (Canberra: Australian Government Publishing Service).

Marx, K. and Engels, F. (1973), *The Communist Manifesto* in *Selected Works*, vol. 1 (Moscow: Progress Publishers).

Meier, H. (1988), *The Lesson of Carl Schmitt* (Chicago, IL: University of Chicago).

Merrick, J. (2008), 'Security Bill for London's 2012 Olympics to Hit £1.5bn – Triple the Original Estimate', *The Independent*, 28 September 2008, http://www.independent.co.uk/news/uk/politics/security-bill-for-londons-2012-olympics-to-hit-16315bn--triple-the-original-estimate-944766.html (accessed 14 January 2009).

Mestrovic, S. (2006), *The Trials of Abu Ghraib: An Expert Witness Account of Shame and Honor* (Boulder, CO: Paradigm Publishers).

Michaels, A. (2008), 'Silvio Berlusconi Calls in the Troops to Reassure his Countrymen', *Telegraph*, 6 August 2008, http://www.telegraph.co.uk/opinion/main.jhtml?xml=/opinion/2008/08/06/do0603.xml (accessed 8 August 2008).

Ministry of Defence (2002) *Strategic Defence Review: A New Chapter* (Cm 5566), (London: The Stationery Office), http://www.mod.uk/DefenceInternet/AboutDefence/CorporatePublications/PolicyStrategyandPlanning/StrategicDefenceReviewANewChaptercm5566.htm (accessed 12 May 2009).

Ministry of Defence (2003), *Delivering Security in a Changing World* (Cm 6043), (London: HMSO).

Ministry of Defence (2005), *Operations in the UK: The Defence Contribution to Resilience* (London: HMSO).

Ministry of Justice (2007), *The Governance of Britain: Constitutional Renewal* (London: HMSO).

Moore, C. (2005), '"To Execute and Maintain the Laws of the Commonwealth": The ADF and Internal Security: Some Old Issues with New Relevance', 28 *University of New South Wales Law Review* 523.

Moore, J. and Williams, D. (2000), 'Further Safeguards for Defence Bill', Department of Defence joint news release, 23 August 2000, http://www.minister.defence.gov.au//2000/22900.htm (accessed 31 August 2000).

Moore, M. (2008), 'Silvio Berlusconi Declares Naples Street Rubbish Dumps "Military No-go Zones"', *Telegraph*, 21 May 2008.

Morgan, M. (2008), 'London Olympics Terror Threat Used to Vastly Increase Surveillance Powers', *World Socialist Web Site*, 3 May 2008, http://www.wsws.org/articles/2008/may2008/lond-m03.shtml (accessed 12 May 2009).

Morris, E. and Gourevitch, P. (2008), *Standard Operating Procedure* (New York: Penguin).

Muller, J. (2003), *A Dangerous Mind: Carl Schmitt in Post War European Thought* (New Haven, CT: Yale University Press).

National Archives of Australia (1978), *1978 Cabinet Records: Selected Documents* (Canberra: National Archives of Australia), http://www.naa.gov.au/Images/1978_Cabinet_Records_Selected_Documents_Security_tcm2-16435.pdf (accessed 16 January 2009).

National Archives of Australia (2009), 'The 1978 Cabinet Records', http://www.naa.gov.au/collection/explore/cabinet/by-year/cabinet-records-1978.aspx (accessed 16 January 2009).

National Security Australia (2005), http://www.nationalsecurity.gov.au/agd/www/nationalsecurityHome.nsf/headingpagesdisplay/9F291545F46DC7B9CA256E43000565D4?OpenDocument (accessed 1 December 2005).

National Security Australia, National Counter-Terrorism Committee (2003), *National Counter-Terrorism Plan* (Canberra: National Security Australia).

Nations Encyclopaedia (2008), 'Germany: A Country Study', http://www.country-data.com/cgi-bin/query/r-4999.html (accessed 1 December 2008).

Neumann, F. (1942), *Behemoth: The Structure and Practice of National Socialism* (London: Victor Gollancz).

Nicola, S. (2006), 'Germany Debates World Cup Security', United Press International, 5 January 2006, http://www.upi.com/InternationalIntelligence/view.php?StoryID=20060105-122459-5392r (accessed 12 January 2006).

North, D. (2004), *The Crisis of American Democracy* (Detroit, MI: Mehring Books).

Osiel, M. (1999), *Obeying Orders: Atrocity, Military Discipline and the Laws of War* (New Brunswick, NJ: Transaction Publishers).

Paoletti, C. (2008), *A Military History of Italy* (Westport, CT: Greenwood).

Parliament of Australia (2005), *Defence Legislation Amendment (Aid to Civilian Authorities) Bill 2005* (Cth), Explanatory Memorandum, http://parlinfoweb.aph.gov.au/piweb/view_document.aspx?ID=2144&TABLE=OLDEMS (accessed 16 May 2006).

Parliament of Australia (2006), Senate, *Hansard*, Wednesday 8 February 2006.

Pashukanis, E. (1978), *Law and Marxism: A General Theory* (London: Ink Links).

Pempel, T. (1992), 'Political Parties and Representation: The Case of Japan', 25 *Political Science and Politics* 1.

Povoledo, E. (2009), 'Italy Tones Down Berlusconi's Vow to Increase Military Presence in Cities', *International Herald Tribune*, 26 January 2009.

Prime Minister's Office (2008), *Report of Inquiry into National Recognition of our Armed Forces* (London: Prime Minister's Office), http://www.ppu.org.uk/ref/recognition_of_our_armed_forces.pdf (accessed 14 January 2009).

Privacy Commissioner of Canada (2002), news release, 'Amendments to Bill C-55', 18 June 2002.

Pugliese, D. (2002), *Canada's Secret Commandos: The Unauthorized Story of Joint Task Force Two* (Ottawa: Esprit de Corps Books).

Quick, J. and Garran, R. (1901), *The Annotated Constitution of the Australian Commonwealth* (Sydney: Angus and Robertson).

Rasmussen, M. (1999), 'The Military Role in Internal Defense and Security: Some Problems', Occasional Paper No. 6, The Center for Civil-Military Relations, Naval Postgraduate School, Monterey, California, http://www.ccmr.org/public/images/download/defense.pdf (accessed 23 July 2008).

Reid, R. (1989), *The Peterloo Massacre* (London: William Heinemann).

Reindl, J.C. (2008), 'Mayor to Marines, Leave Downtown', *Toledo Blade*, 9 February 2008, http://www.toledoblade.com/apps/pbcs.dll/article?AID=/20080209/NEWS16/802090394 (accessed 12 May 2009).

Robertson, G. (2008), *Crimes Against Humanity* (Camberwell: Penguin Books).

Rowe, P. (1985), 'Keeping the Peace: Lethal Weapons, the Soldier and the Law', in Rowe and Whelan (eds).

Rowe, P. (2006), *The Impact of Human Rights Law on Armed Forces* (Cambridge: Cambridge University Press).

Rowe, P. and Whelan, C. (eds) (1985), *Military Intervention in Democratic Societies* (London: Croom Helm).

Royal Commission Sheraton Hotel Report (1984), *Royal Commission on Australia's Security and Intelligence Agencies: Report on the Sheraton Hotel Incident*, Mr Justice Hope, Royal Commissioner (Canberra: Australian Government Publishing Service).

Rudd, K. (2008), 'Appointment of Duncan Lewis as National Security Adviser', Prime Minister of Australia media release, 4 December 2008, http://www.pm.gov.au/media/Release/2008/media_release_0661.cfm (accessed 10 December 2008).

Ruddock, P. (2004) 'A New Framework: Counter Terrorism and the Rule of Law', Address to the Sydney Institute, 20 April 2004, http://152.91.12/www/MinisterRuddockHome.nsf/Alldocs/RWPB046617DB0869 (accessed 29 June 2004).

Saul, B. (2005), 'Speaking of Terror: Criminalising Incitement to Violence', 28 *University of New South Wales Law Journal* 868.

Sevastopulo, D. (2009), 'Intelligence chief warns of security threat', *Financial Times*, 13 February 2009, http://www.ft.com/cms/s/0/ca60312e-f965-11dd-90c1-000077b07658.html?ftcamp=rss&nclick_check=1 (accessed 22 June 2009).

Shalom, S. (1993), *Imperial Alibis: Rationalizing US Intervention after the Cold War* (Cambridge, MA: South End Press).

Singer, P. (2003), *Corporate Warriors: The Rise of the Privatized Military Industry* (Ithaca, NY: Cornell University Press).

Snell, K. (1970), 'The Extra-Parliamentary Opposition in Postwar Germany', *Comparative Politics*, July 1970, http://www.marcuse.org/herbert/booksabout/70's/70schell/schell70.pdf (accessed 17 December 2008).

Solomon, D. (2009), 'Some Secrets Too Sensitive to Release', *The Courier-Mail*, 1 January 2009.

Southern Highland News (1978), 15 February 1978, 1.

Squires, N. (2008), 'Italian Government May Use Soldiers to Crack Down on Mafia', *Telegraph*, 21 September 2008.

Stephen, N. (1984), 'The Governor-General as Commander-in-Chief', 14 *Melbourne University Law Review* 563.

Stretton, A. (1976), *The Furious Days: The Relief of Darwin* (Melbourne: Collins).

Sugita, A. (2002), 'Security Legislations and Human Rights in Japan', paper presented at the Australian National University, 8–9 October 2002, http://rspas.anu.edu.au/pah/human_rights/papers/2002/sugita.rtf (accessed 21 June 2008).

Sullivan, B. (1984), 'A Thirst for Glory: Mussolini, the Italian Military and the Fascist Regime, 1922–1936', PhD thesis, Columbia University, New York.

Sutton, M. (1994), *Bear in Mind these Dead: An Index of Deaths from the Conflict in Ireland 1969–1993* (Belfast: Beyond the Pale Publications).

Sydney Morning Herald (1978) Editorial, *Sydney Morning Herald*, 14 February.

Symonds, P. (2008), 'Japanese Government Pushes Through Law to Allow Naval Support for Afghan Occupation', *World Socialist Web Site*, 18 January 2008, http://www.wsws.org/articles/2008/jan2008/japa-j18.shtml (accessed 9 February 2009).

Templeman D. and Bergin, A. (2008), *Taking a Punch: Building a More Resilient Australia*, ASPI Strategic Insights 39, May 2008.

Tharp, D. (2008), 'To Send or Not to Send: Japanese Military Disaster Relief Assistance', The Nippon Foundation, 4 February 2008, http://www.nippon-foundation.or.jp/eng/current/20080204APIMilDisasterRelief.html (accessed 6 January 2009).

Trebilcock, C. (2000), 'The Myth of Posse Comitatus', *Journal of Homeland Security*, October 2000, http://www.homelandsecurity.org/journal/articles/Trebilcock.htm (accessed 25 August 2008).

Tucker, R. (1975), *The Lenin Anthology* (New York: Norton).

United Kingdom Parliamentary Papers (1893), *Parliamentary Papers*, vol. 17 (1893–94).

United Nations (2005), *Report on the World Social Situation 2005: The Inequality Predicament* (New York: United Nations), http://www.un.org/esa/socdev/rwss/media%2005/cd-docs/media.htm (accessed 23 June 2008).

US Federal Reserve (2009), *Flow of Funds Accounts of the United States* (Washington DC: Board of Governors of the Federal Reserve System), http://www.federalreserve.gov/releases/z1/Current/z1.pdf (accessed 2 February 2009).

US Northern Command (2007), 'Exercise Vigilant Shield '08 Slated for October', NorthCom News, 30 August 2007, http://www.northcom.mil/News/2007/083007.html (accessed 1 September 2008).

US Northern Command (2008), 'US Northern Command, Canada Command Establish New Bilateral Civil Assistance Plan', NorthCom News, 14 February 2008, http://www.northcom.mil/News/2008/021408.html (accessed 1 September 2008).

US Northern Command (2008b), 'Top Army Leader Visits Newly Assigned Consequence Management Force', NorthCom News, 15 September 2008, http://www.northcom.mil/news/2008/091508.html (accessed 5 December 2008).

US NSPD (2007), National Security and Homeland Security Presidential Directive, NSPD 51, HSPD-20, http://www.whitehouse.gov/news/releases/2007/05/20070509-12.html (accessed 20 June 2008).

US President's Commission (1970), *Report of the President's Commission on Campus Unrest* (Washington, DC: US Government Printing Office).

Vadarlis (2001), *Vadarlis v MIMA and Ors* M93/2001 at http://www.austlii.edu.au/au/other/hca/transcripts/2001/M93/2.html (accessed 30 November 2001).

Vallely, P. (2002), 'The Airey Neave Files', *Independent*, 22 February 2002, http://www.independent.co.uk/news/people/profiles/the-airey-neave-files-661625.html (accessed 12 May 2009).

Van Auken, B. (2007), '*New York Times* Public Editor Repudiates MoveOn.org Ad on General Petraeus', *World Socialist Web Site*, 25 September 2007, http://

www.wsws.org/articles/2007/sep2007/move-s25.shtml (accessed 12 May 2009).

Victoria State Coroner (1989), Investigation into the Death of Jedd Malcolm Houghton.

Wade, E. and Phillips, G. (1970), *Constitutional Law*, 8th edition (London: Longmans).

Walker, C. and Broderick, J. (2006), *The Civil Contingencies Act 2004: Risk, Resilience and the Law in the United Kingdom* (Oxford: Oxford University Press).

Walton, M. (2005), 'The Anti-Terrorism Bill (No. 2) 2005: An Overview', *Human Rights Defender* 3.

Ward, E. (1997), *Call Out the Troops: An Examination of the Legal Basis for Australian Defence Force Involvement in 'Non-Defence' Matters*, Parliamentary Research Paper No. 8 (Canberra: Parliament of Australia).

Watching Brief (1986), Interview with Clyde Cameron, for 'The CIA in Australia', Part 2 (Sydney: Public Radio News Service, October 1986).

Watt, N. (2000), 'Paratrooper Lee Clegg Cleared of Last Charge over Death of Teenagers', *Guardian*, 1 February 2000, http://www.guardian.co.uk/uk/2000/feb/01/northernireland.nicholaswatt3 (accessed 1 August 2008).

Western Australia State Coroner (n.d.), Investigation into the Death of Daniel Mark English.

Wheate, R. and Wheate, N. (2003), 'Lawful Dissent and the Modern Australian Defence Force', 160 *Australian Defence Force Journal* 20.

Whelan, C. (1985), 'Military Intervention in Democratic Societies: The Role of Law', in Rowe and Whelan (eds).

White, M. (2005), 'The Executive and the Military', 28 *University of New South Wales Law Journal* 438.

Windeyer, V. (1979), 'Certain Questions Concerning the Position of Members of the Defence Force when Called Out to Aid the Civil Power', in Hope (1979), Appendix 9.

Winterton, G. (1992), 'Dissolving the Communists: The Communist Party Case and its Significance', in *Seeing Red: The Communist Party Dissolution Act and Referendum 1951: Lessons for Constitutional Reform*, ed. Elsa Atkin and Brett Evans (Sydney: Evatt Foundation).

Winterton, G. (2003), '1975: The Dismissal of the Whitlam Government', in Lee and Winterton (eds).

Wootten, H. (1991), *Report of the Inquiry into the Death of David John Gundy* (Canberra: Australian Government Publishing Service).

Workers News (1976), *The Canberra Coup* (Sydney: Labour Publications).

Zinn, H. (2002), *Terrorism and War* (New York: Seven Stories Press).

Index